TO HELL AND BACK

NIKI LAUDA

AN AUTOBIOGRAPHY

TO HELL AND BACK

Written in collaboration with Herbert Völker
Translated from the German by E.J. Crockett
Introduction and Postscript by Kevin Eason

1 3 5 7 9 10 8 6 4 2

Virgin Books, an imprint of Ebury Publishing
20 Vauxhall Bridge Road
London SW1V 2SA

Virgin Books is part of the Penguin Random House
group of companies whose addresses can be found
at global.penguinrandomhouse.com

Originally published in Great Britain by Stanley Paul & Co. Ltd in 1986
Published by Corgi Books in 1987
This edition published by Virgin Books in 2020

www.penguin.co.uk

A CIP catalogue record for this book is available from the British Library

ISBN 9781529106794

Printed and bound in Great Britain by Clays Ltd, Elcograf S.p.A.

Penguin Random House is committed to a sustainable future for our business, our readers and our planet. This book is made from Forest Stewardship Council® certified paper.

CONTENTS

INTRODUCTION

THE LEGEND

Kevin Eason

HIGH ABOVE THE phalanx of fans clad in their red caps and shirts was a banner with a haunting picture in stark monochrome of a pair of eyes, scarred by heat and flame, staring down at the bare racetrack below. After the picture was a simple yet heartfelt message: 'Ciao, Niki.'

The occasion was the 2019 Italian Grand Prix, a race steeped in memories and the history of a team that dates back to the very start of the modern era of Formula 1. Ferrari arrived at the fabled Monza circuit celebrating ninety years since Enzo Ferrari founded his eponymous team, the most famous and successful in the world.

This theatre of speed, carved between the trees of the royal park and the sporting home to Ferrari, has provided the stage for some of the team's greatest acts, from Alberto Ascari's first victory at Monza for Ferrari in 1951, the second world championship year, to Michael Schumacher's tearful (first) retirement in 2006, just minutes after winning his final race for a *Scuderia* that he had helped transform into a powerful and dominant force.

This time, victory belonged to the freshest of Ferrari faces, Charles Leclerc, a stripling of just twenty-one years, who provided the champagne toast for the ninetieth birthday celebrations. The man whose eyes adorned that poster – and was missing from the Italian Grand Prix for the first time in more than forty years – would have grinned and revelled in one of the greatest sights in all of sport as Leclerc clambered onto the elevated podium to see the faithful Ferrari fans, the *tifosi*, turn the main straight into a river of red with their flags to cheer their new hero.

The memories of many of those teeming fans would have turned to the past, though, and appreciation of the man who looked down on their revelry: Niki Lauda, who died on 20 May 2019, as preparations for the September celebrations reached their climax.

Niki Lauda would have been central to the anniversary party as a key character in the Ferrari story. But he was more than a racing driver, more than a Ferrari driver and more than a man who presided over a team dominating Formula 1 in his final years. He was a symbol of extraordinary courage and determination, whose story was so shocking that even the scions of Hollywood were taken aback when it was committed to celluloid.

The word 'legend' is bandied about too easily in sport: a footballer scores a goal and is instantly crowned a 'legend', or a boxer knocks out an opponent and becomes a 'legend' because of just one fight. The quote attributed to Ernest Hemingway perhaps comes closest to an explanation of Lauda's elevation beyond these lesser legends, beyond even the greatest. 'There are only three sports – bullfighting, mountaineering and motor racing. The rest are merely games,' Hemingway said. The intent of his analysis was to show that kicking or hitting a ball or running 100 metres might well be a worthy test of strength or skill, but it is not a contest of mortality.

Niki Lauda drove a car for sport, but crossed the line between life and death and fought back to even greater glory. Lauda really was a legend.

Even people who know nothing of Formula 1 have heard of his crash at the Nürburgring in 1976 when he was dragged from the inferno of his Ferrari so badly injured that he was given the last rites. It was here at Monza before the astonished *tifosi* that he came back from the dead, racing barely forty-two days after a priest attempted to usher him into the afterlife. His wounds bled, he had no eyelids and couldn't blink, so he could hardly see the track ... and he was terrified. Enzo Ferrari was horrified by the publicity that surrounded a comeback that seemed beyond human endurance, but the fans descended on Monza in hordes, encouraged by an hysterical Italian press heaping superlatives on this astonishing hero.

There was no heroic return in Lauda's mind, though. For him, there was simply no alternative. He disguised his fear behind the fireproof balaclava through which blood seeped, and clamped his red helmet firmly onto his raw skull. Now no one could see the fear, trace the trembling and realise that Lauda was not just pitting his skill against the best, but probing the recesses of his mind where the darkest dread waited. A year later, he reclaimed his world championship for Ferrari.

Lauda's first stab at an autobiography came in 1978 with *For the Record – My Years with Ferrari*, translated from the German into English by Diana Mosley, the mother of Max, who provided Lauda's first Formula 1 cars from his March factory and later became the controversial president of the Fédération Internationale de l'Automobile (FIA), which governed Formula 1.

His second and last autobiography, *To Hell and Back*, was published in 1986 after his final retirement, and it was typically Niki – to the point with no frills and fancies, no doubt dictated at breakneck speed. It covers the years from his childhood to his accident and the battle for the 1976 title with the charismatic James Hunt, and then his departure from Formula 1 and motor racing as a three-times world champion and one of the most successful drivers in the sport, starting at the bottom with BRM and March, then Ferrari, before moving to the Brabham team run by Bernie Ecclestone, and finally McLaren. But Lauda never updated the book, nor told the story of life after Formula 1 as an airline magnate and then his extraordinary return to the track as chairman of the all-conquering Mercedes team that brought an astonishing five world championships for Lewis Hamilton, plus one more for Nico Rosberg, in successive years.

That was to be my job, and I have attempted to focus on the stories, events and anecdotes that would have been in his mind, which means that this book is part-autobiography, part-portrait of the man behind the mask of scars that became a trademark thanks to the Nürburgring.

I had the privilege as motor-racing correspondent for *The Times* to meet Lauda on many occasions at racetracks around the world, and there was one thing a journalist could rely on – that Niki would have an opinion on almost anything to do with motor racing. His opinions carried unique weight, though, because he had been there, done that and got the scars to prove it. Lauda's image was of a bombastic, curt, driven, even impolite man, and he was all and none of those things, but the measure is that he was adored around the world, could charm even the grumpiest of associates and became one of the most revered of countrymen in his homeland of Austria. John Hogan was the mastermind behind the Philip Morris Marlboro sponsorship that invested hundreds of millions of pounds in Formula 1, including backing Lauda. According to him, Lauda was incredibly well-mannered, 'particularly to women', Hogan said. 'He was always interested in people and put them at their ease. Women of all ages adored him. I think it was his upbringing because, despite his image, he was always courteous and polite.'

Lauda loved pranks and jokes, and would be a fascinating dinner companion with anecdotes that ranged through a life that refused to bow to rules and regulations or respect for authority. Lauda simply did not do rules – unless he could break them. He was his own man, struggling from the suffocating correctness of his privileged childhood to defy his family, who thought motor racing beneath their status in society; standing up to the fearsome Enzo Ferrari, who dominated Formula 1; and then taking on an airline cartel. It was as if he needed life to be a battle against authority and convention.

Hogan, who knew every driver and senior figure in Formula 1 from the early 1970s, including sponsoring and becoming close friends with James Hunt, put it simply: 'You would have to call Niki a maverick. That's the best description.'

Lauda loved a deal and could wring cash from even the tightest of fists to finance his motor-racing career and airline businesses. He started life in Formula 1 with massive debts as he inveigled cash from sponsors persuaded by his assurances of instant success, and ended his life with a fortune estimated by some of almost 500 million euros. He was never driven by money, though, only the deal, the battle and the victory.

'Niki was always restless, always looking for the next thing,' according to Bernie Ecclestone, who lured Lauda from Ferrari to his Brabham team. They had sat in a car among the trees of Monza's royal park after the 1977 Italian Grand Prix, away from prying eyes, to stitch together a deal worth $1 million a year – a huge price in that era. Lauda secured his second world championship with the *Scuderia* in the United States and then walked away with two Grands Prix of the season remaining to join Ecclestone. Typically, he saw no point in prolonging his association with Ferrari, no matter the success he had enjoyed with them.

And he knew his worth. Before his second season with Brabham, Lauda demanded a pay rise to $2 million from Ecclestone, who blanched and refused point blank – until they had to attend a meeting with Parmalat, the team's main sponsor. Ecclestone made the introductions and told executives that the team was prepared for the new 1979 season and that Lauda would be his Number One driver again. 'No, I won't,' Lauda said, stunning the room into silence. Ecclestone and Lauda retreated to a backroom to argue over the $2 million, but Ecclestone was over a barrel: no pay rise, no lead driver. He paid up.

'Niki didn't stand on ceremony. He just got to the point,' Ecclestone told me. 'He couldn't understand why people made a fuss. If something went wrong, he just got on with it and did something else. He didn't have time for emotion and looking back. He learned a lesson and moved on. People understood that when Niki said good morning, it was before twelve o'clock. They felt comfortable that they could talk and what they got back was just how it is. That's where he captured a lot of people to support him, because he was straightforward. He didn't mind criticism.'

Ecclestone had already got his payback after the Nürburgring and from a man who could easily have claimed to have kick-started Formula 1 as a global television event. Grand Prix racing on television was a hit-and-miss affair with broadcasts in Europe controlled by the European Broadcasting Union. But Lauda's crash and spectacular comeback had turned Formula 1 into must-see television and broadcasters were lining up for deals. Ecclestone, who also negotiated for the F1 teams, took on the European Broadcasting Union and started signing contracts with individual broadcasters for the first time – with the proviso that they came back to show the entire 1977 season, not just a pick-and-mix of whatever they fancied. It was the start of Formula 1's drive to becoming a $1 billion-a-year sporting and entertainment giant – and made Ecclestone a billionaire.

'In the old days, the broadcasters would just show Monaco and something else and that was it,' Ecclestone said. 'But Niki was suddenly a massive star and everyone wanted to know how the 1976 season would end. It was a breakthrough for

Formula 1, otherwise we would still be stuck in Europe with very little coverage. I suppose it was all down to Niki and that crash.'

Lauda wasn't remotely interested in stardom and hated being noticed in restaurants or in the street. He had no time for gushing tributes or emotional moments. There was, perhaps, no better demonstration of his lack of sentimentality than his attitude towards his many trophies. Some found their way straight to the bin, but the man who ran his local garage showed some interest, so they struck a deal: he could have a trophy in return for free carwashes.

'That's what I did,' Lauda told the Reuters news agency. There was, however, a downside to this deal. 'The guy died, unfortunately, and his son was running the petrol station, so a friend of mine took them away, polished them and then my kids put them on eBay. Now I have to pay for the carwash.'

That lack of sentimentality reached every part of his working day, even for those closest to him. Paddy Lowe, Lauda's chief technical officer for three years at Mercedes, remembered: 'One Christmas, I had a Christmas card from Lewis [Hamilton] for him, a personally written card expressing his thanks to Niki for all he had done and wishing him all the best. Niki read it and threw it in the bin. I thought he could at least have taken it home. It was just like everything in his life – it was bullshit, and he didn't have time for bullshit.'

Even the scars that covered his head became an emblem to be exploited. Lauda had no vanity, no desire to look like James Hunt, the tall, blond Englishman he had competed against for the 1976 world championship. He accepted his scars and, apart from some work to replace his eyelids, he never bothered with plastic surgery, simply putting on a red baseball cap to cover the burn marks on his bald head, which he then turned into a $1 million-a-year advertising hoarding. Every setback could become a deal. He was matter-of-fact about his scars where others, such as Ian Wooldridge, were filled with horror. The celebrated *Daily Mail* sportswriter, who had witnessed the Nürburgring accident, wondered whether Lauda's return at Monza was an act of extraordinary courage or of stupendous folly. 'Is one man, aged 27, so unwilling to concede an earthly title that he is prepared to wager life against death when most men would be hiding their desperate injuries in a darkened room?' he wrote. Lauda was simply phlegmatic. 'I have reason to look ugly,' he told one interviewer. 'Most people don't. The cap is my protection from stupid people looking at me stupidly.'

The lack of an ear was also a source of both amusement and simple reality: 'People ask me, "Why did you never have an operation?" to which I would say, "Where the fuck do I find an ear?" It's a very simple answer,' he told Reuters.

His favourite story was of trying to recruit someone with acute observational skills. According to his narrative, he has each candidate come into the room to face the first question. 'What's the first thing you notice about me?' Most of the candidates fail, immediately pointing out his burnt ears, but one says: 'You are wearing contact lenses.' Lauda is surprised and pleased, but wants to know how the prospective employee figured it out. The answer came: 'If you had ears, you would be wearing glasses.'

Actually, there was one attempt to find Lauda's missing ear. After a fashion. Years after the 1976 crash, Bernie Ecclestone decided his old friend Lauda should return to the scene. They took along Karl-Heinz Zimmermann, Lauda's fellow Austrian who ran Ecclestone's motorhome at Grands Prix. Like Ecclestone, Zimmermann was an inveterate prankster and he guided the three of them around the old circuit – known as the Nordschleife and closed to Formula 1 after the 1976 accident – until they arrived at the Bergwerk turn where Lauda crashed and his Ferrari burst into flames.

The three stopped and wandered around the grass verge as if searching for something until a group of German passers-by spotted them and recognised Lauda. 'Hey, Niki Lauda,' one said. 'What are you doing?' Zimmermann was already prepared and shouted over: 'Looking for his ear, of course.' The Germans thought that Lauda and his friends were taking the mickey, but Zimmermann nudged Lauda and pointed at the ground in front of them. 'Look there,' he hissed. A quick scour of the verge uncovered a fresh, pink ear. Lauda emerged triumphant, waving it in the air at the Germans like a Formula 1 winner's trophy. It was, in fact, a pig's ear, which had been secreted in Zimmermann's pocket. The laughter was long and hearty, though the memories for Lauda must have been raw.

That fiery crash in 1976 deep in the forest of the Nordschleife could never leave him. It could have claimed his life in seconds there and then; instead, it took forty-three years to snuff out the irrepressible and undaunted Niki Lauda. This is the account of a life lived at speed, a life that went to hell, but came back to glory and fulfilment.

CHAPTER ONE

EARLY DAYS

COMING FROM A 'good' family has its advantages, although I question this at times when I think back to how angry I used to feel at being thrashed so often. In Austria, the Laudas are a 'good' family. At any rate they were. These days, Laudas of the captain-of-industry variety are something of a dying breed.

The most striking personality in the family was my grandfather, 'Old Lauda'. Even now, after his death, the 'old' sets him apart from all the other Laudas (who, I imagine, also have hopes of living to a ripe old age). What I particularly liked about him was his physical presence, his sumptuous Vienna town house complete with liveried manservant, his sprawling estate in Lower Austria, his fabulous place in St Moritz.

Old Lauda saved his most original and graphic expletives to describe Socialism and all it stood for. One evening – I must have been about twelve at the time – I caught a glimpse of him on television. There he was in the front row at some ceremony or other, and there was Austria's (then) Number One Socialist in the process of draping a ribbon and medal round his neck. I sat down at once and wrote grandfather a letter. I couldn't understand (I wrote) how a person could rant and rave a lifetime long and then calmly accept an *Orden* from his worst adversaries. No reaction.

Months later, during one of his annual visits to our house, we came face to face. I was very pleased to see him because he always let me park his Jaguar in our driveway. By this time most of our visitors let me take care of their cars – it saved them the trouble and they knew I was capable.

Anyway, after half an hour of small talk, Grandfather Lauda pulled my letter out of his top pocket. I was in for a dressing-down. What did I think I was playing at? How could I have the effrontery, etc., etc.? Pointing an accusing finger at my parents, he read the whole text out loud, every single phrase offering fresh evidence of my insufferable insolence. My mother was furious with me; my father took it more calmly.

As for myself, that was when I opted out of the we-Laudas-are-something-special way of thinking, such as I understood it then. As soon as I was more or less old enough to stand on my own two feet, I came back at Old Lauda with a vengeance: I pointedly kept my distance from his Christmas Day lunches at Vienna's most aristocratic hotel, the Imperial, when the entire clan was duty-bound to attend. At the time, Young Lauda considered no gesture more defiant.

Family background and education clearly explain much about my temperament today. I was brought up in a distinctly cold environment, in a milieu where certain truths are self-evident. Take horse-riding, for example. Although everything about it disgusted me, I had to learn to ride. Even the clip-clop of the hooves as the horse came out of the box would get on my nerves, and the stench literally got up my nose to the point where, in the early days, it made me physically sick.

However, not one single member of the family was flexible enough to suggest that a ten-year-old might be excused riding lessons and encouraged to take them up again later. There was no concession, no way out. Looking back, of course, my parents were right. Despite everything, I shook off my phobia and learned to ride impeccably. Today, when the mood takes me, I ride my brother-in-law's horse on Ibiza, and I have a way with the children's ponies.

This proper but severe upbringing probably accounts for my addiction to excellence, my need to do things better than other people. It certainly helped in one respect: it gave me a lot of self-confidence.

Have you never noticed how, in an expensive restaurant, with bow-tied waiters slaloming from table to table, some people seem to change personality completely? They look different, they act differently, they make all kinds of outlandish gestures, crook their little fingers, etc. Not me. No matter where I am I have learned to be myself and act naturally, and feel totally confident in handling all manner of social situations.

My schooldays were highly enjoyable because I was careful not to let education get in the way. From my very first day at school I felt no sense of involvement, no commitment whatsoever. I simply couldn't see the point, particularly once I reached twelve or so and started taking a real interest in cars. I failed my first and third years in senior school, and had to repeat a year on both occasions. By then I already had wheels – a vintage-year (1949) drophead Beetle. It cost me £65 in saved-up pocket money, but it was a car I could drive around the courtyard and do a paint-job on, with an engine I could strip down and reassemble.

I had the VW towed out to my grandparents' estate, which had its own private roads where I could drive to my heart's content. I also built a take-off ramp to see how far the Beetle would travel through the air: the record was twenty-four yards, with the springs popping out right, left and centre.

When I failed my third-year examinations for the second time, my parents enrolled me at a special school to do a university entrance course. Once there, I found I had a free hand, so I studied even less than before. I didn't sit one single examination; all I did was mess about. It finally dawned on my parents that the situation was getting out of hand, so they sent me off to do an apprenticeship as an auto-mechanic. I was coming up to seventeen. By Lauda family standards all this was very *infra dig.*

I ended up in a Volvo/BMW garage and thought to myself, hey, this is not too bad. Sadly, my new career soon took a sharp turn for the worse.

Early one morning, an agitated businessman brings in his Volvo. It is only about seven o'clock, but he has to have a quick oil-change because there's an important meeting at eight and he needs the car.

As far as the foreman is concerned, an oil-change is all that Lauda is fit for in life. I drive the Volvo downstairs and get it up on the ramp. I clamber down into the pit and try to loosen the nut on the sump. Unfortunately, I turn it too hard the wrong way and strip the threads. Back I go to report that I'm having a problem draining the sump – can the foreman come down and have a quick look? It doesn't take him a second to realise what has happened. There is one godawful row, because the whole engine has to be lifted out to get at the sump and remove it up through the hood. In goes a new sump, back goes the engine – two days' work, the customer going bananas (he's the type who tends to get really emotional).

The other mechanics threw everything they could lay their hands on at me – screwdrivers and monkey wrenches went whizzing past my head. From that day on, I was the resident idiot. I wasn't allowed to lay a finger on any of the cars; the only job I was fit for was running errands.

During the summer vacation I took my driving test at my parents' place in the country. It was a fair distance from there to the driving school, so I used to drive myself to lessons in one of the various cars we had about the place, being careful to park round the corner out of sight of the driving instructor.

After a year of running errands I confessed to my father that I felt ready to return to college. Father took the point but, as a penance for all my transgressions to date, decreed that I would have to attend courses in the evening and continue working during the day.

I took studying a bit more seriously this time and managed to major in a couple of subjects. My grandfather promised me a small car if I passed English, but when I challenged him about this – in his twenty-bedroomed garret on the *Schubertring* – he told me not to be so impertinent. Couldn't I see for myself what a frugal life he led? And poor *Tante* Helga (his second wife), having to wear the same clothes year-in, year-out?

I asked my father about this and he said I shouldn't become too disappointed. Time and again, it appeared, Grandfather Lauda had promised him a horse, but had never delivered.

It was the height of humiliation for a nineteen-year-old in my social circle not to have a car. Everybody had wheels. It was particularly embarrassing where girlfriends were concerned, because I could hardly expect them to travel by public transport.

There finally came a point when the whole situation got on top of me: the special school with all its upwardly mobiles, not to mention the fact that I had already wasted a precious year of my motor-racing career (which I had settled on a long time previously). I racked my brains for some way of speeding things along a bit so that I would never again have to worry about tiresome academic qualifications. I was absolutely convinced that I would never get myself into any profession that needed that sort of thing; it was all just a sop to my parents' ambition.

As it turned out, there *was* something I could do to hurry things along. A girlfriend at school had just graduated, and one of my schoolfriends thought he might be able to retouch her diploma so that my name would appear on it. The girl would then say she had lost hers and would apply for a duplicate.

Imagine my astonishment when I clapped eyes on the retouched diploma. My talented graphic-designer friend had dabbled with erasers and ink-remover so amateurishly that you could tell the thing was a fake from a hundred yards away.

I quickly reviewed the legal ramifications of what I had in mind, coming to the conclusion that a forgery executed for purely 'domestic purposes' couldn't be all that serious. Come what may, I decided to take the scrap of paper home with me. Standing at a safe distance from my audience I held the paper up, waved it about, tucked it back in my pocket and, leaving the room as quickly as possible, immediately destroyed it.

It worked like a dream. The news coursed through the Lauda dynasty like wildfire: OUR NIKI HAS GRADUATED! At long last I could concentrate on the things that really mattered in life.

I used graduation gifts from relatives to buy a VW Beetle that was going for £650. Then, one evening, Peter Draxler, my old schoolfriend, who still didn't have a driving licence, suggested that we go for a drive. Not in my boring old Beetle, of course, but in a chic Mini Cooper S which his dad has in the garage and is trying to sell for £1,750.

Draxler Jr duly 'borrows' the car. I drive it.

We are shifting along quite nicely – no doubt, as Draxler now maintains, the first signs of a future world champion were in evidence – until we blast into the *Höhenstrasse* in Vienna at about four in the morning. I hit a patch of frost on one of the bridges, skid, and the car slams sideways against a high kerb. The near-side wheels buckle, and the bodywork is bent and twisted out of all recognition.

Draxler's father was an imposing figure. Draxler Jr and I were in deep trouble – until Peter suddenly had a bright idea: 'If you buy the car, he won't have to know anything about what happened.'

I dash down from the *Höhenstrasse* to my grandmother's apartment, ring the bell, get her out of bed and tell her I have just written off a set of wheels – to the tune of £1,750 – and that it's prison for Niki if I don't pay up. Grandmother gets dressed, drives me to the bank first thing in the morning, and gives me that amount in cash. I hurry round to Draxler Sr.

'... Incidentally, sir, I wouldn't mind buying your car.'

So, overnight, I become the proud owner of two cars – a clapped-out VW and a smashed-up Mini. I sell the VW and apply the proceeds to a repair job on the Mini.

Those were the days of the great Fritz Baumgartner, the 'Mini-King' and, for me, one of the great personalities of Austrian motor-sport. He had just advertised in *Autorevue* that he was selling his racing version Mini Cooper S. There I was, no academic qualifications, no job prospects, no money, no nothing. But I drove out to Baden where Baumgartner's car was garaged and looked it over. A dark-blue racing version. Minus engine.

Baumgartner saw me nosing around the car and came over to say hello. To me, he was some sort of god. We seemed to hit it off, and one day he visited me at my parents' house. That was an eye-opener for him; it seemed to convince him that I was someone he could do business with.

We pieced the racing engine together in my parents' garage and struck a bargain: he would trade me the Racing S for my street Mini (now repaired) plus £650; naturally, there was no need for me to worry about paying him the cash right away.

Within the shortest time imaginable, I had gone from zero to racing car. My non-existent diploma had underwritten the VW; the VW had metamorphosed into a Mini; and the Mini had been swapped for a racing version (albeit not fully paid off).

My family got wind of the fact that I was out in the garage tinkering around with a racing car. I told them that all I was interested in was the mechanical challenge which would help develop my engineering skills. I did have to promise, however, that I wouldn't race.

My first race came a couple of days later, on 15 April 1968. I travelled with my new sponsor (Baumgartner) to a place called Mühllacken in Upper Austria. A hill climb. In the first run I stuck to the 9,000-rev limit Baumgartner had recommended, eased up and finished third. I had a word with Baumgartner and he advised me to red-line (exceed the recommended rpm) in short bursts. I did this on the second run and won. When the two times were aggregated, however, I was only placed second overall.

Meanwhile Fritz Baumgartner's conscience had been playing him up, or maybe he was getting jumpy about the money I still owed him. Either way, he went behind my back and confessed all to my father: I had taken part in my first race, I was actually very talented, but Baumgartner would move heaven and earth to stop me entering the next one on the calendar. This was the Dobratsch Hill Climb, he explained, a very difficult one; a European Championship event with dangerous corners and a sheer drop to the valley floor. At all costs I had to be talked out of it.

With this ploy, Fritz Baumgartner contrived to act the concerned friend; he probably also contrived to collect the £650 he had coming to him, since I assume my father paid up.

My father made a tremendous song and dance, furious at my lies and deceit. He brought the full weight of paternal authority to bear to ensure that I would not enter the Dobratsch Hill Climb. I was to have no illusions on that score, he warned.

I found myself in a ridiculous situation. I didn't have a car that I could drive around town in, I had to suffer the indignity of my girlfriend travelling by public transport, I had a racing car without plates sitting around in the garage, and now I had been forbidden to race again. I analysed the situation from every angle and decided *que sera, sera*: I would be at Dobratsch on 28 April.

A friend from school lent me his father's BMW V8, which had a trailer attachment. Another friend lent me £125 for gas. In the middle of the night I wheeled the Mini out of the garage and loaded it onto the trailer. Then, with Ursula Pischinger, my girlfriend, I made tracks for Dobratsch.

The Mini choked and spluttered abominably at first, so I asked yet another friend if his mechanic could tune it for me.

I got in, drove smoothly, and won my class.

By the time I got back home my father had already seen the results in the newspaper. That was it: he'd finally had enough of me. As soon as I could afford to, I moved – out of the parental home and in with Mariella Reininghaus in Salzburg.

It took years for us to reconcile our differences. It was not until I was well on my way in Formula 1 that my father finally gave in and admitted there was nothing more he could do to stop me. However, in the period leading up to his death we grew very close. As for my mother and grandmother (who had stood by me in my hour of need), our relationship is still very close to this day, although we all too seldom see one another. Grandfather Lauda, the old patriarch himself? More about him later.

I suppose the question might as well come up now: *why* was I so completely and utterly determined to be a racing driver?

Answer: I don't know. That's just the way it was. There was not one single thing in the world that interested me even a fraction as much. Studying or having a 'normal' profession was totally alien to my way of thinking. Once in the sport, however, my approach has always been very level-headed and pragmatic: I have always thought my career through one step at a time, starting with the need for a driving licence and dealing with each subsequent problem as and when it came up.

I never craved stardom, I never identified with anyone (although there was a real candidate for hero-worship in those days in the person of Jim Clark).

Clark died in a shunt exactly one week before my first race. I can remember it to this day. I was watching a race in Aspern. Just as the race was finishing, it came over the PA system that Clark had been killed at Hockenheim. The news went through me like a knife and I was very depressed: what a shame, I thought, he'll be missed, the world will be a poorer place without him. I had no sense of drama about his death, no feeling of awesome tragedy. It never crossed the mind of a nineteen-year-old that the weeks, months and years ahead would be just as dangerous for me.

Jochen Rindt was another individual I didn't identify with, although, of course, he really impressed me. In November 1969, as part of a public relations exercise to promote the Jochen Rindt Show, he took the incredible Green Monster out on the apron at Aspern airport. I was in the crowd that day and saw Jochen in a superb full-length fur coat. A coat like that would have looked incredibly stupid on any other man, but on him it looked truly majestic. He came right across to where I was standing and shook hands with me. This came as a total surprise and I was naturally delighted and proud. His death a year later hit me very hard.

My first year in racing – 1968 – was an important one for the sport. Changes were coming fast and furious. I told myself I'd better not hang about too long wasting valuable career time.

Eight weeks after my first outing in the Mini Cooper I was already behind the wheel of a Porsche 911 (financed by trading in the Mini, a quick pilgrimage to my two grandmothers and a further – inevitable – bank loan). I seemed to have an easier time raising cash than most youngsters of my age; one look at my parents' villa seemed to put a creditor's mind at ease.

I raced in hill climbs and round airfields and did fairly well; well enough at least to draw attention to myself. I was offered a Formula Vee spot in 1969 in Kurt Bergmann's Kaimann team; the same team in which Keke Rosberg was to make a name for himself two years later.

My Formula 3 year, 1970, saw me up to my ears in debt and without a care in the world. Fact is, you can't afford worries when you're in Formula 3 because you have to keep your wits about you to cope with the utter madness of it. Technically speaking, there is precious little difference between one Formula 3 car and another. There are some twenty-five drivers in the field, all as fast as each other. And nobody gives an inch. We used to come over the top in formation at 125mph plus, jostling and banging into each other like dodgem cars in the *Prater* fairground. You had to be crazy to drive in Formula 3 at all. Back in 1970, I fitted the bill.

My first start in Formula 3 was typical of my whole season. I travelled down to Nogaro in the South of France with another

Austrian driver, Gerold Pankl – thirty-six hours on the road with a flat-bed trailer toting two racing cars.

We are the only two Austrians in a field of thirty mad Frenchmen. First training lap: I slot into Pankl's slip-stream, close up and scissor out past him. Just that instant, his engine dies on him. My left front wheel catches his rear right, I take off, hurtle through the air, come down just ahead of the guard-rail, lose all four wheels, and plough some hundred yards along the rail. There isn't too much of the car left after that. So much for my first five minutes of exposure to Formula 3.

Even so, I had absolutely no problem clearing my mind of images like that and stopping myself worrying about them. Just as well, since I spun out time and again.

We drove back at breakneck speed from Nogaro to Vienna, and I went over into Germany to buy myself a new chassis. I got the car back together (more debts) and made my way to the Nürburgring: I'm lying fifth, with no one in my sights and no one coming up behind me, and I suddenly spin out. To this day, I've never been able to figure out why.

Then came another thirty-six-hour haul to France. During the race something gets snarled up when I'm changing gears, I shift down instead of up, and bang go gearbox and engine.

Brands Hatch: Alois Rottensteiner, the photographer, asks me before the race which corner I think he should position himself at. 'Just ahead of the pits, somebody's bound to lose it there.' No sooner said than done: Lauda tries to outbrake someone, cuts in too sharply ahead of him, the driver behind clips his rear wheel and, whoops, there he goes, smack in front of Rottensteiner. A total write-off.

Now and again, though, I did finish a race, placing anywhere from second to sixth; not bad in the tight conditions of Formula 3 with people like James Hunt up against you.

The shunts didn't worry me at first. It wasn't until 5 September 1970 that I started to see things differently. That happened to be the day Jochen Rindt was killed at Monza, but what triggered my change of heart had nothing to do with him. Thinking about his death made me extremely sad, but it didn't influence me one way or another.

What did influence me was a Formula 3 outing at Dolder.

Lap three: Hannelore Werner becomes involved in a shunt somewhere out on the circuit. We come over a crest in formation doing 130mph. Right in front of us is an ambulance doing 30. The first three cars squeeze out to the right and through. James Hunt among them. And Gerry Birrell. Then a fourth tries, doesn't quite make it, oversteers and goes into a spin. I go out left, but the car that's spinning swings across in front of me. We collide, I spin, the car behind catches me on the volley. All of this is happening right out in the middle of the track. I sit in my wreck and here comes the next wave in tight formation over the crest of the hill. Yellow flags are out by this time and all kinds of signals are being flashed, but none of the pack coming through even considers easing off. All I can do is sit tight and wait for them to ram me: left, right or dead centre. One shoots straight over the nose of my car. That's it. I jump clear and make a run for it.

This incident was the high point of my third racing season (or should I say, non-season?). The day I started to develop one of my special talents: thinking things through, analysing, setting one goal at a time.

What it boiled down to was this: yes, I wanted to be in racing, always had done. But I didn't want to be one nutcase in a field of two dozen other nutcases. There was one logical conclusion – get out of Formula 3 and move up a class to Formula 2 as fast as possible.

There would be a lot of financial hardship involved. It would mean doubling the ante without having won a single game.

CHAPTER TWO

DEALS AND WHEELS

ONE ASPECT OF Grand Prix racing now accepted as commonplace did not in fact creep in until the early seventies: I refer, of course, to 'buying in'. To the best of my knowledge, Spain's Alex Soler-Roig was the first driver to use his own cash to buy himself a few Formula 1 starts. This was the other side to a new professionalism in motor racing. More and more money was pouring into the sport, everything was getting bigger, more elaborate, more expensive, and the weaker teams could afford only one driver. The cockpit of car Number Two had to house a paying guest.

March was one of the most interesting Formula 2 teams in those days. They had young superstar Ronnie Peterson as their Number One and, as a result, did not feel the need for anyone particularly good in the Number Two slot. They were prepared to take aboard someone like myself, providing, that is, that I paid my way. After all, I didn't have too bad a pedigree, I was competent, and I could probably argue my candidacy better than most other twenty-one-year-olds anxious to get out of Formula 3.

I signed for March before I actually had their asking price – just over £20,000. I then put together an advertising deal with the *Erste Oesterreichische Spar-Casse*, a leading Austrian bank; needless to say, the family name was not exactly a handicap in this particular instance.

During 1971 I learned a lot from Peterson but, by the end of the season, two thirds of my debts were still outstanding and I needed a fresh injection of capital to buy in for 1972. In for a penny, in for a pound, I thought to myself, and tried for a combined Formula 2/Formula 1 deal with March, who, admittedly, were quite happy to have me but by no means prepared to let me drive for free, let alone pay me for my services. This time March pegged the buy-in price at £100,000.

My answer was short and to the point: no problem, gentlemen. I came over as a young man who could handle any difficulties that came his way.

The *Erste Oesterreichische* had been pleased with the return on their investments in terms of exposure, and a further year's backing was on the cards. The managing director told me that the bank was agreeable, and I flew over to England to sign the contract at March. When I got back I discovered that the bank's board of directors had turned the project down: it seems that the old tycoon Mautner-Markhof had felt an obligation to do a favour for his friend of many years, Old Lauda. The latter was overjoyed at this turn of events which would 'bring the lad to his senses'.

I telephoned Old Lauda and asked him what on earth he thought he was doing. Back came the classic response: 'A Lauda should be written up on the financial pages, not the sports page.' I slammed down the receiver and never once spoke to Old Lauda again. As for the mighty Mautner-Markhof, I wrote him an irate letter, berating him with all the insolence a youngster can muster. I have never written a letter like that since. Incidentally, at that time Mautner-Markhof was himself going through a sticky patch as President of the Austrian Olympic Committee, with Karl Schranz and Avery Brundage at loggerheads over the former's amateur status.

I approached another bank, the *Raiffeisenkasse*, where I made the acquaintance of a man who has a very acute 'feel' for what is feasible and what is not: Karlheinz Oertel. He set up a £100,000 line of credit, with a piggy-back sponsorship package whereby the bank would waive any interest on the loan and pay for my obligatory life insurance cover. I handed the money over to March, leaving myself with no cash in hand and enormous debts. The one positive feature was that I didn't lose any sleep over the situation; it seemed to me that this was the right way to get myself quickly into the big league.

At the time I was living with Mariella Reininghaus in a tiny apartment in Salzburg. I had met Mariella when skiing at Gastein. She was with a group from Graz which included Helmut Marko. I had just fallen spectacularly – and I do mean spectacularly – and was lying spreadeagled, half buried in the snow. Mariella extricated me and asked if I was hurt. I said 'No' and, by the way, how would she like to go to the *Jägerball* with me? (In those days, the Hunt Ball was just about the most exciting event that Vienna had to offer its *jeunesse dorée*.) She said yes, and a couple of days later she came down from Graz to Vienna.

We stayed all of ten minutes at the *Jägerball*; it was a total drag. Although we were both in traditional peasant costume – Mariella in a *Dirndl* and yours truly in knicker-bockers and bow-tie – we left and went for coffee in a traditional Viennese *Kaffeehaus*.

We hit it off immediately, and from then on were in each other's company more or less twenty-four hours a day. We soon moved into the Salzburg apartment.

Why Salzburg? There were several reasons. First, Salzburg is, quite simply, a beautiful town. Second, I had really had enough of Vienna, my family and so-called Viennese society, young and old alike. And third, Salzburg was a good 175 miles west of Vienna, which meant 350 miles less driving to and from the major race events.

Mariella was a very pretty and intelligent girl, level-headed and composed. Her reasoned approach to life and her self-control rubbed off on me during those early, hectic years in racing, and being around her had a pronounced influence on my character. I have much to thank her for.

We were on the road most of the time: Mariella came with me to virtually every race. One of her remarkable traits was her ability to remain silent, to retreat into herself. She would sit next to me in the car for hours on end without opening her mouth and, if I left her on her own somewhere at the track, the odds were that I would come back to the same place hours later and find her in exactly the same pose as when I left.

I had never before and have never again since driven in so many races in one season as I did in 1972. Formula 1, Formula 2, Touring, Endurance – thirty starts in all. Even so, it was a nightmare season, because my main drive, the Formula 1 March, was a colossal mechanical fiasco.

The 721 X, with its transmission up ahead of the differential, was looked upon as a revolutionary design. The people at

March saw it as a passport to world championship success, a machine to complement the incomparable Ronnie Peterson.

The 721 X was test-driven for the first time at Jarama, in the run-up to that year's Spanish Grand Prix. Peterson was at the wheel, of course, but I was allowed to watch. Right from the start Ronnie was posting lap times up with Jackie Stewart in the Tyrell and, in those days, Stewart was the universal yardstick. The March team were ecstatic, none of them seeming to allow for the fact that Stewart had been plagued by shock-absorber trouble for a whole two days, the upshot being that his lap times did not really have all that much relevance. I listened in as Ronnie enthused about the new car and Robin Herd worked himself up into a frenzy of excitement.

I finally had my crack at the car the next day. For me, it was undrivable. I immediately spun out – not once, but twice. The car was incredibly aggressive; the rear end especially vicious. I just could not come to terms with it at all, and my lap times were appreciably slower than Peterson's. That evening, as we were sitting around in the hotel, Robin Herd said to me consolingly: 'Once you have Ronnie's experience, you'll be able to handle her too.'

I had a chat with Ronnie, who repeated that the car was fine and that the problems had to be of my making, not the car's. Depressed, I took Mariella off to Marbella for a couple of days. The break did me precious little good, however, because I racked my brains day and night while I was there, trying to work out why it was that the 721 X and I didn't hit it off. For the first time ever, I felt unsure of myself: maybe I wasn't the fantastic driver I believed myself to be? (Up to then, the first direct comparison with Ronnie Peterson had been encouraging – I had sensed that I was within spitting distance of him, although no doubt I was the only person who thought as much at the time.)

Ronnie and the March team elaborated some excuse to explain our subsequent poor showing in the Spanish Grand Prix. However, by Monaco it had finally dawned on them that the miracle machine left a lot to be desired. After a further round of tests, it was obvious that the car was wrong from top to bottom and that no amount of re-designing would help. The only solution was to ditch the 721 X and chalk it up to experience.

The experience was certainly salutary for me. I learned first of all, that I should have more faith in my own technical judgement. Second, that there are designers who go off at a tangent, carried away by their own euphoria. And third, that there are well-known drivers who would rather try to tame a vicious car than attempt to explain to the designer where the car's faults lie and how one can perhaps correct them.

Peterson left the sinking ship and joined Lotus. Lauda faced triple bankruptcy: a season of terrible results (hardly calculated to inspire confidence among my creditors), debts of £80,000 (I had managed to pay off £20,000 out of my Touring Class earnings), and no prospect of a new contract. True, March had recognised some potential in me, but would only race me in Formula 2 and keep me as a test drive back-up for their latest signing, Chris Amon.

This last piece of devastating news did not filter through to me until late October – by which time a driver has no hope of securing a contract for the forthcoming season, let alone a driver who has had to shell out a fortune to buy himself in and hasn't placed better than the back rows of the grid.

When I drove away from Bicester after a final confrontation with March, the thought went through my head for the first – and only – time in my life that I could end it all right there and then. I knew there was a T-junction a few miles ahead and that all I had to do was keep my foot to the floor: there was a solid wall on the other side.

I clicked my brain back into gear in time. However, returning to civilian life was not a solution. I had no formal education to speak of, no real trade. I would feel miserable and it would take years to pay off my debts (twenty or thirty at least, and closer to forty, I reckoned, taking interest payments and salary prospects into account).

That was it, then. Motor racing it would be, and for the same reasons as before: it was the only future I could conceive of, the only one that made sense. But 'Project 1973' would have to be accomplished without forking out more cash, that much was clear. There was simply no way I could accumulate more debts.

I had had brief contact with Louis Stanley, the boss of the BRM racing team. He knew my name, at least, and had heard some good reports about me. The team itself was middling, with good technicians and an impressive, albeit complicated, 12-cylinder engine. BRM's heyday had been back in the sixties – and the early sixties at that. Graham Hill had won the world championship for BRM in 1962, and that was the cornerstone of BRM legend.

I was invited to test drive at Paul Ricard. I asked the illustrious Clay Regazzoni, BRM's Number One driver, to show me the circuit. He gave me a guided tour in his own Ferrari Dayton, and at 125mph on the second lap we went into a spin! I was of an age when that sort of thing appeals.

Testing itself was something of a frustration, because only Regazzoni and Vern Schuppan were allowed behind the wheel for the first two days, and I was given a measly twenty laps only on the third and last day. Despite this, I was faster than Schuppan.

I had cleared the first hurdle and was summoned by Louis Stanley to his permanent suite at the Dorchester in London. No illusions: Stanley would only take me on if I paid my way; he was already paying two drivers (Regazzoni and Beltoise). He would let Schuppan go.

I gave the impression that my 'sponsor', Dr Oertel and his *Raiffeisenkasse*, would continue to back me, although I suspected this was not going to be the case. I had got myself into a progressively tight spiral of debt ever since that first £1,750 escapade when Grandmother bailed me out. I was well on the way towards a lifetime of indebtedness. It was time to review my plan of action.

This time, I realised, I would not have a whole season's grace, but would have to do something spectacular within the first three races. So spectacular, in fact, that I would be graduated there and then from the ranks of the buy-ins and join the paid élite. My tactics would be to schedule my (as yet nonexistent) 'sponsorship' payments in such a way that the first instalment would bridge the debt repayment gap. By the time the next instalment was due, I would already be established as a star.

Louis Stanley travelled out to Vienna shortly before Christmas 1972 to finalise the contract. Clearly my 'sponsor' was obliged to put in an appearance, and I managed to persuade Dr Oertel to come along; his English was such that I had to act as interpreter. I kept the real plan to myself: what I was going for was repayment of a new £80,000 advance in three instalments, the first of these falling due at a point where I could meet it myself from my BRM and Touring Class starting money. By the time the second instalment was due I would already be a star in the making and would be able to renegotiate the loan conditions accordingly.

The negotiations took place at Vienna airport. They were tricky, but it was finally agreed between Stanley and myself that I would go off and get the okay from my 'sponsor'. In his book *Behind the Scenes*, Stanley describes how he spent the intervening hours in Vienna:

> Lauda went off to get approval and promise of funds. I went into Vienna, to Christmas carols sung by the Vienna Boys Choir in St Stephen's Cathedral, walked along the *Kärnterstrasse,* indulged in Vienna's favourite pastime of coffee at Sacher's, and sampled *Kastanien mit Schlag* – boiled and sieved chestnuts with whipped cream. Back at the airport, Lauda signed a contract on the terms agreed.

I was now a further £80,000 in debt, making a grand total of £160,000 outstanding at the end of 1972.

Today I would certainly answer in the affirmative if asked whether I thought that getting behind the wheel of a racing car at all under this kind of financial strain was simply madness. It *was* madness, of course, to allow debts to pile up like that and to allow myself to become more and more entangled financially. But it had absolutely no effect on my performance as a driver. You don't give money a second thought when you get into the cockpit of a racing car. In fact, I gave as little thought to my precarious financial position then as I was to give a couple of years later to the fantastic amounts of money I was earning. Money – whether on the credit or debit side – never affected my driving style.

The 1973 season was anything but a triumphal one for BRM's three drivers. The best we could do in fifteen starts was a fourth place by Beltoise. I managed to place fifth once – in Zolder – picking up the first two world championship points of my career.

From a technical viewpoint, BRM was by now well into its decline. Up to the time it was scrapped, it never won another race. We were plagued by mechanical problems and shortcomings, some a result of out-and-out carelessness, others attributable to inadequate research and development. In every sense, the team was firmly anchored in the halcyon years of the sixties.

Louis Stanley was a veritable caricature of the sporting philanthropist. There were only two possible times you had a chance to talk with him. Either he called you in the middle of the night (according to him, it was too difficult getting through during the day), or you were invited for afternoon tea at the

Dorchester. I cut a dashing figure there, partly because – in the course of my wonderful upbringing – I had mastered the Viennese *Handkuss* and could kiss *Frau* Stanley's hand to great effect.

What I wanted was to get things moving; to focus Stanley's interest on matters technical. In the course of yet another audience at the Dorchester, I explained to him (yet again) that the monster which was his pride and joy was delivering too little horsepower for a 12-cylinder engine. He listened patiently and answered so quietly and formally that I had to strain to catch every word. Meanwhile, he was drinking tea at an astonishing rate. When he had put away so many cups that a visit to the bathroom was necessary, he remarked on leaving the room that 'right away' he would find a solution to this technical matter I had brought to his attention. Ten minutes or so later, he came back into the room and announced: 'I've just been on the telephone to the test bench. We've found another twenty horsepower in the exhaust system.'

The technical discussion was at an end. To question the veracity of his pronouncement would have been unthinkable. No additional twenty horsepower materialised in the course of the next race, either in the exhaust system or, for that matter, anywhere else.

While I was with BRM I always had the impression that owning a Grand Prix marque was an indulgence that was firmly held in check by certain financial constraints imposed by the Owen family; I can think of no other explanation to account for the lax technical approach. Our fuel pumps, for example, packed up with monotonous regularity. The mechanics claimed they were World War II issue and, when I asked them if they were the same ones Pedro Rodriguez and Jo Siffert had used, back came the answer that, yes, very probably they were.

Given this situation, it was pointless trying to motivate Louis Stanley. He had no interest in technical matters at all, but relished his role as owner and appeared at all the social events which are part and parcel of the sport. He was one of a dying breed, and certainly not the right man – technically or commercially – to lead into a new era a team that once had boasted Fangio, Hawthorn, Behra, Brooks, Trintignant and Stirling Moss.

My Touring Class earnings with the successful BMW-Alpina Team were just barely enough to pay BRM their first instalment. A second instalment was due in May, but I was penniless. The Monaco Grand Prix came just before the creditor's axe was due to fall. I was sixth fastest in training, ahead of the other two BRM drivers. In the actual race, I held third place behind Jackie Stewart and Emerson Fittipaldi for no less than twenty-five laps before my gearbox blew. However, it was *my* race.

That evening, Stanley suggested that we forget the instalment payments. He proposed that, henceforth, I would be paid to drive for him, provided that I committed myself there and then to a further two seasons with BRM.

I had no option. I signed.

It appears that I had caught the attention of Enzo Ferrari, who had watched the Monaco Grand Prix on television. To be absolutely sure he wanted me, he turned up at Zandvoort, where, in the wet, I was fastest in training.

Zandvoort 1973: the tragic race where millions of TV viewers watched Roger Williamson slowly burn to death. So much has been said and written about that day that I would like to take a moment to clear up certain misconceptions.

It was said after the race that I was ruthless, that I didn't give a damn that another driver was burning to death. Roger wasn't just 'another driver', by the way, he was one of the nicest people around. I liked him as a person and I was close to his sponsor, Tom Wheatcroft, a gentle and intelligent man. Our friendship went back to Formula 3 days and our relationship was close, not just a casual Grand Prix familiarity.

To understand what transpired, the tragedy has to be examined from three entirely different perspectives.

First, what actually happened. It is lap eight. Williamson's car suddenly shoots off the track on a fast, but otherwise unproblematic stretch of the circuit. Subsequent investigations reveal marks on the concrete which suggest suspension trouble, but it could just as easily have been a tyre defect; driver error can effectively be ruled out. The car smashes into the guard-rail, is hurled back across the track, somersaulting several times. It comes to rest upside down against the safety barrier opposite.

Second, what David Purley saw. Purley, Williamson's closest friend, is immediately behind him when it happens. He sees it all. He hits the brakes, drives up onto the grass verge, leaps out and dashes over to his friend's car. By this time it has caught fire, although the flames are not, as yet, all that alarming. Purley tries frantically to right Williamson's car, but he doesn't have the strength to do it on his own. Track marshals and firemen keep pulling him back instead of trying to help. Television clearly records how Purley repeatedly drags them over to the wreck, but is still left to tackle it alone. In vain. Anxious spectators try to climb the safety fencing to help but are pushed back by the police. Drivers passing the start and finishing line signal to race officials, but the officials don't know what to make of it. There is no telephone hook-up, no signal to abort the race, nothing. Except the lone struggle of David Purley, live on television.

Third, what we drivers saw. The flames and smoke leave no room for doubt that there has been a serious shunt. But the driver is obviously clear of the wreck and is trying to put out the flames. In fact, it is Purley trying to save Williamson's life, but there is absolutely no way we can know this, because Purley's car is parked up on the grass out of our field of vision (perhaps shrouded by the smoke, it's difficult to recall).

When we discovered later what had really happened, we were all devastated. For as long as I live, I'll never forget the sight of Tom Wheatcroft's crumpled figure, tears streaming down his cheeks. What became apparent afterwards was the clear discrepancy between the drivers' perspective and that of the television public. Millions watching 'sport' on television had witnessed a degrading spectacle, where – with David Purley the sole exception – the contestants did absolutely nothing to save one of their own but, instead, piled on lap after lap, passing the scene of the tragedy three or four times without stopping.

We may often be regarded as cold-hearted, egotistical and calculating, but there isn't one driver among us who wouldn't do everything in his power to pull another driver clear of a burning wreck. In the case of Roger Williamson, however, all sorts of factors came together: woefully inadequate track marshals, cowardice, confusion, incompetent race administration, and drivers who totally misinterpreted the evidence of their own eyes.

Some ill-considered remarks I myself made immediately after the race have long been held against me. Now, so long after the event, I can only say that I did not intentionally appear to be cynical or arrogant. We were all extremely upset and, seconds later, were being mobbed and jostled by reporters. In such circumstances it is very easy to give some brusque reply to get rid of an unwelcome interrogator. I look back on Zandvoort 1973 as one of the darkest days of my entire professional career.

As of July 1973 Enzo Ferrari had no further doubts about wanting me to drive for him. He sent an emissary to say as much.

Ferrari and BRM – what a contrast! The journalist Helmut Zwickl remarked at the time that it was like comparing NASA to a group of kite enthusiasts ...

Obviously I wanted to go to Ferrari, but I was committed to BRM for a further two years. I turned the situation over in my mind and came up with three good reasons for breaking the BRM contract in the autumn of 1973. I rationalised the situation as follows: first, Louis Stanley was behind in his payments to me (it was well known in those days that BRM payments were a long time in the pipeline); second, you can buy your way out of any contract providing you have the money (and

Ferrari was prepared to give me cash to pay the breach of contract penalty); third, the whole BRM set-up was demotivated and technically clueless (the team's demise was quite clearly only a matter of time).

It would have been asking a bit much to expect Louis Stanley to send me a good-luck telegram. His team disappeared from the racing scene, leaving only the proud record of the ace drivers of the sixties. Stanley himself popped up regularly and, after my Nürburgring shunt in 1976, he offered the services of a leading British surgeon. Later, in London, I had an opportunity to thank him personally for his most generous offer. When I think back on my dealings with Louis Stanley, I remember him less as the imperfect racing impresario and more as the perfect gentleman.

CHAPTER THREE

FERRARI

JOHN SURTEES WON the world championship for Ferrari in 1964. In the years that followed, Ferrari won an average of one race per season. By 1973 the team was in a shambles. Jacky Ickx and Arturo Merzario had a thankless task. Halfway through the season, when Ickx barely made qualifying with a nineteenth place on the grid at Silverstone, Ferrari made it to the start only in every other race.

Colombo was the technician held accountable, so – in mid-season 1973 – the brilliant Mauro Forghieri was called back from the wilderness. I have no notion why Forghieri was sent packing in the first place but, in all events, Ferrari gave him a second chance. Colombo concentrated on Ickx's car and Forghieri did what he could with Merzario's. To the world at large, however, the blame for Ferrari's disastrous showing rested squarely on the drivers.

I was invited down to meet Enzo Ferrari in the autumn of 1973. I was to drive a few laps of the test circuit in Fiorano, then tell the Old Man what my impressions were. (In those days I couldn't speak Italian, so Ferrari's son, Piero Lardi, was called in to interpret. Piero was illegitimate and, as such, not entitled to bear the Ferrari name, so sacred was the memory of Ferrari's 'real' son, Dino, who had died of leukaemia at the age of twenty-four. It was not until some time in the eighties that

Piero was fully acknowledged as a Ferrari and permitted to change his name accordingly.)

Back to autumn 1973. Well, asked Ferrari, what do you think of the car? A disaster, I replied. Piero cut in immediately: 'You can't say that.'

'Why not? The car understeers and doesn't corner worth a damn. It's undrivable.'

'No,' said Piero, 'you can't say that either.'

'All right then, tell him the car isn't quite set up properly, it has a tendency to understeer, and the front axle may have to be looked at.'

Piero translated for Ferrari's benefit.

Ferrari to Forghieri: 'How long will it take you to make the changes Lauda suggests?'

'One week.'

Ferrari to Lauda: 'If you are not one full second faster this time next week, you're out.'

Of course, I knew that Forghieri was already well on the way towards revamping the front axle to give the car a deeper roll centre, so I wasn't particularly alarmed by the Old Man's ultimatum. But I did realise what a can of worms I had opened. It was taken for granted that it couldn't conceivably be the cars that had made such a mess of the season; it had to be the drivers, Ickx and Merzario. By definition, a Ferrari was perfect. Telling someone like Enzo Ferrari that his cars are badly set up is simply not on.

I spent twenty-four hours a day for the whole of the next week looking over Forghieri's shoulder. His re-designed front axle proved such a substantial improvement that I had no difficulty at all saving my neck (for the first but by no means last time *chez* Ferrari).

One of Ferrari's minions once said of him: 'He is the figurehead, he is the marque, he is life itself.' That was entirely valid in the seventies and even in the eighties: it catches the spirit that fuelled the Ferrari legend and was a very real part of it.

When I first met Ferrari in 1973 he was already seventy-five years old – and looked it. He could exude great dignity making a public entrance but, in a more intimate circle, he was less impressive. He had a couple of odd habits: he would scratch himself in the most unlikely places, and hawk and spit for minutes on end, with obvious relish, into a gigantic handkerchief which, unfolded, was the size of a flag. He still had all his wits about him, however, and his remarks were perceptive and amusing. In the midst of all the dog-like devotion he seemed to engender, he retained a fine sense of gentle irony. A journalist once asked him how he, Enzo Ferrari, looked upon himself. 'When I look in the mirror in the morning,' replied Ferrari, 'even I don't understand myself.' (He added that some things in life are truly inexplicable.)

The tactless but nonetheless burning question all Italy asked – What would happen to the firm after his death? – would provoke the supremely imperious response: 'I feel no excitement at the prospect of what may come after me.'

For all this, Ferrari was thoroughly capable of the most unadulterated *schmaltz* and prone to declaiming like a latter-day D'Annunzio. When it was time to motivate the troops – notably in the course of the so-called 'Annual

Address' – his imagery would run to 'oaths of loyalty' and the 'anvil of work on which are forged the weapons of ultimate victory'.

Central to the Ferrari legend was his refusal to attend a race or even, except on the rarest of occasions, leave the Modena/Maranello region. Since Ferrari's house guests were few and far between, he tended to live in a world of his own, totally dependent on information supplied by his lackeys and gleaned from the press. It seems that it is completely impossible in Italy to say anything objectively or dispassionately on the subject of Ferrari, with the result that personal prejudices on the one hand and vested interests on the other spawned great mounds of newsprint which, every now and then, had an unfortunate tendency to collapse on top of one Ferrari employee or another. Enzo Ferrari was never in a position to sift these newspaper reports for truth and accuracy; accordingly, Ferrari drivers, Ferrari team bosses and Ferrari technicians were continually pressurised by the media. The upshot was that virtually no newcomer to Ferrari could arrive under normal, calm conditions. There was always furore at Ferrari – from Fangio to Alboreto.

When all the temperamental aspects of sport and life with Ferrari were channelled in the right direction, the potential was enormous, particularly when you consider the technical back-up available and the possibility of direct and immediate access to the Fiorano test circuit no more than a couple of hundred yards from the factory gates in Maranello. No other Formula 1 squad has such facilities permanently at its disposal.

When Clay Regazzoni and I were test driving at Fiorano, *Il Commendatore* would almost invariably put in an appearance, often sitting there the whole day devouring newspaper after newspaper. The sound of his cars in the background seemed to have a therapeutic effect on him. Frequently, he would lunch in the tiny restaurant he had had installed at the circuit. He always knew what the tests were about – front axle, exhaust, whatever – and made sure that he was kept continuously in the picture. Not that there seemed much point to this, for he never came up with any technical advice. Nevertheless, the decision-making process ran its regular course all the way up the hierarchy to the boss and back down again to technician, manager or driver.

In a situation like this, it was clearly imperative to speak directly to Ferrari and circumvent his lackeys and informers. In the final analysis, all he really knew about what was going on in the world was based on snippets of information fed to him by his 'sources'; the technique of keeping the Old Man happy was often more important than technique *per se.* He wasn't the avuncular type: he was the Lord and one feared His wrath.

Every day we test drove I would make a point of making direct contact with the boss and, if he didn't happen to show up at Fiorano on the day in question, I would drive over to the factory and go straight to his office, unannounced. I would knock discreetly, hear the command to enter, and open the door to the famous grotto with its impressive dark-blue walls and the portrait of Ferrari's late son on the wall opposite his writing desk. No one else in the outfit seemed to have the nerve to seek a direct audience in this way, but the Old Man didn't appear to mind in the least. In any case, it certainly made my life at Ferrari a lot easier, and unquestionably paved the way for technical improvements to the extent that I was able to influence Forghieri and keep the development impetus going.

Luca di Montezemolo, Ferrari's team chief, was a fully fledged protégé of the Agnelli (Fiat) dynasty; he was very young but he was good. Because of his social background he was largely proof against the daily round of intrigue, and this meant that he could concentrate on the real job in hand, something of a privileged position for a Ferrari team chief. Off the top of my head, I can't think of anyone in that position before or after who enjoyed the same freedom.

The public image of a dynamic, forward-looking and totally integrated squad was marvellously rounded off by the presence of Clay Regazzoni. For me, he was the ideal team partner; our relative positions in the Ferrari stable were to develop as time went on.

Off duty, I always got on incredibly well with Regazzoni. We led a pretty hectic life. To the Italian public he was the original macho man, a no-holds-barred womaniser, and I must say that it was anything but dull being in his company. I have never since had a teammate whom I hung around with so much after hours. He was honest and direct. You could tell what was going through his mind by the expression on his face: when something didn't suit him, he let you know at once. To be honest, though, I have to admit that he was a little in the shadow of the Lauda/Montezemolo pairing.

We could have won the world championship in 1974. I had my chances and threw them away, then Regazzoni lost a last-ditch battle for the title because of technical problems. Fittipaldi took the crown for McLaren.

The following year, 1975, saw the magnificent Ferrari 312 T, a permanent monument to Mauro Forghieri's skill, a gem of a car. As of Monaco, I had the world championship by the scruff of the neck. Monaco was the first in a golden series of wins: Monaco, Zolder, Anderstorp, Le Castellet and, once the title was in the bag, Watkins Glen.

In many respects, my life changed almost overnight. On the surface, the main difference was in terms of popularity. Two wins in the previous season (the 1974 Dutch and Spanish Grand Prix) were enough for everyone in Austria to know me simply as 'Niki'. The Germans adopted me to some extent. And in Italy, of course, it was a case of Lauda, Lauda, Lauda, because of the Ferrari connection.

Right from the start being famous did not mean all that much to me. At most, it changed me in the sense that I tried to keep my private life intact by withdrawing into specific enclaves – a tighter circle of friends, a very small number of favourite restaurants, spending more time at home.

My newly discovered passion for flying fitted in perfectly. What had first appealed to me only from a technical point of view had suddenly acquired practical value. A small plane of my own would at least dramatically shorten travelling time between Salzburg and Modena. I started to take flying lessons and bought myself a Cessna Golden Eagle (for which I initially had to hire a pilot). By 1975 I could afford this kind of expenditure, because my income from Ferrari was spectacular by comparison with anything I had previously earned (although it was ridiculously low by present-day standards), and I was still doing well in terms of starting money from the BMW-Alpina Team.

Between Mariella and myself, however, things were going less well. I would be hard pressed to give any specific reasons, that's just the way it was. Nevertheless, I was determined to move with Mariella out of the tiny Salzburg apartment, and we commissioned an architect to build a house in *Salzburgerland*, on a superb site between Fuschlsee and Thalgau in the commune of Hof, a mere ten minutes from Salzburg airport. Mariella spent her days discussing plans with the architect.

One summer day in 1975, the actor Curd Jürgens threw a party at his home in Salzburg. I had as little time for that sort of thing then as I have now but, one way or another, Mariella and I went along. Karajan was there and we chatted about cars. Curd Jürgens couldn't have been more friendly, and everything was far more enjoyable than we had anticipated. A young lady caught my eye, very attractive and vivacious, her deep tan beautifully accentuated by a white dress. At one point during the evening she came over to where I was sitting, knelt down in front of me, and put her hands on my knees. Although we had never clapped eyes on each other before that evening, it seemed perfectly natural for her to use the familiar *Du* form of address: 'What can I get you to drink?'

I asked for some mineral water and she brought me a glass. I was taken by the nice, open way she had spoken to me and the warm friendliness of her expression. I asked someone who she was. 'Oh, that's Marlene, Curd Jürgens' girlfriend,' came the reply. In other words, the hostess. That was all there was to it.

The next day I bumped into Lemmy Hofer. He told me to wait for a second, he had a surprise for me. He left me in the garden of the Friesacher Hotel and came back moments later with Marlene. I was too shy to say much to her and the whole situation was decidedly awkward. Lemmy and I rattled on about some trivia or other, then I said I had to leave for a flying lesson. The young lady had somehow deduced from our conversation that I was a racing driver. (The previous evening she had been told that I was the well-known sports personality Niki Lauda, but her first guess had been that I was probably a tennis player.) As I was leaving, she asked: 'And what does a racing driver do in his spare time?'

I mumbled some kind of sophisticated reply: 'It all depends. Nothing much. Why?'

'Oh, I was just curious.'

I couldn't keep my mind on the flying lesson that afternoon. The following day I got Curd Jürgens' telephone number and called his house. Luckily he wasn't there. Marlene was. How did she feel about going out somewhere with me?

I was already something of a public figure and, as a result, had to watch where I went and with whom, so we drove out of Salzburg to Freilassing.

When Marlene contracted pneumonia I went to visit her in hospital in Salzburg. She told me that she was being discharged that day. Nothing could have been further from the truth; in fact, she was supposed to stay obediently tucked up in bed. She skipped through an open window and we drove up the *Gaisberg* to an ancient inn, where I seem to remember five peasants sitting round playing cards.

From then on, everything was settled.

Marlene flew back to her family on Ibiza. I rounded up my pilot, Herr Kremetinger, and told him that we had to fly to Ibiza urgently. That's a bit far, he said (we only had the Golden Eagle at the time), but I replied that I couldn't care less, we were taking off at four that afternoon. I told Mariella some story about a jeans advertising contract I had to negotiate in Barcelona.

Off we flew to Ibiza. We landed about midnight and Marlene was there waiting at the landing strip. She dragged us off to see Ibiza by night. Then I was introduced to the marvellously chaotic Knaus family: mother, sister Renate and brother Tilly. Her mother was Spanish, and the children had been born in Venezuela (Marlene), Chile and Spain. Everything about them was somehow 'southern': incredibly warm and relaxed – in short, a total contrast to my everyday life up to then, with all its self-discipline, ambition and drive. I was captivated.

For the time being nothing would be said until I could clear up the situation between myself and Mariella. First I had to spend two weeks in the States test driving for Ferrari before the US Grand Prix in Watkins Glen.

It rained and rained in Watkins Glen and I did very little driving, so I sat around kicking my heels and had ample time to think things out. After the race I flew back immediately to meet Marlene at the Friesacher. I must go home, I told her. I can't stay out the first evening back here after two weeks in America. In that case, she said, I'll drive up to Vienna, because Curd has asked me to check how things are at his place.

I went home, draped my jacket over the back of a chair, looked at Mariella and suddenly it hit me: this won't work. My God, I said, I've forgotten to go to the bank in Vienna (by this time, it was already evening). I snatched up my jacket and left. I screeched down to the Friesacher, panic-stricken that Marlene might have already set off for Vienna. I caught up with her just as she was getting into her car. 'Hold everything. I'm here – and I'm staying here.'

Our secret wasn't kept for very long. The Austrian press got wind of it and the *Kurier* ran a spread on Niki Lauda and Curd Jürgens' girlfriend.

Marlene and I married in spring 1976 at the registry office in Vienna-Neustadt. They were most helpful there: the registrar set a time for the ceremony outside normal registry hours so that there wouldn't be any circus with the press. He was scandalised, however, that I hadn't bothered to wear a tie. I borrowed one from my best man, Dr Oertel, and the whole affair went off beautifully.

The 1976 season started with a bang. The Ferraris left all the other marques standing. I won the first two races and Regazzoni the third. With hindsight, everything was going just a shade too smoothly.

The first hint of trouble came with the departure of my friend and ally Luca di Montezemolo, who had to make a career for himself and couldn't afford to stay on the lower rungs of the ladder as team chief indefinitely; Luca was promoted closer to the seat of power in the Fiat dynasty.

His successor, Daniele Audetto, as fraught a personality as any surrounding Ferrari, promptly got involved in the day-to-day intrigues in an effort to carve out a niche for himself.

Then came the ridiculous business with the tractor.

I was trying to shift a mound of earth from the meadow in front of my house when I somehow managed to tip the tractor right over on top of myself. A couple of inches either way and it would have been really serious. As it was, I was pinned to the ground and ended up with two broken ribs – all things considered, not too bad for a shunt with a 1.8-ton tractor, but the pain was excruciating.

What was worse, the press got hold of the story – you can hardly blame them; a Formula 1 world champion crushed by a tractor makes pretty good copy.

At Ferrari all hell broke loose. There were frantic comings and goings. All the races I had won for Ferrari had still not silenced one particular section of the Italian press which constantly clamoured for an Italian driver behind the wheel of Italy's best-known marque. As soon as the news leaked out about my accident with the tractor, they sensed an opportunity to promote an Italian into the cockpit. There just happened to be a young lad called Flammini around who had had a good result in Formula 2; he would be an automatic choice.

Tempers ran high and, in the heat of the moment, I paid scant attention to what I said. I came out with a few choice remarks, notably to the effect that Ferrari could take a long walk off a short pier. The *Gazzetta dello Sport* ran that in a banner headline and all Italy was up in arms.

Ferrari despatched a personal ambassador, Sante Ghedini (later to be a close colleague of mine and, as PR director at Parmalat, the man behind the logo on my cap). Ghedini was driven flat-out overnight from Maranello to Salzburg. He arrived *chez* Lauda in the early hours, brandished a broom handle to chase off the reporters round the front door, and fired off communiqués to Ferrari.

I was lying there in bed in absolute agony when a Salzburg radio reporter called Klettner appeared with a man called Willy Dungl in tow. I had never met Dungl, but had heard a tremendous amount about him: masseur, guru, dietician, layer-on-of-hands, the miracle-worker behind the then sensational exploits of Austria's ski-jumping squad.

My first encounter with Dungl went more or less as follows. I am lying in bed, hardly able to move because the pain is so intense. The miracle-worker is announced. Bring him in, say I. In comes Dungl. Badly dressed. Grumpy. A grunted *Guten Tag*. He looks me over and listens to what has happened. He makes no move to touch me. He offers his diagnosis: 'Can't do a thing for you. If you want me to try, you'll have to get yourself over to Vienna.' Exit Dungl. There, I thought to myself, must be the world's biggest pain in the ass.

At the time, I had a comfortable lead in the world championship (24 points after three races, with the second-place man on 10). But there were panic stations at Ferrari and I felt the pressure. I was determined to do everything I could to start in the next race. So, ignoring the additional discomfort involved, I 'got myself over to Vienna' for treatment at the hands of Poigenfürst, a superb surgeon in accident cases, and Willy Dungl (who frequently worked with him on problem patients).

Dungl told me that I had rehabilitated myself in his eyes because I had made the effort to come to see him in Vienna; up until then, he had always regarded me as an arrogant type of sportsman who neglected his body. If I would categorically state that I was willing to do something for my physical well-being from then on, he would treat me.

From that moment, Willy Dungl has been one of the most important people in my career and my life. There is no one to touch him; he is simply a genius. His knowledge, his sensitivity, his touch, his methods – I simply cannot imagine that there is another like him anywhere in the world. He has helped me rediscover my own body and, at thirty-six, I'm in better shape physically than I was ten years ago. He convinced me to alter my eating habits and, in each instance, explained the reason for the change in a way that I could understand and accept.

This said, Willy is still one of the most bad-tempered people in the world. It is virtually impossible to hold a telephone conversation with him: he is so unfriendly that you feel like hanging up after a couple of seconds, because you don't know what to say next. Those who like their conversations on the spicy side would revel in the repartee between Willy and his wife. However, seeing that Willy and Gusti have just celebrated their silver wedding anniversary, I can't imagine that there is all that much wrong. What is more, very few people knew that, for years, Willy suffered from a serious kidney complaint. He had a successful kidney transplant in the summer of 1985, so we'll all have to wait and see whether his moods improve.

Let me divulge one astonishing fact about Willy Dungl: those golden hands of his turn into brass the moment he puts them on a steering wheel. He has an unerring instinct for selecting the wrong gear and a delightful stubbornness in staying with it. Of course, there is no way you can discuss his driving with him; he is as contrary as a mule and it only makes him more bad-tempered.

There was a classic instance a couple of years ago when we were in South Africa together. The local Mercedes dealer let me have a beautiful metallic-gold Mercedes 380 SE to run around in. I turned it over to Willy to do the daily shopping for fresh fruit and vegetables, on the strict understanding that he would acknowledge three simple facts: first, in South Africa, you drive on the left; second, when you're driving, the lever is moved to the 'drive' position; and third, when you park, you put on the handbrake.

For the first few days everything worked out a treat. Every time Willy came back from the stores I would casually stroll around the Mercedes and check. No visible damage. I have always had enough self-respect to want to return a borrowed car in pristine condition – hence my enthusiasm at Willy's remarkable progress.

Then, at Saturday qualifying, no Willy. I am already strapped into the McLaren cockpit. I call out to Ron Dennis, 'Where's Willy?' Ron makes a placatory gesture: 'I can't tell you that now.' Of course, this is just about the most stupid answer of all. I'm worried. I have to know what has happened. Eventually, the truth emerges.

Willy is shopping at the greengrocer's when suddenly – quite inexplicably – the metallic-gold Merc decides to inch forward, gather speed, plough through the display stands outside and smash through the shopfront. The damage is considerable, the commotion huge. I don't understand it, says Willy, as he is taken to the police station, furious with the Mercedes.

Later, he embellished the story: two men, intent on holding up the greengrocer's, pushed the car through the shopfront display to create a diversion. Any explanation will suffice, other than that Willy simply forgot to apply the handbrake. I dropped the subject as quickly as I could – I was getting nowhere and Willy's mood was darkening by the minute. Anyway, when all is said and done, I'm supposed to be the driver in this partnership and he looks after everything else. A genius. I have an infinite amount to thank him for.

Back to 1976. Dungl actually managed to get me fit for Jarama, although we pushed right to the limit and it could very easily have gone wrong. In a tight manoeuvre – jockeying for position with James Hunt – a broken rib popped out in the wrong direction and just missed piercing a lung. The pain was unbearable. After the race, Willy carefully massaged the rib back into position again. Magic.

My second place in Jarama was worth six valuable championship points. But I had really had to struggle desperately for them. It was a foretaste of things to come both in my personal life and in my relationship with Ferrari.

Meantime, however, I was on a winning streak: Zolder, Monaco, Brands Hatch. After the first nine races of the 1976 season I had amassed 61 world championship points. The two drivers running neck-and-neck behind me in second place were James Hunt in the McLaren and Patrick Depailler in the Tyrell – and they were way back on 26 points each.

In a major departure from standard Ferrari practice, I was urged to extend my contract right there and then, in the middle of the season. Ferrari wanted to forestall any unpleasant surprise later on. As a rule, Enzo Ferrari had the nasty habit of keeping his drivers on the hook until there were no other rides available – this was his way of exerting pressure on the contract price, and the Old Man looked on himself as a shrewd tactician. In 1976, however, *Il Commendatore* had every interest in settling things with me as soon as possible.

I described the pantomime that ensued during the contract negotiations in an earlier book – *For the Record** – and I can do no more than repeat now what I said then.

I am sitting with the Old Man and his son, Piero Lardi, in a back room of the Cavallino Restaurant opposite the Ferrari factory in Maranello. By this time my Italian is quite serviceable but, for this kind of negotiation, Lardi is always called in to interpret between English and Italian.

The Old Man starts by saying that he would like me to stay on for the 1977 season. What would that involve? 'A team with two drivers,' I reply. 'On no account three, because that

* *For the Record* (William Kimber, London, 1977).

will be too much for the technicians and mechanics to handle.' I add that I would like Regazzoni to stay on in the Number Two slot. That won't be easy, says the Old Man, because I intend to suspend him. The conversation goes back and forth and I keep repeating that I would be happy if Regazzoni stayed on.

Suddenly, Ferrari brings up the subject of money. How much am I asking? I give him an amount in schillings: so-and-so many million. He says nothing, stands up, goes over to the telephone, calls his accountant Della Casa, and asks him how much so-and-so many million schillings are in lire. He waits for a reply, replaces the receiver, walks back across the room and sits down facing me. Then he *screams* at me – I've never heard anything like it in my life. 'You insolent pig, how dare you? Are you crazy? We have nothing more to say to each other. We are parting company as of this minute.'

He pauses for breath as Piero rapidly translates the last in a string of obscenities (it is handy having an interpreter in this kind of negotiation; his interposition somehow makes the expletives a shade more abstract).

I turn to Piero. Please tell him that as we are parting company I'll be flying home immediately. Piero says: 'Sit where you are,' and on it goes, back and forth, to and fro, until I finally say that Ferrari should make me a counter-offer.

No, says Ferrari, he can't make a counter-offer, because he only wants his drivers to be happy and any counter-offer he makes will only make me unhappy. In that case, I say, I really will fly home, because there's surely no point to this if he won't accept my price and he won't make a counter-offer.

At last Ferrari names a figure, a good 25 per cent below mine and expressed in lire. I blow my top and say to Piero he should tell him that his team chief has already offered me a few million more lire than that. Is he trying to make a fool of me? I am genuinely angry now because of the lack of mutual respect: we are equal partners – he wants to buy my services and that is what they cost.

'What's that you say about Audetto?' yells the Old Man.

'Call him in and ask him.'

Audetto is called. How much did he offer me? Is that the amount? 'That's right,' says Audetto. 'That's what I offered him.'

'Well,' says Ferrari, 'if one of my employees is mad enough to offer that kind of money, I guess I'll have to go along with it.' Audetto is sent out of the room ('I'll talk to you later').

'But that's my final offer,' bellows Ferrari.

As a sign of goodwill, I come down a percentage point from my original demand. Very calm. Ferrari calms down too: 'You're incorrigible. It's mad, it's too much, enough is enough. Think about my nerves. What are you trying to do, kill me?'

I turn to Piero: 'Tell him that Ferrari would never have been world champion without me.'

Piero: 'No, I can't translate that, I won't.'

'Go on, don't be a coward. Tell him. Now.'

Piero braces himself. He is blushing. He translates.

Ferrari starts his bellowing again. We go at it for another hour or so until he finally asks again: 'How much do you want?' And I drop another 4 per cent. My final offer.

'Okay, *ebreo*,' says Ferrari. Okay, Jew-boy.

He's entitled to say that – he's paying.

The next moment he is pleasant and friendly again. A charming old man, the most delightful company anyone could imagine.

CHAPTER FOUR

NÜRBURGRING

I CRASHED AT the Nürburgring on 1 August 1976.

The media have played it up as some kind of personal vendetta or overdramatised the whole business along the lines of a Man and his Destiny. They contrived to make a mystery out of something that never existed. Let me start from the beginning.

I first came into contact with the Ring in 1969 as a twenty-year-old driving Formula Vee. We all thought being there was fantastic and went at it hammer and tongs. If you spun out, you ploughed through the shrubbery and it swallowed you up. When all that greenery closed in behind you, no one knew where you were. We didn't think that was at all bad, only exciting.

By the early seventies I had become more and more involved with the Ring – technically, that is, not emotionally. My ambition was to drive the Ring perfectly and, because it is such an enormously long circuit, it offered so much more in the way of a challenge than any other.

I drove the Ring in my Touring Class days and, in 1973, I clocked 8:17.4 in a twin-valve BMW, sending shivers down the spectators' spines.

I had shunts on the Ring, too. In 1973 I went for a 300-yard sleigh-ride along one of the embankments. And, in 1974, I collided with Jody Scheckter. Well, that's all part of the sport.

By then, however, a lot of drivers were being killed – on the Ring as well as on other circuits all over the world. It was increasingly plain that, as lap times got faster and faster, we were endangering not only our lives but the sport of motor racing itself, by failing to do something about track safety. Responsible drivers, responsible journalists and responsible race officials started working to improve matters, with Jackie Stewart as standard-bearer.

The problems posed by the Nürburgring were obvious at a glance. Its layout made it the most difficult circuit imaginable. It was well-nigh impossible to render safe 14.2 miles of tree-lined track. In the long term, a circuit like the Ring couldn't survive. However, a three-year programme (1974–76) was launched to make some improvements, as regards guard-rails, for example. Even so, it was certain that the FIA, as the sport's governing body was known then, would subsequently withdraw the Ring's licence.

The year I won my first world championship – 1975 – saw the ultimate madness: a first-ever Nürburgring lap under seven minutes. This came during Saturday qualifying and was possible only because I was in a special sort of mood that day and ready to go for broke to an extent I have never permitted myself since. As I flashed past the pits I glanced in my rear-view mirror and saw the mechanics waving their hands in the air. I knew then that I had cracked the seven-minute barrier. To be exact, my new Formula 1 lap record was 6:58.6. And that's how it stands to this day – no one has ever driven the Ring faster. (The record books show how times improved over the years: the ten-minute barrier was broken by Hermann Lang in a Mercedes in 1939; Phil Hill clocked under nine minutes in a Ferrari in 1961; and Jackie Stewart came home in under eight minutes in a Matra in 1968.)

I steeled myself to drive that fast lap in 1975 although my brain kept telling me it was sheer stupidity. The antithesis between the modern-day racing car and the Stone Age circuit was such that I knew every driver was taking his life in his hands to the most ludicrous degree.

At a drivers' meeting in spring 1976 I proposed that we boycott the Ring. I was voted down and I accepted the decision; after all, I had to admit that a considerable amount of money had been spent to step up safety precautions. However, the mere fact that I had made such a proposal was enough to spark off the legend of Lauda and the Ring and the antagonism I felt towards it. That was nonsense – I had merely expressed a professional opinion.

My shunt came later that season. At the end of the year the FIA licence for the Nürburgring was automatically withdrawn. These two facts were wholly coincidental. The FIA move had nothing to do with what happened to me.

Reporters have urged me repeatedly to return to the scene of the shunt, to act out, as it were, some kind of pious ritual. God knows what they expect of me: that I'll let my emotions run riot and burst into tears? Or that, by being back at the scene again, all the minutiae of the drama will come flooding back? Unfortunately for them, when I do go back and look at that harmless left-hander that we always took flat-out, I'm more liable to say, 'Ah, yes, the Grill Room.' And they'll go away thinking what a cold bastard that Lauda is.

Returning to the spot where it all took place stirs no emotions in me at all. Even if I go back fifty times, it will always leave me cold.

I recall bits before. I recall bits after. But I recollect nothing during, not a damn thing. Except a big, black hole.

I arrive the previous Thursday and drive through the team trailer park in my own private car. I am caught in a small traffic jam. A man comes over to the car and shoves a picture through the open window: Jochen Rindt's grave. He is plainly quite delighted with himself because he has been able to show it to me. What is he trying to say? What kind of reaction am I supposed to have? I have no idea.

That scene comes to mind because there was a lot of talk about death then, and the idea seems to have given certain people a kind of perverse pleasure.

Next, I remember a sports programme on television. I am watching it in my hotel room in Adenau. Someone is ranting about that cowardly so-and-so Lauda who is at the root of all this anti-Nürburgring campaign. What it comes down to is this: if Lauda is so chicken-hearted, so terrified, then he should get out of Formula 1. Sitting there alone in front of the TV set, I was absolutely livid, knotted with rage at my inability to defend myself.

I remember bumping into Helmut Zwickl, the journalist, early on Sunday morning. He tells me that the *Reichsbrücke* has collapsed. This is simply incredible: the biggest bridge in all Austria has toppled into the Danube, just like that. But because it happens in the early hours of a Sunday morning, only one life has been lost, not a couple of hundred as might otherwise have been the case. I don't know what to make of this grotesque piece of news. I am stunned. I have to get it out of my mind as quickly as possible.

My last recollection before the race is of changing from wets to slicks and driving away from the pits.

Next, the chatter of a helicopter. I'm lying in bed. I'm tired. I want to sleep. I don't want to know any more. It will all be over soon.

Only after four days in intensive care did it emerge that I would pull through. Serious damage had been done to my lungs and blood as a result of inhaling the smoke and petrol fumes. The burns on my face, head and hands were severe but not critical, although the scars they left are more permanent.

Mercifully, I wasn't in a fit state to read a newspaper. *Bild* ran one headline which asked: 'My God, where is his face?' The piece explained: 'Niki Lauda, the world's fastest racing driver, no longer has a face. It is no more than raw flesh with eyes oozing out of it.' Once I was over the worst (but, fortunately, still unable to read the newspaper reports), *Bild* ran a follow-up: 'Niki Lauda has survived … but how can a man exist without a face?' The story then went on to forecast what life would be like for Lauda: 'How can he *face* life *without* a face? Horrible as it may sound, even if his body recovers completely, he will not venture into public for six months at least. It will be 1979 before they can build him a new face. By then, nose, eyelids and lips will have been refashioned. But the new face will not bear the slightest resemblance to the one he had before. Lauda the racing driver will only be recognisable to his friends through his voice and his gestures.'

Admit it, I seem to have done a bit better than they predicted.

As soon as I had been discharged from hospital in Mannheim and brought back home to Salzburg, I was shown a film of the shunt taken by a fifteen-year-old boy with his 8-mm movie camera. It showed my Ferrari jerking right, crashing through the safety netting, slamming into the embankment and bouncing back onto the track. The whole incident must have taken place at or around 125mph. As the car rebounded onto the circuit, you could see the petrol tank flying through the air. The Ferrari was straddling the ideal line as Brett Lunger came through, smashing into it and pushing it some hundred yards down the track. It burst into flames.

Other photographic evidence uncovered later shows how powerless the safety marshal was without fire-proof clothing. Also how other drivers – Guy Edwards, Brett Lunger, Harald Ertl – tried to rescue me. But my real saviour was Arturo Merzario, who plunged into the flames with total disregard for his own life and unbuckled my safety harness.

When I saw the first film, I obviously knew that that was *me*, that something was happening to *me*. But, somehow, I felt completely detached from it – it was a horrendous shunt that *someone* was involved in, but I couldn't relate what I was seeing to *myself*. I didn't remember. There was no correlation between the film and my present state; the driver on the screen was a total stranger. There it all was: jack-knife, impact, slide, flames. 'Look at that. God Almighty, look at that.'

No official statement was ever released as to the cause of the shunt. No comment was forthcoming from Ferrari and I clearly could contribute nothing because my memory had been erased. Today, I would hazard a guess as to the probable cause. It is very close to the theory propounded right from the start by Ferrari's head mechanic at the time, Ermanno Cuoghi.

The engine unit in a modern racing car is a load-bearing component. It is connected to the suspension via a magnesium tie-rod, part of the car's steering mechanism. Cuoghi thought that the tie-rod rear left detached from the engine unit. When this happens, the rear wheel mounting goes, and the wheel angles out and blocks. This would account for the sudden jerk to the right. Cuoghi knew that Ferrari had encountered problems with this before.

I seem to remember now, however, that, just before the shunt, I had driven over a kerb with my left front wheel. This was unintentional, of course, but the lapse was an insignificant one to the extent that the kerbs at the Ring are shallow and, as such, comparatively harmless. It is feasible, however, that the shock of the impact went right through the car.

I have always claimed that Nürburgring had no lasting effect on my state of mind, my attitude, my performance. This is true, although I am uncertain as to what extent having gone through that inferno affects me subconsciously.

Basically, my talent for overriding my emotions by staying detached and objective has served me well. There is really no point in having a complex about losing half an ear. Take a good look at yourself in the mirror: that's you, that's the way you are. And if people don't like you that way you might as well forget them. (I even capitalised on my semi-baldness by signing with Parmalat to wear a cap with their name on it;

even now I'm retired, that cap still has the same promotional value.)

Waking or sleeping, the shunt doesn't haunt or obsess me, since I did not consciously experience the flames. Once, and only once, was there any throwback to my fight for survival. That was in 1984, on Ibiza.

A friend of ours had left a joint at our place. Cannabis is quite popular on Ibiza, although Marlene and I don't normally touch the stuff. Nevertheless, there must have been something that night that persuaded us to light up.

We are sitting upstairs in the living room. Nothing happens for twenty minutes or so, but then it hits me so intensely that I realise afterwards that the stuff we are smoking must be something special.

We are speaking about this and that, and start laughing at the most trivial statements. Eventually, the laughter gets so bad that Marlene can't stop. I am lying on the couch and my body starts to feel so heavy that I can't move a muscle. It is beautiful lying there in a stupor, my tongue lolling out of the corner of my mouth.

Marlene clearly feels the effects less than I do. Suddenly, she is completely lucid – and concerned about my condition. Concentrate, she keeps saying, concentrate, do something. But I just lie there, blissfully happy, saying over and over: 'Got to get out of here.' Somewhere at the back of my mind I know that something is wrong, but the way I feel is too pleasurable to want to do anything about it.

Marlene won't let go. Do something! DO SOMETHING! Click your fingers! I hold up two fingers, focus and try to click them.

They move in the wrong direction. Marlene is getting more and more alarmed. Panicking. Let's talk about something, she says. Anything. Say the first thing that comes into your head. Who invented penicillin?

'Mr Penicillin.'

I am completely out of my mind.

Suddenly, it hits me. Nürburgring. Intensive-care unit. I am falling into a big black hole. I am slipping backwards, somersaulting into a huge void, and that will be the end of it. Please let me die, I say to Marlene. It's such a beautiful feeling. I am falling. Weightless. Exactly like it was in the intensive-care unit.

Cut it out, says Marlene. Get on your feet. I have great difficulty standing up. Then I start to play the fool. After what seems like a long time Marlene suggests we get some sleep.

I go into the bathroom and become fascinated by the hole in the washbasin. Another hole. I gaze down into it. There it is again. Let me fall into it. But Marlene hasn't left me on my own, she is right there behind me. She boots my behind. That's enough, you idiot.

For me, however, the situation is not in the least bit funny – it is deadly serious. There is the hole and I want to fall into it, just the way I felt after Nürburgring.

In the intensive-care unit it was snatches of conversation – the surgeon, Marlene – which forced me to start thinking again, gradually piecing together the situation I was in and beginning to will myself out of it. I had to live. I had to get my brain working. I must not give in to this beautiful feeling of slipping into the hole. Clinging desperately to a tiny scrap of reality – a conversation between two human beings – helped me to survive.

I slept very badly that night in Ibiza and was still in a daze the next morning. I went into a café in Santa Eulalia and grinned vacantly at all the customers. The seriousness had deserted me: I was feeling gregarious, *gemütlich.*

Once I returned to normal I swore that I would never touch that stuff again. Even though the experience was fascinating to the extent that it had allowed me to recapture exactly my mental state after Nürburgring. That was the only time in the ten years since the shunt that any involuntary associations had caught up with me.

I made a quick recovery as far as damage to the vital organs was concerned, but my superficial injuries turned out to be more complicated.

Both eyelids had been burnt away, and six different surgeons volunteered six different opinions on how best to effect repairs. I finally opted for an eye surgeon in St Gallen, Switzerland. He took skin from behind the ears to graft on new eyelids. They worked perfectly for a few years, but the right eye started playing up towards the end of 1982. The lower lid wouldn't close completely, not even when I was asleep, and the eye became seriously inflamed.

I went to the most celebrated man in the field, Ivo Pitanguy, the Michelangelo of plastic surgery, or so I once read afterwards. He lives in Rio, but I made contact with him initially by going up to Gstaad, where Michelangelo was skiing.

He took one look at me and his eyes lit up. He spent only a second or two examining the real problem area, the lower lid of the right eye, but everything else had his rapt attention. The missing half of my right ear, the eyebrows, the scar tissue. Beautiful, he said. We'll take out some rib cartilage and build you a completely new ear; we'll take hair from the back of your head and fix up some new eyebrows; we'll fix the bald patch on the right-hand side while we're at it; we'll transplant from here, and so on. He was in his element.

It took me a good half-hour to make him understand that I would be racing again when the new season got under way in three months' time and that the only thing I was concerned about was having my right eye fixed. That would take time enough on its own, and I didn't want a new right ear made of rib cartilage.

Pitanguy was visibly dejected that he couldn't talk me into a complete overhaul but would have to settle instead for a 500-mile service. We finally fixed a date and I flew down to Rio with Marlene and Lukas. That was Lukas' first flight, which helped make the trip more pleasant.

At the clinic they anaesthetised me. I woke up four or five hours later with both eyes bandaged, feeling nauseous. After three days I was allowed back to our hotel, with only the repaired eye still bandaged. A strip of skin just under an inch long and a ¼-inch wide had been transplanted from the back of my head to the lower eyelid. To immobilise it, upper and lower lids had been sewn together.

I healed quickly. The transplanted skin was not rejected and, after a week, the stitches were removed. I couldn't see a thing. The problem was that the pupil, for the first time in years, had been in contact with an eyelid and had become severely irritated. After a few days, however, everything was working normally and my eye problems ceased.

As for all the other damage – ear, forehead and head – that can stay. I'm not going to have cosmetic surgery; as long as they function unimpaired, I don't feel the need.

CHAPTER FIVE

LIFE GOES ON

MANY PEOPLE WOULD have thought it fitting for me to spend the first few months after Nürburgring 1976 in a darkened room surrounded by peace and quiet. My matter-of-factness in automatically resuming my career as soon as all systems were go was disconcerting: some thought it betrayed a lack of dignity, others found it downright unappetising.

At Ferrari, of course, my return caused some confusion. It seemed to me that there wasn't a single person in the entire Ferrari set-up who could take a pragmatic line and stick to it. Daniele Audetto thought he was 'acting in my interest' by making clandestine overtures to have the Austrian Grand Prix cancelled. What I really needed from the squad was a sense of composure, a feeling of continuity, trust. Fat chance. To the outside world, Enzo Ferrari and his company were standing by their slightly singed world champion but, from the inside, the pitiful insecurity of each and every one of them was palpable. Tactics took precedence over trust.

As far as trust was concerned, I had to knock some together by myself, aided and abetted by Marlene, who was simply wonderful, and Willy Dungl, who put my body back in shape for walking, running and, finally, racing.

The only logical step appeared to me to get back into the world championship arena as soon as I could hold a wheel properly. Some of the newspapers said at the time that I must have burnt out a few circuits in my brain as well, but my chosen course of action was the best I could have taken for my physical and mental wellbeing. Lying in bed ruminating about the Ring would have finished me. Accordingly, I went back to work as soon as I possibly could – at Monza, thirty-three days after the shunt. I had missed two races and ceded 12 world championship points of my lead over James Hunt. Those points were to prove costly.

I said then and later on that I had conquered my fear quickly and cleanly. That was a lie, but it would have been foolish to tell the truth and play into the hands of my rivals by confirming my weakness. At Monza I was rigid with fear. Training in the rain on the Friday before the race was so terrifying that I got out of the car at the first available opportunity. Naturally, I had to play the hero to buy myself enough time to sort things out. The fact is you have to play the hard man on occasions, whether you actually feel like one or not. It is really all a game of mental hide-and-seek: you would never be forgiven if you blurted out the truth at an inopportune moment. You would be finished.

The Monza situation was a new experience for me. I had employed my standard tactics – objective review of emotions, establish causes, dismiss any illogical and irrelevant items – and I was well primed mentally. I had also shrugged off the Nürburgring shunt, or at least I thought I had. I said to myself: you could drive before, so you can do it exactly the same way now. And, since nothing has changed, there is nothing to be worried about.

Great, but in the event it didn't work out that way. When I climbed into the cockpit at Monza, fear hit me so hard that all my self-motivation theories flew out the window. Diarrhoea. Heart pounding. Throwing up. I made it back to the peace and quiet of the hotel and went over the situation in my mind, trying to identify what I had done wrong.

What I *had* done wrong, in fact, was attempt to drive as fast as I had done before the shunt, quite irrespective of my weakened condition on the one hand and the rain on the other. I had felt insecure and had overreacted. I hadn't held the car in check as I usually would have done; I simply hadn't used my expertise to take control of it. I had over-corrected, hit the brakes too early and got myself into a stupid tangle.

This analysis helped me reprogramme for the following day, Saturday. Don't put yourself under so much pressure, take it easy, drive more slowly. And that's what I did. I started slowly, then gradually built up speed until, suddenly, I was the fastest of the Ferraris – faster than Regazzoni and the newcomer Reutemann. I had managed to prove in practice what I knew in theory: I could drive as well now as before the shunt.

In this way, I managed to repress the anxiety I had felt, at least enough to place fourth. Which is not too bad, all things considered.

Ferrari kept telling the world how solid they were behind me but, in private, they were at sixes and sevens. They didn't know what to make of a defending champion with a disfigured face (it really did look bad those first weeks) who carried on as if everything was quite normal. Instead of taking pressure off me, they put even more on by bringing Carlos Reutemann into the team. We never could stand each other.

It was a terrible struggle to keep my head above water, both physically and mentally.

Ferrari sent Reutemann across to Paul Ricard to do some important test driving, but decided he wanted me to stay in Fiorano to check out some brake blocks or some other such rubbish. I had to raise the roof and perform all sorts of antics to make him get his priorities right. My one piece of good fortune was, of course, that Ferrari had been so anxious to get me under contract for the following season. If I hadn't had that contract, they could have ground me down mentally and turned me out to pasture.

A technical problem put me out of the Canadian Grand Prix, and I placed third at Watkins Glen. Hunt won both races. I went into the final race of the season – at Fuji, near Tokyo – with a 3-point lead.

In retrospect, I see the loss of the 1976 world championship differently from how I did then, although I do not reproach myself. *If* I had been a little less tense at the decisive moment, *if* I had taken it easy and coasted to the couple of points I needed for the title, then I would have four titles to my credit today instead of three. But, to be candid, I couldn't care less. I have no regrets on that score. And Ferrari needn't feel cheated about losing the world championship. It was their fault that the title came to be decided in the last race of the season at Fuji: we had crankshaft trouble at Paul Ricard, when I was well out in the lead, and a broken rear suspension in Canada. At Monza all that would have been needed was a word to my teammate Clay Regazzoni reminding him who was Number One. But the only thing that Ferrari could say was that Lauda had thrown in the towel at Fuji and lost a world championship.

Fuji, 24 October 1976. In normal circumstances, the last two or three races in a season are madness, even for a strong and healthy driver. In my case, the physical and mental trauma of Nürburgring is an added burden, not to mention the pressure piled on by James Hunt, who is sweeping all before him in his bid for the title. By the time I arrive in Tokyo I am clearly showing the strain. I need to charge my batteries, I need peace and quiet, I need time. Instead, what do I get? Rain. And, in the wet, you have to call on additional reserves of motivation and endurance. I have no such reserves. I am finished. The rain has totally destroyed me.

It rains and rains and rains. A whole day. Rivers course down across the circuit. Doing no more than 20mph in a warm-up lap you are simply flushed away at the corners because the tyres cannot cope with that volume of water. With the exception of Brambilla and Regazzoni, we all refuse to drive in the prevailing conditions. We sit in the race official's trailer and tell him no go.

Getting on for four o'clock in the afternoon, some clown arrives with the news that it is getting dark outside. If we don't start soon, the last few laps will have to be cut, and what about the television coverage, etc., etc. The race must start.

Brambilla troops out in the lead, and all the others follow. Fittipaldi, Pace and myself know we have no intention of racing. We'll go to the start so that our respective teams can pick up their starting money, but then we'll pack it in. Because nothing has changed: everything is just as dangerous as before, and the fact that it is getting dark can hardly help matters.

As it turns out, the feeling is absolutely unbearable, sitting there panic-stricken, rain lashing down, seeing nothing, just hunched down in the cockpit, shoulders tense, waiting for someone to run into you. Everybody is skating and spinning; it is crazy. Looking at it this way, it seems only sensible to drive into the pits and give up.

Then comes the miracle: after twelve hours of solid downpour the rain stops – about a quarter of the way into the race. If I had only held out that long, driven slowly and avoided being hit, there would have been no problem putting my foot down and working through the field to whatever place was necessary to clinch the title. As it turned out, fifth place would have been enough.

Sadly, hanging on patiently was more than I could manage that day, the last of the 1976 season.

Enzo Ferrari's behaviour in this rather special instance was less than dignified. He reacted like any other team boss who sees his chance slipping away. There was none of the legendary Ferrari greatness about him. Officially, he supported me and accepted my decision. But even the telephone conversation I had with him from the airport lounge in Tokyo was non-committal, heartless. He never seemed to wonder how I was, never asked, 'But what about you?' He never seemed to want to understand the anxiety felt by a driver who had been through a serious shunt, never gave any indication of wanting to go on together towards a new and better season. Nothing.

'Do you want to go on driving? What's wrong? What happens next? What can I do? What's our next move?' All of these are questions that Enzo Ferrari never once asked. At seventy-eight years of age and with a lifetime of intrigue and distorted information behind him, he was too far removed from the essential issue. He could only sit and read his newspapers. They reported that Lauda was yellow, Lauda was scared, Lauda was finished, Lauda was done for.

As soon as I got back to Europe, Enzo Ferrari called me in and offered me the job of team manager. A switch clicked on in my brain. What's behind this? What does he hope to achieve? I was about to play for time, but then the answer hit me: he had found a sure way out of his pathetic dilemma (*Is* Lauda done for or not?). He would put me on ice as a driver, but make sure I didn't sign elsewhere. It would have been a major embarrassment to him if I had won the title driving for somebody else. Offering me the team manager's job must have struck him as a shrewd tactic.

As soon as the penny dropped, I ran out to my car and got the contract that we had signed prior to Nürburgring – the *ebreo* contract for 1977. I threw it down on the table.

'And what do we do about this? Forget it? Shall I tear it up?'

'How come?' asked Ferrari.

'Because then I can drive for McLaren.'

He was completely taken aback. What would I do driving for McLaren? They have made me an offer, I said, and all I have to do is say yes. There was not a single shred of truth in this, of course. I just decided on the spur of the moment to play it this way. I tossed in McLaren because they were the best team around in those days apart from Ferrari.

I was sent out of the room. A few cronies were quickly summoned, and a huge discussion got under way. Then I was called back. I could stay on as a driver, but Reutemann would be the team's Number One. That was hogwash, because we would both be driving the same car. Who emerged as Number One and who emerged as Number Two would soon be apparent – this would automatically depend on our respective performances and I had no particular worries on that score.

By this time, however, I had pretty much had my fill of Ferrari – *Il Commendatore* and all his entourage.

The 1977 season turned out to be tough. My first priority was to put Reutemann in his place and secure the Number One slot in the team. By the third race of the season – the South African Grand Prix – this had been more or less accomplished, and I was able to concentrate all my efforts on pushing for technical progress. But the Ferrari was no longer the fast car of years gone by: we managed only two pole positions in the season as a whole. The biggest rivals in this department were Hunt in the McLaren, Andretti in the Lotus, and Scheckter in the Wolf.

I stored away in my mind the memory of Ferrari's breach of trust, just like a rogue elephant. Leaving would be a relief. At Zandvoort, the thirteenth race of a seventeen-race season, the time was ripe: I signed for Bernie Ecclestone and Brabham. It had to be kept secret, of course, otherwise my brilliant prospects in the title race would be in jeopardy. *Il Commendatore* was again very anxious to get me to sign a contract for the forthcoming season, and I had to come up with one lame excuse after another to postpone negotiations.

I was happy that my departure would be like a slap in the face for Enzo Ferrari. Today I see things in a slightly different light. It wasn't really a fair fight. I was young, I was strong, I could make my own decisions; Ferrari was seventy-nine, surrounded by self-serving 'advisers', and got his information second- or even third-hand.

At the time, however, my anger was so much to the fore that I simply didn't give him a chance. I really enjoyed turning down the most generous offer he has surely ever made. I was very cool, very curt, and offered no explanations: 'I don't want to stay, that's all there is to it.' Over and out.

I was happy when I left.

Once I had secured the world championship for a second time, I didn't feel like putting up with the ridiculously strained atmosphere, so I declined to start in Canada and Japan. Mind you, I had a worthy replacement – Gilles Villeneuve.

Enzo Ferrari was indeed very put out and he tossed a few choice remarks my way.

For my part, the chapter was closed, my anger dissipated. I was left with the fact that Enzo Ferrari had made it possible for me to race in one of the top teams. I was left with 15 wins, 12 second places and 5 third places. I was left with 23 pole positions, 3,292 miles in the lead in Formula 1, 248 world championship points and two world championship titles. And I was left with a great love for Italy and much of what is Italian.

When Enzo Ferrari sent me a congratulatory telegram when Lukas was born, I assumed that his attitude towards me had changed much as mine had changed towards him. With the passage of time, my respect for this giant of motor racing and his achievements eclipsed all else.

The day of reconciliation came six years after I had left Ferrari. It was pure coincidence: on one of his very rare trips away from home, Ferrari had come to Imola to run some tests. He was just driving out of the trailer park in his Lancia when there I was, directly in front of him. He got out and clasped me to him like a prodigal son. He asked after Marlene and the children and, quite simply, was a warm, charming old gentleman of eighty-four.

Today I even own a street-version Ferrari – I must be getting sentimental in my old age. When I had a company car it used to get on my nerves: I hardly ever drove it and used to leave it parked for someone else to pick up. Now I own one of the 213 GTOs in the world and, for the very first time, I have a car that I want to keep and maintain for the rest of my life.

CHAPTER SIX

BRABHAM

MOVING TO AN English set-up did me good. Bernie Ecclestone and designer Gordon Murray were easy-going or, at least, more easy-going than anyone had been at Ferrari. There did not seem to be that overwhelming compulsion to succeed, and the media pressure eased off. Everything was more natural, less abrasive – and much more direct. Gordon Murray was a technician who came in early and got down to work: a quick 'Good morning' and that was that, no verbalising, no drama.

Everything would have gone like a dream if only we had had a different engine. The 12-cylinder Alfa simply couldn't hack it, and there were problems and crises round the clock. We missed finishing race after race because of some nonsense or other, an oil-seal defect or similar. There were truly theatrical confrontations between Gordon Murray and Alfa's technician Carlo Chiti. (I visited Chiti a couple of times in Milan and was always fascinated by the forty or so stray dogs that ran around the workshops. Chiti seemed to be looking after every stray in Milan and the surrounding district: he fed them and had them checked out by the vet. All this care and attention didn't seem to apply to the engines that were being put together in that chaotic kennel, however, and I always felt that nothing good would come of it.)

In those days, Bernie Ecclestone had already emerged as the big promoter in Formula 1, and he seemed to worry about his own team only sporadically. I didn't think that was particularly sensible, because it meant that there was no tandem driving force to complement Gordon Murray.

Ecclestone really is the coruscating character they all say – and completely unpredictable into the bargain. When you have to negotiate with him, it's best to be on top form. He will use any excuse, any half-truth to give a new twist to the conversation. He'll argue that black is white and two plus two equals five – or vice-versa – whatever comes into his head, if it happens to suit his purpose and fit in with his negotiating strategy. He twists and turns to such a degree that there is no thread running through his conversation that you can grasp.

However, immediately you have reached an agreement with him, you can be sure that the deal is cast-iron. If Bernie shakes on something, you can take it as read. Over the years, everybody in Formula 1 – from race officials to drivers – has come to learn what Bernie's handshake stands for, and that naturally makes it easier working with him. The question is frequently asked as to whether Ecclestone is a genius when it comes to business matters. I don't believe he is a genius exactly, but I do think he is the best man around when it comes to Formula 1 politics.

The most exciting event during my two-year stint with Brabham was the introduction of the 'vacuum-cleaner' car halfway through the 1978 season. Of course, there had been previous models along similar lines – such as the American Chaparral of the sixties – but the new Brabham version was a unique product of Gordon Murray's vision.

Technically, the timing was right: Lotus had already taken the wing-car concept* much further than anyone else and, as a result, was well ahead of the rest. Murray cast about for a technical solution of his own to increase the car's ground-effect. There was nothing in Formula 1 regulations to preclude the use of fans *per se*, provided they were used to cool the engine. Murray was able to conform to current regulations by shifting the coolers to the back of the car. The main function of the rear-mounted fan was, of course, to suck air up from underneath the underbody – although Brabham and Gordon Murray never officially admitted as much. The competition suspected that Murray had a powerful ace up his sleeve, and the atmosphere was pretty strained. Bernie Ecclestone applied to the sport's governing body for an affidavit attesting the legality of the new design.

In fact, the new Brabham was unpleasant to drive. It understeered massively, all the more so when you took your foot off. The fan was powered by the engine, with the result that the suction effect fell off when the revs dropped. After a couple of test laps at Brands I started to adjust my driving style. Whenever the car failed to respond going into a corner, you had to

* The wing-car concept has nothing to do with visible wings, although spoilers do play a modest role. What the concept really refers to is what occurs when air flows over wing-shaped profiles. Just as lift is generated by the wing surfaces of an aircraft, ground-effect is generated when these profiles are mounted upside down. ('Wing-car' and 'ground-effect car' are two expressions describing the same phenomenon.)

In a car, ground-effect is achieved via external aerodynamic aids on the one hand – spoilers – but on the other hand, much more significantly, by designing the car underbody in such a way that a suction effect is developed, i.e. increased downthrust. The 1978 Lotus was going in that direction, although there were still major technical problems to be resolved – such as underseal (the plastic skirts first used abraded too quickly).

put your foot down rather than ease off. This way, the car would be sucked down tighter against the track and would corner at incredible speeds. This was a foretaste of what was to come in the wing-car era proper.

It went without saying that the competition didn't stand a chance against this kind of car – not even the brilliant Lotus design with top-notchers like Andretti and Peterson behind the wheel. The vacuum-cleaner was ready in time for the Swedish Grand Prix in Anderstorp, and our biggest worry was giving the game away by demonstrating its undeniable superiority. John Watson and I drove the qualifying laps with full tanks and did our level best to avoid pole position.

When it came to the race proper, I let Andretti go into the lead, playing cat and mouse with him. Damage to Pironi's Tyrell resulted in a patch of oil on the circuit and I could see Andretti up ahead of me slithering about as if he were on black ice. I scarcely checked to see where the oil patch was, I just stubbornly held my line and ignored it. I overtook him without the slightest difficulty and finished with embarrassing ease, being careful not to let my lead appear too great.

There was no protest about that win, but the powers-that-be promptly outlawed the fan. Technical developments continued to pursue the same goal – increased ground-effect – but step by step and by more subtle means (underbody design, abrasion-resistant running strips, etc.). It all came down to the same madness in the end but, in 1978, this was something we could barely foresee. Even so, the Brabham vacuum-cleaner remains one of the curios of Formula 1 history, with £200,000 worth of research and development wasted.

That year the Lotus was an impossible nut to crack, and I managed to win a second race – at Monza – only because Andretti was penalised a full minute for jumping the starter's gun. Otherwise, the season was a bit wearing, sitting there with our Alfa engines, trailing the field or dropping out. The following year was even more infuriating: I finished only twice and my new teammate Piquet was only once among the points.

In fact the Ferraris carried all before them in 1979, thanks to Scheckter and Villeneuve and the then magnificent Michelins.

I was asked at the time if it wasn't annoying to see Ferrari win without Lauda. All I could say in reply was that I couldn't care less about what happens to a team I have left behind me. And why shouldn't Ferrari come up trumps again? It was quite logical, particularly given the ideal pairing with Michelin. There was, however, absolutely no question of my having any regrets.

Our son Lukas was born in Salzburg in 1979. At that very moment, I was in a Learjet somewhere between Las Vegas and Long Beach. I was happy when the news came through, but being so far away made the event somehow abstract – at least for the time being.

By this time Marlene had long since shut herself off from motor racing. It is true to say that she hated it, and she hasn't had a change of heart since. The Nürburgring business, coming as it did only five months after our wedding, had shocked her to an extent she would never be able to forgive. She had been brutally jolted out of her utterly devil-may-care attitude to life, so much so that she was never again capable of seeing motor racing in a detached way.

Accordingly, Marlene had long since dismissed the sport as mad, together with anyone who had anything to do with it, including yours truly. She had also developed an acute awareness of the callousness of the sport and would react to trivial irrelevancies that someone like myself doesn't even register. Small, everyday occurrences, part of the daily ritual of motor racing and, as such, of no consequence, take on meaning when seen through her open and generous nature. Marlene remembers banal situations, such as the morning of a Grand Prix weekend spent in one of those characterless lookalike hotels. You get into the lift, recognise someone, force yourself to exchange some meaningless greeting, and can't wait until the lift stops and you can get out. Those seconds, when we are standing around in the lift waiting for the door to open and seemingly incapable of communicating with one another, irritate Marlene intensely. 'Can't you sense how sad and empty that is?' she asks me. And I reply: 'No, I don't sense anything at all.'

She finds certain things that are part of my life as a racing driver ridiculous. For example, that there are no celebrations after a race, no get-togethers where people can eat, drink and swap anecdotes. In fact, Marlene would have adapted much more readily to the chivalrous age of motor racing, when certain human qualities counted just as much as a fast lap time. To her, our uptight, artificially intense approach is shabby. Such as the way we take off as soon as possible on the Sunday afternoon once the race is over, as if we can't bear the sight of one another one second longer (which is often true). Superficialities like these – which to me are a blessing (no time-wasting, no gossip, no fraternisation) – are things that Marlene notices.

As a result, you can imagine how little time she has for motor racing itself, with all its hype and the opportunity it affords to cripple yourself for life.

It was only her innate tolerance which made it possible for us to be together at all: if I really believed that racing was what I needed out of life then, okay, I had to do it. That is her view of individual freedom, even within marriage.

I had always made myself my number one priority and convinced myself that family life was one side of things and racing another. Even the birth of my son changed nothing on that score. However, by the middle of the 1979 season, racing had started to pall, and I began to take stock of the situation.

In order to rekindle some small spark of excitement, I decided that I would hold out for a ridiculously high fee, a record sum in those days. The recent run of poor results had not diminished my PR potential – everyone realised that it wasn't my fault that the Alfa engine wasn't up to scratch. Ecclestone was still very much for me and, since the switch to a Cosworth engine had already been confirmed, would need my valuable services as a test driver. Also, I was very acceptable to his main sponsor, Parmalat.

All in all, the situation seemed ripe to negotiate a fantastic contract.

Bernie and I started haggling early that summer. I demanded $2 million and not a cent less. He thought I was off my head. I had to be joking. One day he would rant and rave, the next he would be conciliatory, but all I did was repeat my price.

This dragged on for four months or so, and I refused to budge an inch. The whole situation was a challenge: I had a lousy season behind me and was slowly losing interest in the game. Beating down the financial wizard was a damn sight more fun than driving.

By the time autumn came everything fell into place. Bernie needed me desperately, so he capitulated. The contract was officially signed at Parmalat, in Italy, and that was the moment I realised that the bubble had burst. Scarcely had I won the day against Bernie, when I found that the whole business no longer interested me. And the prospect of $2 million didn't really change matters. Previously, I had hoped that a fortune like that would motivate me again and bring a new sense of excitement to my career. I clung to the hope that the switch from Alfa to Cosworth would set up some positive vibrations.

Brabham entered its 8-cylinder Ford Cosworth for the first time in Canada, at the Montreal Grand Prix. By this time, all the other teams except Ferrari and Renault were using Cosworths. The switch had meant re-designing the entire car, and I drove out to the circuit on the Thursday before the race to examine the machine. It looked splendid; just the way a Formula 1 car should. Gordon Murray had the hit of the decade on his hands. In normal circumstances I couldn't have wished for more – the fascination of having an obviously successful new design, a new beginning, a super-contract. I felt nothing, however, least of all a sense of euphoria, and I was very conscious of this fact.

The next day I looked over towards the circuit from my room in the Bonaventura Hotel. Miserable weather. What a drag. I go across to training, but the feeling persists. I look the car over. Nothing. No thrill. I've spent my last eight years driving 12-cylinder machines – BRM, Ferrari, Alfa – and they have always given me a sense of pleasure, with their high revs, shrill note and sheer aggression.

I start the Cosworth. A strange feeling: in the small of my back. The exhaust rasps as I drive away from the pits. Brrrm, brrrm. The noise is flatter, muted. Everything seems slower; boring somehow. There is nothing special about this. There is no substitute for the 'feel' of a 12-cylinder engine.

All at once the curtain comes down. I have only one thought: you don't belong here, you don't belong here at all. Go and do something else. Now. Another inner voice tells me to calm down, not to panic, to drive a lap or two and see what happens. Yes, that's it, drive a lap or two, take your time. Maybe I should bring the car in and tell them to set this or that up differently? That might give me time to think. I struggle through for fifteen minutes or so, finally come in to have some adjustments made, then drive out again. And I know: it is over. Finished. Enough is enough. I drive back to the pits, climb out, and tell them to bleed the clutch and brakes. I go up to Bernie: 'I need to have a word with you.'

I don't like it any more, I don't want to any more, I can't do it any more. I'm getting out.

Ecclestone took this in immediately. For his own peace of mind he asked if I wanted to drive for another team. No. We tore up my lucrative 1980 contract. No problem. Bernie agreed with me totally. If someone wants to stop, he should do so right there and then and shouldn't be prevented from doing so. 'It's a big decision,' Bernie says, 'but a good one.'

I stripped off my gear, put my helmet and overalls down in a corner of the pits, and went over to the office to call Marlene.

'We're cutting down on washing powder. You have washed your last overall.'

Marlene was happy. And so was I. I drove back to the hotel and booked a seat on the late-afternoon flight to Los Angeles.

Meanwhile, Bernie Ecclestone was keeping the media off my back. You need peace and quiet, he said, and I'll buy you enough time to get clear of Montreal. All manner of frantic explanations were trotted out. A terse communiqué was issued: Mr Zunino would be driving the Brabham that afternoon, car number five. (Ricardo Zunino, an Argentinian with a little experience in Formula 1, had come to Montreal to watch the race. Ecclestone grabbed him and gave him my gear. Poor devil, stuck in a new car on what, for him, was a new circuit, and wearing a crash helmet with Niki Lauda painted across it. And the others, who hadn't been told, kept asking themselves: what's up with Niki, he's driving all over the place.)

Only a couple of reporters guessed what was going on and cornered me in the hotel. I told them that it all came down to one thing: 'I'm fed up driving round in stupid circles.'

It was totally incorrect to extrapolate from this that I was calling motor racing stupid, not least because that was equivalent to saying that I had squandered ten years of my life. All I was trying to convey was the reality of my situation. I was not attacking the sport, or my team, or my fellow drivers, or my fans; all I was saying that September day in Canada was that it wasn't for me.

That afternoon Parmalat's PR man, Sante Ghedini, drove me to the airport, crying his eyes out all the way. There was nothing to cry about, I told him, he should be pleased. I was alive, I had a life to live and I was going to live it to the hilt.

When I arrived in Los Angeles I drove out to a hotel in Long Beach, where no one recognised me. It was marvellous.

The only thing that interested me now was flying. I set up a meeting with Pete Conrad and the people at McDonnell-Douglas.

CHAPTER SEVEN

COMEBACK

THE FIRST THING that struck me after I retired was how slow everything was out in the 'real' world. The fact that the pressure had eased off was, of course, marvellous; doubly so because I felt no pangs of regret or nostalgia at leaving the chaos of Formula 1. On the other hand, motor racing had created within me a certain rhythm, a sense of speed which applied not only to driving. You recognise the performers in today's competitive society by the pace they set – be it in sport, technology or commerce. And, for the past ten years, I had been exclusively in the company of top-notchers who all wanted exactly the same thing as myself – to win, to be the best, to be the fastest.

When I had left the 'real' world, I was a good-for-nothing youngster without a penny to his name and with no formal education and no job prospects. When I came back, it was as if I had skipped not ten but a hundred years. I was convinced that I could transpose some of what I had learned in the interim into everyday business life. And, if the wheels of industry were grinding too slowly for my taste, then I would simply put my shoulder to the wheel and speed things up.

The intention was there, but it was a totally different matter putting it into practice. This was true not only with regard to my dealings with the authorities and state-owned concerns, but also my own colleagues at Lauda Air, which had got off the ground in 1978 (see Chapter 15). I used to say to myself: so-and-so thinks differently, he doesn't understand what you are getting at, or doesn't want to understand. All too often, there would be a hiatus between pinpointing the solution to a problem and taking the prompt action required to put that solution into practice. As a result, I had to put on my own mental brakes and do things at a pace that was practicable.

It is perhaps naive on the part of a racing driver to expect short braking distances and top speeds in the world of commerce. The fact is, motor racing is very clear and very direct. Any excuse or half-truth is immediately shown up in the next race. This aspect of competition and measuring your own performance is really incredible. It could be valid in any occupation, but there is no chequered flag in the real world, no means of measuring one's performance fifteen times a year. Many people go through life without ever catching a glimpse of that chequered flag.

Those were the lessons I learned in autumn 1979 and throughout 1980. There was nothing for it but to throw myself into my new profession.

Marlene and Lukas stayed on in our house in Hof, near Salzburg, but I spent most of my time in Vienna. I didn't rent an apartment, however. I slept in hotels, in the office or at Lemmy Hofer's. It was a strange interlude; neither fish nor fowl, as they say.

I didn't miss racing in the slightest. Even TV coverage left me cold and totally uninterested. After a couple of months, however, I did switch on, but got no enjoyment out of it. At the start of each race I was afraid there would be a collision; it was an unpleasant sensation, almost as if I myself were physically involved.

I fought tooth and nail to get Lauda Air on its feet, but ran into progressively tougher opposition from the state airline AUA. At the same time, the overall economic picture was getting worse and worse, which didn't help matters. My commitment was exclusively to Lauda Air rather than to Niki Lauda. The money I poured into the business initially was not crippling, however, and neither were the subsequent periodic injections of funds. The amounts involved were never such as might endanger my future.

Mathias was born in 1981. That was a beautiful experience. Marlene and her sister drove down to the clinic in Salzburg and I stayed at home with Lukas, who was barely two years old at the time. That, in itself, was quite something: we fell asleep together and didn't hear the telephone ringing for the best part of two hours. We finally drove down to the clinic and found that all was well. The baby was lying on Marlene's stomach and I was very moved. No comparison with Lukas' birth, when I was over the States at 35,000 feet.

In essence, however, not much had changed. The family stayed in Salzburg, I stayed on in Vienna. It was a curious period of transition. I believe we were all waiting for something to happen.

My aversion to watching TV coverage of Formula 1 had gradually dissipated. In summer 1981 I accepted an invitation for the first time from the Austrian television service to act as back-up commentator alongside Heinz Prüller at the Austrian Grand Prix at Zeltweg. Looking down on the grid from the vantage point of the commentary box was quite pleasant: for the first time in ages it all looked quite nice. It smelt good again, it *tasted* good again. The start of the race didn't make me feel tense; instead, there was a lovely tingling sensation.

I went over to see Willy Dungl, who happened to be holding a training course at Bad Tatzmannsdorf. It was just possible, I said, well, you know, the new cars, g force and that sort of thing, I mean to say, what kind of physical shape am I in?

Willy said something like: 'Mmmmmmh. As long as you're here, you might as well come on a little bike ride with us.'

Willy knew exactly what he was doing. His seminar was made up of a group of well-trained, clean-living females, who proceeded to humiliate me over a twenty-mile course up hill and down dale. I got the message: in the state you're in, you needn't bother trying any sport, cycling included. To drive the point home, Willy asked, 'I suppose you noticed how those women ran you into the ground?' I had noticed.

I got him to prescribe me a short- and medium-term fitness programme that would be good enough to get me into a racing-car cockpit again, if I should perchance feel so inclined. I had a sneaking suspicion that this would soon be the case, because I had to get to the bottom of certain feelings which were suspiciously irritating. I drove down to the Italian Grand Prix at Monza. Watching the race felt good. I liked it again.

McLaren's Ron Dennis had kept in touch with me after I retired and had always made it clear that he was lying in wait for me. He would call up every other month and ask if I didn't feel like coming back, waiting for the moment when I said yes.

Accordingly, it seemed logical to have a word with him at Monza. There is something bothering me, I said, and I'd like to get to the bottom of it. Could he possibly set things up for me? No problem.

Above all, what I wanted to find out was whether I would be *capable* of coming back. If I could click back a little switch in my brain enabling me to change to a different level of consciousness. I knew that, if I *could* reach that frame of mind, there was no reason to be intimidated by the new drivers who had made their mark in the interim – Pironi, Prost, Villeneuve, Rosberg, Piquet, the 'young lions', as they were known by the media. They would not have the edge over me.

Some reference to money is appropriate at this juncture, if only for the simple reason that so much was written on that subject at the time. When I embarked on the experiment with Ron Dennis, I was under no kind of financial strain. True, Lauda Air was not going well, but the losses were being held down and, furthermore – as Austria's finance minister had suggested – I could have got out of the business any time I liked. I do not see how money can possibly be the sole motive for racing: either you are in the right frame of mind and feel the spirit move you or not, as the case may be.

I had to approach my first attempt to compete in Formula 1 again with the greatest conceivable caution – from every possible angle.

Ron Dennis took pains to ensure that the whole affair was kept as secret as possible. It was for this reason that he chose Donington, the rather odd circuit near Nottingham, to allow me to try out. I had never driven there before, but the circuit is completely walled in, which was clearly advantageous.

As far as my wife was concerned, I also had to exercise some caution. At that time Marlene seemed to have got a better bargain – a new-model Niki, less self-centred and less ruthless than his predecessor. Over the years I had developed a mechanism for coping with the pressures of being in the public domain. The Lauda System had ensured that everything happened logically, rationally and painlessly (painlessly for yours truly, of course). Family life had been one fairly smooth component of the System, and Marlene would have been too proud a lady to have indulged in nit-picking – one fine day she would simply have left. It was only on the final straight that it dawned on me how much had been wrong in all this; it was only then that I really put my strongest talent to work – to reconsider, analyse, probe for error, work out how things could be better. These various arguments were all very, very persuasive – and the notion of making a comeback was scarcely supported by them.

There had been regular rumours and newspaper reports that I was planning a comeback. Marlene would often ask me about them, and I would convince her they were absolute rubbish. This was easy enough because she was used to the drivel written about me, about her, and about our life together. I took her to England with me, but left her in London. I was off to test drive some car or other – nothing serious, of course, just for fun.

Donington, 16 September 1981. Beautiful weather. Ron Dennis is there. Plus John Watson, a few mechanics, an ambulance, a fire tender. No reporters. The secrecy has certainly paid off. Watson gives me a hand to set the car up, everything is so new to me. There have been incredible changes in the two intervening years: we are now in the middle of the wing-car era, in that technological one-way street where only ground-effect and senseless cornering speeds are important. (It was unfortunate that Formula 1 had allowed itself to be manipulated into this idiocy, but you had to live with it.)

The first thing I notice is that I don't have the strength to drive three consecutive laps. I come into the pits after two and ask for something to be looked at. I am inwardly embarrassed at my shocking lack of condition, but not really worried about it because I know that Willy Dungl will have me as fit as any racing driver can be within a couple of months. Right now, it's a question of lasting out the day and gradually building up speed to the point where I can make some meaningful assessment.

By the afternoon I am handling the car a little better. I go for a couple of fast ones and am only one tenth of a second behind Watson's best lap time. That settles it: if I do come back, I'll have the speed.

It was pure coincidence rather than the bush telegraph that brought Frank Williams to my London hotel that very same evening. He told me that Alan Jones had announced his retirement. How did I feel about taking his place? I told him I would think it over.

There wasn't much to think over. Ron Dennis had set the whole thing up so cleverly that I already felt almost at home with McLaren.

I didn't tell Marlene until I had definitely made up my mind to go back. She sensed that there was no way of challenging my decision, no point even in discussing it. All she said was: 'You're mad.' She choked back any further comment and only gave vent to her feelings every six months or so thereafter.

The burning question for me now was: how much? There was absolutely no question of my selling myself short or settling for the norm. The people to deal with were McLaren's sponsor, Marlboro. I promptly asked for more money than anyone had ever earned in Formula 1. There was a deathly silence, then they trotted out their main counter-argument: there was no way of knowing if I would still be fast enough. I was ready with my reply: 'My PR value alone is worth that much. You'll be paying only one dollar for my driving ability, all the rest is for my personality.'

In the event, this was the basis of our contract, albeit with the proviso that Marlboro and McLaren would have the right to declare it void, subject to appropriate compensation, after one third or two thirds of the season. This was presumably to allow for the possibility that I would put up such a miserable showing that my public relations value would also be zero.

There was no doubt in my mind that physical fitness would be immeasurably more important in the wing-car era than it had been in previous years. I weighed 143 pounds (thirteen too many, as was established later) and was in terrible condition. However, I had adjusted mentally to the programme that Willy Dungl had created to put me back on my feet, and I put myself totally in his hands.

Not only in his hands: Willy has a way of taking on the mantle of spiritual masseur, working not only on his protégés' bodies but also on their mental attitudes. I must say, however, that one or two of his methods didn't work as well with me as with some of the others. According to Willy, he had had tremendous success with concentration exercises developed for the Austrian ski-jumping squad; however, whenever he tried to get me to murmur to myself such magic incantations as 'Relax, relax', I relaxed so completely that I would fall asleep on the bench.

One of the routine situations Willy trained me for was 'Accident', the point being to reduce the effect – in some instances fatal – that shock can have on the human body. I had an early opportunity of proving to him that I was a willing pupil.

We were driving a first series of tests at Le Castellet when part of the rear suspension went. I happened to be on the Mistral straight at the time, so I must have been pushing 190mph. Then, suddenly, I headed for greener pastures. There were rows and rows of safety netting and I knocked them down one after another. Meanwhile, the car was falling apart at the seams.

My first reaction was to duck down, making myself smaller. Hope this doesn't hurt, I thought to myself. However, when I finally came to rest and discovered I was still in one piece, Willy's counsel prevailed: sit absolutely still for a moment, breathe deeply, unbuckle the harness, climb out of the car, walk a few yards away, sit down, breathe deeply in and out again.

It took maybe three or four minutes for a car to be sent out from the pits. Willy had come along too. He saw me sitting a safe distance away from the car. He took me by the wrist: 'Ninety. Good lad.' He had quickly taken my pulse and was clearly pleased with the situation. The car was a wreck and, all around, the safety netting had been torn down, but Willy was happy.

On the whole, Willy thinks my nerves are not bad and that I can be trained to accept what is required, provided that I can be convinced of its usefulness. Willy was once asked about the tension experienced by the average driver in this crazy sport. I quote:

> I'm in a position to make certain comparisons to the extent that Niki isn't the only racing driver I have treated. On the morning of a race, when a driver comes up to my room to have a massage and eat a sensible breakfast, his pulse will be between 90 and 100. With Niki, it is between 80 and 85.
>
> We have a piece of equipment that looks a little like a wristwatch and which is designed to take continuous pulse readings and store the peak values. This makes it possible for us to record a driver's pulse-rate during qualifying and in the race itself. Some drivers peak at 220 or even 230; Niki's readout will show a peak of 190. Up in the extreme 220–230 range there is a chance of mini-blackouts – which may well explain otherwise inexplicable shunts to the extent that the driver loses consciousness for a fraction of a second.

While we're at it, here are a couple of other notes my friend Willy has made relating to his work with me:

> Niki was capable of being persuaded that it was important to use his nervous energy sparingly. This can be achieved by

two different approaches – proper nutrition on the one hand and elimination of stress on the other. It is enough for the latter if you can simply and *effectively* tell yourself: I WILL NOT GET ANGRY. All the other techniques are secondary: deep breathing, bringing your shoulders up around your ears, then exhaling strongly, repeating to yourself that you will not get angry. Of course, you have to practise this over a longer period of time until you can switch on this defence against excess adrenaline and a racing pulse.

In Niki's case, it is sufficient for him to reason with himself, telling himself that getting angry is unhealthy. This is why he was able to cope with the most stupid and most irritating moments of his stint with McLaren. Time and again, there were situations in training where nothing seemed to go right, where valuable time was lost or when repairs seemed to take an eternity. Other drivers might have been provoked into losing their temper. Niki, on the other hand, would keep his cool, sit in the cockpit and let them get on with it, as though he himself were sublimely aloof from the situation. He wasn't, because every wasted second really hurt, but he had enough sense to understand that letting his emotions get on top of him would only drain him further.

Let's leave Willy Dungl for the moment and return to the early weeks of my comeback.

I got myself an Austrian racing driver's licence, but then it was discovered that I didn't meet the requirements for the new super-licence that had just been introduced. The super-licence had been dreamt up to prevent any old clown from climbing into a Formula 1 cockpit just because his father had come up with a penny or two. Of late, several dangerous situations had developed because of inexperienced – bad – drivers who got in the way and reacted wrongly. As a result, it was decreed that you had to have won a certain number of Formula 3 or Formula 2 races in the season prior to moving up to Formula 1.

An exception was made in my case (as, indeed, two years later, when Alan Jones made his comeback) and I received a strange application form in the post. I was apparently supposed to fill in how long my contract with McLaren had to run and to acknowledge that I did not have the right to switch to another team. The super-licence was to be granted to Niki Lauda/McLaren.

I couldn't quite follow this. Either you're good enough to be granted a licence or you're not. Surely it has nothing to do with the team you are driving for. I called Didier Pironi, the President of the Grand Prix Drivers' Association.

'What is this funny clause supposed to mean?'

'Don't worry about it. We discussed it at our last meeting. Just go ahead and sign.'

Obviously, I had more of a suspicious nature than my colleagues. I seemed to be the only one to whom it had occurred that we were on the point of being shafted by our respective team bosses. If the super-licence was only valid for Lauda/McLaren, then I would be at the mercy of a third party if I made up my mind to drive for, say, Ferrari the following season. I could envisage transfer fees as in soccer, and all the horse-trading and contract buy-outs that implied. A veritable paradise for the Bernie Ecclestones of this world, who would then have unlimited scope to demonstrate their talents. Deals would be struck between one squad and another, and we would be caught like idiots in the middle, hoping for a handout.

There was no way I was going to sign that form, and I managed to persuade Pironi that we should all get together and do something about it. He made a few calls and was just in time to prevent most of the other drivers from sending their forms, duly signed, back to Paris.

When we all met up in South Africa in January for the first Grand Prix of the 1982 season it emerged that only five drivers had signed out of a total of thirty. The twenty-five that had not signed were required to do so before qualifying. Pironi and I stated our cases clearly: that there should only be contracts that were mutually binding, i.e. if I am not allowed to leave McLaren, then McLaren is not allowed to fire me.

FISA President Balestre and Ecclestone (in his capacity as spokesman for the bosses) had teamed up to show us who was really in charge. We had a choice, it appeared: accept the conditions as set out or go to hell.

It was one of those strange coincidences that this dispute should come about immediately before my first race after coming out of retirement. It gave the impression that, whenever Lauda is around, the fur will fly. However, the issue was far too important for me to stay in the background. Not least because the younger, more inexperienced drivers were in a weaker position and needed an old hand to show the way.

At a meeting of the drivers it was established that, with the exception of Jacky Ickx and Jochen Mass, we were all in favour of holding out. It was decided that we would call a strike and boycott Thursday practice.

Drivers solidarity had never been all that impressive in Formula 1, not even in the days of Graham Hill and Jackie Stewart. There were too many loners. In this instance, however, solidarity was extremely important, because we couldn't afford to let the united front crumble. We had to give the more vulnerable drivers something to hold on to.

The bus was my idea. At seven o'clock on Thursday morning, a bus drew up and parked at the entrance to the paddock. Inside it: a chauffeur, Pironi and the undersigned. As each of the other drivers arrived, they were asked to park their cars and get into the bus. We were going for a ride. Jacky Ickx and Jochen Mass wouldn't go along with this but, eventually, all the others took their places in the bus rather than on the starting grid.

Not surprisingly, there was a great to-do and excitement ran high. Everyone seemed happy and there was a sense of strength through unity. We took the bus the long way round to a beautiful hotel in Johannesburg. In our wake trailed a whole convoy of reporters, photographers and TV crews.

Pironi had a further consultation back at the circuit. No dice. He joined us at the hotel with the news that, if we didn't start training right away, we would all be banned for life. Sure enough, the PA system broadcast all thirty names that afternoon. All disqualified, all banned *sine die*.

We pottered around the swimming pool and had a really splendid day. Any anxieties were camouflaged by high jinks and laughter, although even long-serving drivers knew that the consequences could be drastic. A case in point: Bernie Ecclestone had already issued an ultimatum to his two drivers, Piquet and Patrese. The deadline had expired and, in theory, both of them had already been sacked for breach of contract.

It was the younger drivers, however, that constituted the main problem. They were still accustomed to the team chiefs having the final word, and they were clearly more afraid than we were at the prospect of broken contracts and the possibility of being sued for damages. They were afraid of how their sponsors would react at the thought of hard-earned cash lying idle in the pits losing interest. For many of them, not being able to start in this, the first race of the season, would be nothing short of a catastrophe. I was convinced, however, that there was only one thing for it: hang in there, stay tough and stick together. If we didn't, the opposition would take us on one at a time and make mincemeat of us.

The good mood persisted through dinner, and there was a lot of laughter and carrying-on when we asked the hotel manager for a room – one room for the whole lot of us. If we'd taken single rooms, that would have been the collapse of the united front, I've no doubt about that.

The room we were allocated was a small banquet suite. There was a piano, but no toilet facilities. We had some sheets brought up and we spread them out on the floor.

The first entr'acte came when Ensign team chief Mo Nunn turned up and wanted to speak to his driver Guerrero. He was cunning enough to bring Guerrero's girlfriend along. The two of them looked at each other through the glass door. Guerrero was in tears; his girlfriend was in tears. It was enough to make strong men weep. Okay, I said, go out and speak to her, but I'm coming with you. We went out and I waited while they whispered sweet nothings. When I tried to get him to come back inside, he refused, so I let her in as well.

Villeneuve and de Angelis started playing the piano and the atmosphere picked up again. Then Arrows team chief Jacky Oliver put in an appearance. He had a local rough-neck with him and tried to force his way in. He had even brought the police along, and we had to be very careful to avoid a brawl which would have given them an excuse to step in. They got the door half open and were nearly inside before we pushed them out again – using the piano to block the door and avoid direct physical contact.

The situation was getting critical. The younger drivers were really scared. Most of them came up to me for reassurance: was I really sure that we were doing the right thing? What happens if they have us arrested? If they have to declare the Grand Prix cancelled, can we be locked up as being responsible and held liable for damages? I felt confident and sure of my ground, so I reassured them as best I could. Didier Pironi and Nelson Piquet were also towers of strength.

We tried to get some sleep. Since the bathroom was across the hallway, we each had to have access to the room key. We placed it on a plate in the middle of the room and agreed – cross-my-heart-and-hope-to-die and so on – that anyone who had to leave would unlock the door, go to the bathroom, come back, re-lock the door, and put the key back on the plate. We all solemnly swore to abide by this routine.

It was a clear moonlit night, a perfect setting for conspirators. Every time one of us stood up, a dozen heads would be raised. By early light, nothing had changed. There had been no attempt at reconciliation. Teo Fabi took the key, went out and didn't come back. Our only deserter. Still, the fact that he had taken off made us think again: shouldn't we take a vote to reconfirm whether everyone was staying of his own free will? The vote was unanimous.

It didn't drag on much longer. Pironi came to terms with Balestre back at the circuit. We had won.

The opposition was not man enough to admit as much in public, and rumours persisted all weekend to the effect that we were going to be arrested at the airport on our way out. What *did* happen was that we never heard another murmur about the controversial super-licence clause which would have tied us down to one team indefinitely.

Some people revel in revenge: after the race an announcement was made that all the drivers – with the exception of Jochen Mass – were to have their licences revoked. That 'decision' was as foolish as it was unenforceable, and was eventually substituted with a warning and a vague threat. The powers-that-be then threw a final tantrum and imposed a $5,000 fine on each of us on the grounds that the strike had brought the sport into disrepute. We all paid up and lodged an appeal. It is difficult for me to say whether or not I ever had the money back: I have no idea whether we won our appeal or whether it is still dragging on.

Overall, however, I would say that what we did in Kyalami in 1982 marked an important milestone in the development of professional motor racing. It demonstrated to those who administer the sport that we drivers are not so weak, simple-minded and disunited that we can be manipulated at will. The thing that really soured the opposition was the fact that, for once, we stuck together. That was something they didn't expect from such a motley crew.

As to the race proper, that went reasonably well for me, no more, no less. I placed fourth and, in doing so, had a first taste of the incredible physical demands made on the driver at the wheel of a wing-car. Alain Prost drove a beautiful race, and his victory suggested that Renault had mastered the technical problems involved. Not so, as it was soon proved. The time was not yet ripe for the turbos to take command, let alone those of the Renault variety.

In the second race of the season – in Rio – I collided with Reutemann. The next race was Long Beach.

De Cesaris has pole position and is in the lead. I tell myself to be patient. He comes up behind a driver who has already been lapped. Whoever it is doesn't move over and de Cesaris is held up coming into the chicane. De Cesaris tries to take him on the outside, but there isn't enough room. I tell myself to take it easy or else I'll spin out. De Cesaris overtakes the slower car and shakes his fist at the driver. I see him raise his hand in a threatening gesture and I say to myself: he should be changing gear *now*. I hear the ugly whine of his rev limiter as it hits 11,000rpm. I pull out past him, giving him a wide berth. After all, you have to watch yourself when you pass someone who is so busy shaking his fist that he forgets he has to change gear.

The race was uneventful. Towards the end I was reasonably happy by my standards. Driving the last lap, I felt that the car wasn't going to let me down. I wouldn't let it – it would cross the finishing line even if I had to carry the damn thing. I'd been in similar situations before and had always been afraid that the car would coast to a stop a few yards before the flag. Not this time, though. I was shouting and whistling for joy. Then I thought, watch yourself, you idiot, just watch yourself, otherwise you'll drive into the wall out of sheer stupidity. I have never felt that like before. It was beautiful.

Coming back after two years and winning the third race of the season. I liked it.

CHAPTER EIGHT

ENTER THE TURBOS

MCLAREN IS A good, large and skilfully managed Formula 1 team. In Ron Dennis, it has a manager with courage and ideas. In John Barnard, it has a designer with courage and ideas. The fact that a sponsor as redoubtable as Marlboro feels the same way, emphasises the basics are certainly there.

In 1981–82, when McLaren was in the throes of technical transition and things were going less than well, Ron Dennis had kept pushing for me, and his persistence had made my comeback that much easier. I remember being impressed then by Dennis's vision and far-sightedness in offering McLaren's sponsor a bridge over troubled water.

Ron Dennis also thought big when it came to the next major decision – the choice of a long-overdue turbo engine for the McLaren. Opting for an existing engine or one that was already in development would have implied dependence on the manufacturer. What is more, the McLaren design would have had to be modified to accommodate a ready-made new engine rather than the other way round.

Getting together with Porsche was exclusively Ron Dennis's brainwave. On the one hand, the idea was quite logical, to the extent that Porsche already had turbo experience in sports-car racing and in the Can-Am Series; as a result, development time would be dramatically shorter than with any other firm. On the other hand, it was somewhat presumptuous to approach

Porsche – after all, if a firm like Porsche had wanted to get involved in Formula 1, it could easily have done so under its own steam.

Dennis set up a dinner date with Wolfgang Porsche and myself. At issue were $5 million of R & D outlay to develop a Formula 1 turbo engine. We did our best to convince Wolfgang Porsche to put the proposal before his fellow shareholders, i.e. his family. What we had in mind was that Stuttgart-based Porsche would come into Formula 1 along with us, namely with an engine called Porsche financed (at least in part) by Stuttgart. That proposal was a complete non-starter, because the Porsche family hadn't the slightest interest in putting their own cash into Formula 1. Naturally, they would be delighted to develop any kind of engine we wanted, but – as customers – we would have to foot the bill.

Dennis started looking around for a partner who might be interested in co-financing the Porsche deal. He fixed up a meeting with Mansour Ojjeh, the son of the boss of *Technique d'Avantgarde*. The meeting was to be in Paris and I was invited along.

At the time, TAG was sponsoring the Williams. Ron opened up very neatly by explaining how being a mere sponsor could not do justice to the aspirations of a technological front-runner. There was more involved, he said, than simply painting one's logo on the side of a car; instead, a firm like TAG should see itself as an integral part of a Formula 1 team. Further, TAG should be seen to be associated with the best team going.

Before going this far, Dennis had run a check on the enormous financial resources of the Ojjeh Group. In this sort of situation, Ron leaves nothing to chance. My role in the discussion was to allay any fears the young man might have about making a wrong move. I was able to predict in all conscience that any engine specifically developed by Porsche would indeed be something special and that there was no way it could be a flop.

These two get-togethers – with Wolfgang Porsche and Mansour Ojjeh – represented the sum total of my contribution to the project.

Mansour Ojjeh got his father's blessing for the project and a joint-venture company was formed. As time went on, Ron and Mansour were to become more and more closely involved – to the point where, allowing for various cross-holdings, Mansour Ojjeh now owns an appreciable share of McLaren (along with Ron Dennis). As far as I know, John Barnard has let himself be bought out. Not bad going, when you consider that Dennis and Barnard originally joined McLaren in 1980 with nothing between them but a stack of ideas. At the time, the firm was jointly owned by Teddy Mayer and Tyler Alexander and was heavily dependent on Marlboro sponsorship. It was Marlboro that pushed for Dennis and Bernard to be taken on board – together with the carbon-fibre chassis that was John's brainchild.

In the months that followed, my services were called upon regularly whenever sparks started to fly between the English and the Germans. As a neutral Austrian I played the part of honest broker on at least three or four occasions. In fact, clashes between McLaren, Porsche and Bosch were no more dramatic than, say, those between Brabham and Alfa or between Brabham and BMW or, indeed, between any parties from different countries who have come together to design a car. As one might expect, Porsche thought only of the engine, whereas Bosch had eyes only for the electronics. The one person to focus on the overall design concept was John Barnard.

With progressive technical over-sophistication of Formula 1 marques at the end of the seventies came increased emphasis on overall design harmony: each design component had to harmonise with ten others. Today, the quality of a Formula 1 design hinges on the interplay between engine power, aerodynamics and ride. To this extent, developing an engine in a vacuum is clearly going in the wrong direction. However, there are endless opportunities for friction where a common project is worked on in separate phases in separate geographical locations.

One thing is certain: Barnard had the right idea as far as the overall concept was concerned and was able to specify accordingly right from the beginning. As for Porsche, what was most impressive – aside from all the technical expertise and know-how one can take for granted in a firm of that calibre – was the speed with which they reacted to each new problem as it arose. One major decision was the choice of injection system. Engineer Mezger favoured a reliable, well-established mechanical system, whereas Bosch argued for sophisticated electronics. In line with the spirit of the project, it was decided to opt for the bolder, more progressive solution – and this decision has been 100 per cent vindicated.

We ran tests in summer 1983 at the Porsche circuit in Weissach. First results were very Porsche-like and I felt optimistic right away. The turbos were already dominating the 1983 Grand Prix season (BMW, Renault, Ferrari) and McLaren was nowhere. I strongly advocated getting the new engine into action as soon as possible in order to use the rest of the season – for us already a wash-out anyway – to test the new design. Barnard was very much against this. He didn't want to run a compromise version for the rest of 1983 but, instead, wanted to kick off in 1984 with a completely new car. True to his perfectionism and high sense of professionalism, he dug his heels in to make sure he got his way.

I was very, very annoyed, because I knew we were letting ourselves in for big trouble. We would start the 1984 season with a beautiful brand-new car, but we would have to spend half the season sorting out teething troubles. And that is no way to win a world championship.

John Barnard wouldn't give an inch, so I had no option other than to go through the back door and do some lobbying and scheming at Marlboro. I flew to Lausanne and gave the man in charge my version of how things stood. Marlboro promptly put pressure on Ron Dennis (as they were in an ideal position to do under the contract terms). There was so much money involved that Ron had to give in and, more important, force John Barnard to back down.

As a result, we entered the new turbo in the last four races of the 1983 season. And, right from the first, problems came thick and fast – brakes, coolers, rear wing, etc. By the time we reached Kyalami, however, the car was so fast that I had the race leader – Patrese – in my sights and sensed victory, only for the car to pack up because of electrical failure six laps before the end. That was the race that decided the world championship for Piquet in the Brabham-BMW – the first turbo champion in Formula 1 history.

Certain emotions had been laid bare because of the high-handed attempt by Ron and John to prevent the turbo being entered in the last four races of 1983. I was furious at Barnard's arrogance and the two of them were certainly annoyed by the hard-nosed approach I had used to get my own way. At the same time, there were other, more complicated issues to be resolved, not least of which was that concerning John Watson.

My dear team colleague again had the feeling that he was underpaid, above all by comparison with yours truly, and he set his sights on a princely sum in exchange for re-signing with McLaren. In my view, he massively over-estimated his market value and allowed himself to be manoeuvred into a dead-end street by his financial adviser, Nick Brittan. It was none of my business, of course, although I was obviously anxious to have John as a partner, since we got on well. Watson is a past-master at protracted negotiation and biding his time; once again, he was in no hurry. He felt safe, because all the other viable Formula 1 drivers had already signed their new contracts: McLaren would have to fall back on him and he would cash in on it.

Then, completely out of the blue, came the news that Renault had released Alain Prost. There were all kinds of reasons for this, it appears, including some of a highly personal nature (Formula 1 gossip alleged that there had been rumours of an affair between Prost and Renault team chief Larrousse's wife).

Whatever the cause, the break came at an unusual moment, since most contracts are signed, sealed and delivered by November and there is normally no spare cockpit around.

The situation was tailor-made for Ron Dennis. He was able to dump Watson ('Sorry, we simply can't afford you') and pick up possibly the fastest driver in the world for a derisory sum. Prost changed hands at a bargain-basement price.

By comparison with Prost, I was terribly expensive. I had already negotiated a two-year (1983–84) contract which represented a new all-time high on the Formula 1 stock exchange. I had pointed out in the negotiations that I had only asked for one dollar for my driving ability when I made my comeback, the rest being paid me for my PR value; when it came to a second contract, I was able to argue that a driver who had, after all, won two Grands Prix in the preceding season must of necessity be worth more than one dollar – in addition to his undiminished PR value, of course.

As a result, I had emerged with a contract that was unprecedented and, I must admit, slightly over the top by comparison with the other drivers – and decidedly so when compared with Prost, who had had to settle for what he could get. This was one reason for much of the tension that was around that next season. To Ron Dennis, I was the man who had squeezed him dry, whereas Alain Prost was his talisman, his bargain-basement buy.

I was not happy at the prospect of having a superstar in the team in exchange for the easy-going Watson. I had to play it cool and act as if it were totally immaterial, but I knew deep down that I was in for a hard time. My persistence, my test driving and my modest political triumphs had all played a part in creating a sound basis for the new car; and the thought that someone new might come along and reap the benefits was, at first, irritating. But then, gradually, it motivated me: Prost was someone I had to contend with.

I only knew one thing about Alain – that he was fast. On a personal level, I steeled myself against unpleasant surprises and possible intrigue; I was wary and reserved. Everything Alain did in the early stages only served to reinforce my uneasiness. He had an unerring instinct for consolidating and developing his position within the team: he kept turning up for no apparent reason at the McLaren works in England, he skilfully kept himself in the picture and built up his own PR image. (Not that I could decry that – it is part of a professional's job to create for himself a favourable working environment.)

He said a great many complimentary things to me. I had been his idol when he took up racing and that I had won my first world championship in 1975 – the year he had taken his driving test. At the time, I told myself that he must have something in mind with all this sweet talk. Eventually, however, my suspicions disappeared: it dawned on me that he was simply warm, friendly and straightforward.

And a fast son-of-a-bitch into the bargain.

CHAPTER NINE

THE TOUGHEST YEAR

THE BIG CONFRONTATION had been announced. My motivation was good, and I had programmed myself to win the first race of the season, if possible – in order to teach the young man what life was all about.

Rio, March 1984. Prost is six tenths of a second faster than myself in qualifying and I am not yet aware that this will be the case in almost every race of the season. No matter. I get away beautifully, overtake him, take de Angelis and Mansell, and zero in on Warwick, who is driving his first race for Renault. I come out of his slipstream at the end of the straight, doing about 190mph. Warwick doesn't move over, but I have my nose in front anyway. We squeeze together into a fourth-gear corner. The McLaren hits a bump on the track and moves over fractionally. There is a sharp jolt as Warwick's left front wheel smacks into my rear right. That could have been it for both of us, but I'm still here and I can see him in my mirror, thank God. I have probably damaged my suspension. I check it carefully for the next two laps, but everything feels all right. Alboreto is in trouble, so I take the lead, something I haven't done in a long time. Everything under control – including Prost, who meanwhile has worked his way past Warwick. We're lying first and second, just the way it should be. Prost is more than ten seconds back.

Everything was going to plan. A shade too well, as it happened: after thirty-nine laps, the red light came on in the cockpit. I drove into the pits and got out, choking back my fury. That would have been a very important win.

Instead, there were three points to ponder. First, the hi-tech miracle I had been driving was sidelined because of a battery cable that had been improperly soldered. Second, Warwick's front suspension had been damaged after all during our little contretemps and the Renault had failed to complete. Third, Prost had just won his first race and I was on the defensive as of day one.

I won the next race – Kyalami – with a good sixty seconds to spare over Prost. Neither of us finished at Zolder. Prost won at Imola, where I didn't finish. Then came the French Grand Prix in Dijon.

I start from ninth on the grid and have to drive harder and more brutally than I really want to in case the leader group gets away from me. I work my way up through the field until only Tambay (Renault) and Prost are ahead of me. I am driving like a madman, pushing beyond what the tyres will take. I have to. There is no point in wait-and-see tactics or saving my tyres: all I can see are those two ahead of me. Just as I pull up on Prost, he turns into the pit lane, one wheel loose. Pity he's gone, I think to myself, because he hadn't a hope today. I plant myself in Tambay's rear-view mirror. Pressure, pressure, pressure. Maybe he'll feel it. Maybe he'll get nervous. We lap Laffite in the right-hander between start and finish. Laffite moves over for Tambay, but moves back immediately on line. He obviously doesn't know we're travelling in sandwich formation. We are hitting 125mph. To avoid ploughing into him I veer out right over the kerb. The car leaps into the air but I get it under control again.

When you are driving relatively slowly, moments like these are really terrifying: your heart pounds and you exhibit all the anxiety symptoms of a normal human being. But, when you are concentrating 100 per cent, going for broke, you don't sense the danger and there is no chance of your becoming alarmed. Two, three quick movements of the wheel, everything going so fast that it doesn't really register, simply bounces off. It is a reflex action. The only thing you focus on is the car ahead.

The car ahead is Tambay's. I try four or five times on successive laps to take him on the straight. I even try to take him alongside the pit wall, a fraction away from the guard-rail and with the nearside wheels virtually in the gutter. I am prepared to risk everything. My habitual calm has deserted me.

Nothing works until he makes a mistake, undoubtedly because of the continuous pressure he has been subjected to. He takes one corner slightly wide, opens the gate, and I slip through on the inside and accelerate away faster than he can.

My tyres are deteriorating all the time. When do we reach the halfway point? Surely it must be soon. I was always given countdown signals for the final five laps of a race only; before that, the pits would only signal my race position and flash me a one-time signal that the race was half over. Had I missed the halfway signal because I had been concentrating on the tussle with Tambay? (When that happens in the middle of a race, there is no way you can rely on your own sense of time. You have no idea how many laps you have driven unless they signal you. In this case, it had been agreed that I would be called in for a tyre-change halfway through the race. They *hadn't* signalled, however, because Ron Dennis had persuaded himself that it perhaps wasn't necessary. What he didn't understand was that my 'charge' had been at the expense of my tyres.)

It is not until I suddenly catch sight of a twenty-laps-to-go signal that I realise what is happening. We are already fifteen laps past halfway, the tyres are in a diabolical state, and I am furious at not having been signalled in. I put my hand up to my helmet – the signal that the driver has decided that a change is necessary and will be coming in on the next lap.

I change tyres. Now I am second again, twenty seconds behind Tambay (who had changed tyres at exactly the right moment, of course). I drive like a maniac again, reel him in once more, and pass him two laps before the end. All at once, his brakes go, and I'm home and dry.

I was really angry with Ron Dennis because he hadn't respected our halfway agreement. It always makes me angry when you have to drive harder to win than absolutely necessary. Taking unnecessary risks is always stupid. Never mind, that was the French Grand Prix, when 70,000 spectators saw Niki first and Renault second.

The next race was in Monaco. I don't like Monaco. What gets on my nerves is not the town so much – that doesn't bother me one way or another – but all the trappings that surround the race. I prefer a Grand Prix to be a Grand Prix and not degenerate into some kind of circus. There is an almost perverse contrast between the sportsman there to do his job and the arena in which he must perform. To me it makes no sense at all. I don't find it all that marvellous for someone to be standing outside the Hotel de Paris with a champagne flute in his hand when I'm screaming past through the corner a scant three yards away. I am too much of a purist to enjoy racing in Monaco.

Monaco was the sixth race of the season and the sixth time that Prost was faster in qualifying. My weakness in qualifying had by this time become apparent. It would seem that I was not capable of lifting myself like Prost did in the chaotic qualifying laps. You really have to fly, you have to 'take off' mentally and sometimes even physically. You have to have that extra something, a compound of enthusiasm and madness. Prost, six years my junior, was more capable of it than I was. The figures speak for themselves: in 1984, Prost was on average 1.2 seconds faster in qualifying than I was. That translates as between four and five places on the grid.

At the time I couldn't admit how much this preoccupied and irritated me. To do so would perhaps have made Prost a further two tenths faster. I analysed the situation and came to the conclusion that my slow qualifying times indicated a weakness that no racing driver should have. There was no reason why I couldn't drive as fast as Prost. That had to be possible.

It wasn't. Apart from one single occasion – in Dallas – I couldn't put together that little bit extra. Finally, I didn't even try. I felt every bit as strong as Prost in the race proper, where I knew he didn't have the edge. The only thing was, I had to pay the penalty for poor qualifying times. To make up those places on the grid between Prost and myself, I had to take some additional risks in the race itself and drive with more aggression than I naturally felt.

Back to Monaco, sixth race of the season. Prost heads the world championship. I am second, six points behind. He has pole position, I am eighth on the grid (and, in Monaco especially, that really hurts). It rains during warm-up and I am one second faster than the field: I'll never forget the look of consternation on Ron Dennis's face. That was when it became clear to me that he was on Prost's side and I began to sense a strange sort of hostility towards myself that, at the time, I couldn't explain.

Having to outdrive two Ferraris in the rain is the penalty you pay for being eighth on the grid. Alboreto is fairly easy: I wait for a favourable moment, accelerating away from Sainte Dévote, the first corner after the start and finishing line. I am close up behind him. I accelerate early to build up turbo-charge pressure, taking care to avoid wheel spin on the wet circuit. I am level with him coming out of the right-hander. He can't quite control the wheel spin. I change into third and I'm half a length up. There's nothing he can do about it.

Next, I come up into Arnoux's mirror. I watch him for a couple of laps. His weakest moment comes just before Loew's, where he brakes one or two yards before he really should. I hang in tightly behind him in the Mirabeau and move out to his left coming up to the next corner. He is a car's length ahead, but I brake later than he does. Arnoux glances left, realising at the very last moment that I am there, and pulls right. The most difficult part of the outbraking manoeuvre is over, but I still have to cope with my excess speed (although everything seems to be happening in slow motion). I shift down into first – something of a rarity in Grand Prix these days. Braking so late puts me into a skid. I can't take the ideal line in left and start skidding towards the guard-rail. A couple of feet away from it, the tyres grip again, the car takes the left turn, and Arnoux is behind me.

After pulling off a manoeuvre like that, it is criminal to throw away the points. I am in second position, behind Prost. I have to let Senna past, but there is no problem coasting home in third. Then, on the crest of the Casino Corner, I accelerate too early and slide into the guard-rail. The engine cuts out. It's all over. Driver error that could decide the entire world championship.

I win at Brands Hatch, putting myself back in world championship contention, within striking distance of Prost. Our personal friendship is okay – good even, considering the circumstances. It is a fight to the finish for the championship: one or other of us must win for McLaren, Porsche and TAG. The plain fact is, we have the best car – more reliable than the Brabham-BMW, and better all round than the Ferrari and the Lotus. The Honda-Williams is looking good, but represents no threat as yet.

My relationship with Ron Dennis, however, is going from bad to worse. Somehow, he swings the whole team round behind Prost. We have the same material, of course, and our cars are prepared with the same tender loving care: it's not that I am put at any disadvantage in material terms, simply that I am upset by the unpleasant atmosphere. A lot of people find it odd that none other than Lauda the Computer should all of a sudden start complaining about lack of human warmth. But I believe that I need warmth and consideration just as much as the next person. I too suffer in a chilly atmosphere. I don't get morose about it, however. Instead, I try to find out why and, if possible, how to repair the situation.

There can be no question that Ron Dennis is a diligent professional. He is good at raising cash and he has the wonderful knack of giving his sponsors value for money. The team functions perfectly, and you can sense the perfectionist at the helm. To me, however, Ron's weakness seems to reside in a sort of chip-on-the-shoulder complex. It hurts him to be reminded that he started life as a modest mechanic at Cooper and Brabham. It is for this reason that he overreacts as team boss. His arrogance can be unbearable.

Having two cars home and dry at the head of the world championship table allowed him to indulge in psychological fun and games, something he viewed as a sort of revenge for the fabulous contract I had managed to negotiate for 1983 and 1984. Clearly, he had never been able to forgive me for that, and now he could take his revenge by parading his 'cheap' driver as Number One in the team and putting me on the back burner. Prost, by the way, did nothing to exacerbate the situation: he did his own thing, he fought within the rules, and he was fair and *simpatico* throughout.

The chilly silence between Dennis and myself was increasingly enervating and I wanted to clear the air. I invited Ron and his girlfriend Liza to fly down to Ibiza with me so that we could talk things over in peace. It was a beautiful day, so we took a trip out to sea in my motor-boat. The Balearics were at their best. I cut the engine and struggled to put out the sea anchor (as a nautical man I'm not up to much). Okay, Ron, how can we get things back on an even keel? What are the reasons behind this split between us?

He said that he felt a sort of love-hate towards me. He felt he had been put at a disadvantage because I had virtually blackmailed him with my two-year contract: at the time, he had been in a situation where he couldn't do without me and, accordingly, he had had to grin and bear it. Further, he reproached me on account of my aloofness and egocentric attitude. Somewhere along the way he came out with the rather droll statement: 'If you pay somebody such an amazing amount of money, you can surely expect a little friendship in exchange.'

That rubbed me up the wrong way. What does an honorarium have to do with friendship? Ron isn't the type that attracts me as a friend (as it is, I only have two or three really close friends) and, irrespective of how much money he is paying, that won't change. As far as egocentricity is concerned, he is right: I do try to arrange everything in my life to suit myself. In the specific instance of Lauda/McLaren, on the other hand, I could argue that I had done all in my power to help the common cause; in other words, he too had benefited from my egocentricity. What's more, as far as performance was concerned, I had delivered 100 per cent.

The conversation went quite well and, by the end of it, I had the feeling that a new basis for civility and cooperation had been created. We put in at a small island to have a bite to eat. As we were going up to the restaurant, Dennis said: 'I must change my hat now.' He was no longer my new-found friend Ron, but McLaren team chief Mr Dennis and, in that capacity, he was about to make me a contractual offer. The sum he mentioned was exactly half what I had been getting. I asked if he was sure he hadn't had too much sun on Ibiza. 'I'd rather sit twiddling my thumbs than drive for half price.'

The conversation ran aground: he was adamant, so was I. I knew perfectly well that my last deal had been over the top, that I was getting at least twice as much as the other drivers, but cutting my income by half was ridiculous, almost insulting.

He then said that he would call in Senna the following Monday and offer him a two- to three-year contract. Please yourself, I said, and wished him luck. 'It was nice having you on my boat for a day, even if the whole thing was a waste of time.'

It was at that point that I first toyed with the idea of signing with another team for the 1985 season. I was originally attracted to Ferrari but, by this time, I had outgrown Ferrari fee structures. At any rate, the Italian team had already signed on their drivers for the next season. Renault also appealed to me, because I thought it must be possible to do something to get a decent return on the enormous investment they had made.

In July I had a first meeting with Renault team chief Gérard Larrousse. I told him I was interested. He didn't think there would be any change of drivers at Renault; we would have to wait and see. He rang later to say that the subject of Lauda was now current. We discussed it in general terms and arranged to meet in Paris. I was a little disconcerted by the fact that it took Larrousse a full ten minutes to establish whether or not he should send a helicopter to pick me up at Le Bourget. If he takes so long to decide such a simple matter, I thought, what are things going to be like when it comes down to the complex business of Formula 1?

Clearly, all this took place under a veil of total secrecy. I was afraid that Ron Dennis would mess me around in the remaining races of the season, and that I could miss out on the world championship as a result. Okay, said Larrousse, we'll keep it dark, nobody will get wind of it.

I flew from Ibiza to Paris. We talked and haggled for hours. Finally, he accepted my financial demands which, admittedly, were far from modest. The contract he showed me was standard Renault, an elaborate affair that I couldn't make head or tail of. Couldn't he simply take a sheet of notepaper and set down the main headings: amount, duration, Number One driver, test-drive privileges, Renault as a private car, etc.? That would cover it.

Once the red tape had been taken care of, Larrousse said that we should pay a short visit to the *Président*. I took this to mean some sort of courtesy call, formal handshake, and so on. We went up to Monsieur Hanson's office, and I took an instant dislike to him – he had a cold, calculating air about him. What is more, he didn't seem to be particularly keen on motor sport – or, at least, he didn't find anything good to say about it. Then he told Larrousse and myself that the contract could not, unfortunately, be finalised that day. Something unexpected had come up and we would need a fourteen-day moratorium.

Larrousse himself was also surprised, and it occurred to me then that his standing at Renault could not be all that high. I found him a nice, decent sort of person, but perhaps a bit on the weak side to hold down the job of team chief in a firm like that. However, Larrousse proposed that I should sign the contract in the meantime; Renault would sign later. I naturally refused to go along with that kind of idiocy: what's the point of a unilateral contract? We left it that Larrousse would get in touch with me when the contract was ready for signing by both sides.

I had left Ibiza that morning and I flew back that afternoon. The only people I had spoken to that day were my co-pilot and the boys at air-traffic control. I hadn't been home more than an hour when Ron Dennis called.

'Where were you today?'

'Paris,' I said, taken aback.

'Good of you to admit as much.'

He went on to recount details of the contract I had discussed with Renault. I was simply astonished. It was perfectly obvious that there was a leak somewhere in Renault, whether deliberate or otherwise. Nonetheless, I could say in all honesty that I had signed nothing. Dennis was somewhat mollified.

Larrousse called back in August. Everything was okay, the contract had been approved, management had said yes, we could go ahead and sign. Irritated by the earlier incident, I said that the contract was valid and that I gave my word on it, but I would sign only after the world championship had been decided. I was afraid that, otherwise, Ron Dennis would put one over on me. If he knew for certain that I was leaving, he'd make sure Prost won the title.

Larrousse took the point. He said that a verbal agreement was good enough for him and that he gave the same undertaking that I would drive for Renault in 1985.

This time the secret didn't exactly leak out, although the French press kept rumours alive. Dennis kept on trying to make me sign for half my current fee. He demonstrated his innate sensitivity by telling me two hours before the Austrian Grand Prix at the Österreichring that, unless I settled for half, he would sign Keke Rosberg.

'Suit yourself. Get Keke. And, by the way, thanks very much for buggering me around like this just before a really important race. It's only the world championship at stake.'

Österreichring: I pass Piquet with fifteen laps to go and move into the lead. Prost has hit an oil slick and spun out, so the world championship has taken on a whole new perspective. There is no real danger from Piquet – I have already seen that his rear tyres are on their last legs, so I don't expect any more trouble from that quarter. All I have to do is bring the car home, the race is run. I accelerate out of Bosch Corner in fourth gear, there is a terrific bang, and I lose all power. The engine is still turning but no power is being transferred to the wheels. Differential gone, I think to myself, and hold my hand up to indicate to the others that I'll be driving outside the ideal line. I move out left and am just about to find a convenient place to park on the grass when the thought strikes me: damn it, it's a long walk back to the pits from here. Why not try coasting on a bit longer? I fiddle around with the gears, find third. It is still working. My first thought is, well, at least you can make the pits in third.

In that kind of situation it is hard to think logically. You are so attuned to driving at the limit that you can't improvise once you leave the realm of super-fast instincts and reflexes and enter a much more banal world. I make no conscious effort to check what possibilities are still left – I simply put my foot down in third, shift up to fourth as the revs come up, get no response, and automatically move up into fifth. Fifth is working. Keep going, I think, maybe you can place fifth or sixth and pick up at least one championship point. I stay in third until the revs are screeching, then bang in fifth. This will cut about five seconds off my lap times by comparison with a healthy gearbox. Piquet is seventeen seconds behind me now, so it will take him three or four laps to catch up. I check the pit signal: seventeen seconds ahead of Piquet. I drive as well as I can without a fourth gear. Next lap: seventeen seconds ahead of Piquet. It flashes through my head, of course, Nelson knows the way I drive, he knows that I throttle back in the final stages and don't give a damn how much lead I have when I cross the line. He probably thinks I'm deliberately driving more slowly, that I'm driving a tactical race, and that there is no point at all putting me under pressure because I'll only respond immediately and put my foot down again. What is more, his rear tyres are not exactly in the best condition to mount a real charge.

It is extremely difficult to find the right moment to shift from third to fifth. The tension is unbelievable. When is Piquet going to realise that I'm not playing cat and mouse, that I'm really done for? And what if the fifth gear goes because the synchromesh rings abrade? Will bits of the damaged fourth gear get in the works and make a complete *Salat* of the gearbox? I pray that I will make it to the finishing line. And, all the while, Nelson holds back, keeps position, thinking to himself: Niki is playing it cool.

I can't recall ever cluttering my mind to that degree during a race. By the end, my head was simply splitting.

I take the flag. I am now neck and neck with Prost in the title race. Piquet and I walk up to the winner's rostrum. He asks how things went. Well, I say, my fourth gear was shot. I can tell by his expression how shattered he is that he let his opportunity slip. He could so easily have won this Grand Prix. Of all the races that decided the world championship in 1984, one way or another the Austrian Grand Prix was my most fortuitous. It was a happy coincidence that it should have happened in Austria of all places.

At the beginning of September I received a message to call Larrousse at his holiday home in Brittany. Urgently.

Sorry, said Larrousse, I can't honour the contract. The French trade unions were incensed at the amount of money involved. Also, Renault had all kinds of other problems and the *Président* had said he couldn't make a case to the unions for paying Lauda so-and-so many millions at a time when some of the workforce were being laid off. I asked him if he was insane. What on earth was he saying?

Larrousse: 'I'm sorry, I'm sorry, there's nothing I can do.'

As far as he was concerned, the matter was closed. As for me, I was without a contract, at the mercy of Ron Dennis, and still had two decisive races to drive in the 1984 championship season – Nürburgring and Estoril.

The tension got to me. I had to clear my brain and settle 1985 contract details. Dennis was still adamant, determined to show me who was boss: half what you're getting now and not one dollar more.

There was nothing for it but to fly out to Lausanne and ask the Marlboro people if they still wanted my services. If the answer was yes, then they'd better do something about it. They did. A few days before Nürburgring, Dennis came up with a contract I felt able to sign. I wasn't over the moon about it, because I would be earning one third less than before, but – when all was said and done – I could accept after two over-the-top Lauda years. It was farcical, all the same: there I was, on the brink of the world championship, and I had to accept the most swingeing salary cut of my entire career.

Prost drove impeccably at Nürburgring and won magnificently. I could only manage fourth place (a manoeuvre by Mauro Baldi cost me one or even two places). The title would not be decided until two weeks later. On a hitherto unknown circuit near Lisbon: Estoril.

CHAPTER TEN

ESTORIL

THE HOTEL STINKS. The rooms are terrible, Prost moves out after the first day, but I can't be bothered. Willy is here, performing wonders in the kitchen, and the switchboard pulls the plug in the evening and promises I won't be disturbed again. All in all, I can put up with it. The hotel is right next to the Estoril circuit and everything has been specially built to house the Grand Prix circus.

The situation is ominous: atrocious weather, a brand-new circuit and all the unknown factors that implies; Alain Prost in superb form, attested by his strong showing at Nürburgring, his obvious high, his cosseting by the McLaren squad. I am on the defensive, but I do have one immense advantage: I only have to finish second in this race to clinch the world championship title.

Qualifying is a nightmare. Everything goes wrong. It is like a second-rate movie. Precious time is squandered repairing incredibly stupid defects. Then, probably as a result, I make a series of mistakes. The upshot is that I am in eleventh place on the grid on the Sunday, Prost in second. And this is supposed to be the most important qualifying for me of the whole season? All I can produce is eleventh place – and on a new, unpredictable circuit at that?

The situation is so bad that there is no point in worrying about it. Willy cooks. Willy massages. Some things in life are constant, after all; there are some things you can rely on. Willy is a colossus. I sleep like a baby.

When I wake the next day I rationalise as follows. All the others are nervous, so there is no need for me to be as well. That certainly won't help. I run through my programme for the day: do your best, concentrate, don't make mistakes, and be as fast about it as you can. Everything else is beyond my control, so it can be ignored for the moment. My thoughts focus on the target for today: perform as well as you can, forget what's happening around you, don't get hung up on the prospects of winning – or losing – a world championship title. Be yourself as far as possible.

I manage to psych myself into a relaxed frame of mind. I am relaxed; Prost isn't. I can tell at first glance. He keeps biting his nails; he is pale and haggard. He tells me right away that he hasn't slept well, that he has had a rough night. I can believe that. He goes to the toilet time and again.

His whole demeanour encourages me to run through my early morning checklist once again and to reinforce it: forget how important the world championship is, get it out of your mind as far as possible, focus on *your* performance *today.*

I am three tenths of a second faster than Prost in morning training, but the engine doesn't feel quite right. It is the same one I won with at Brands Hatch. I replace it with the one I used in Dijon, another winning engine.

Marlene turns up two hours before the race is due to start. It is one of her strange, impulsive gestures. She hates racing. She never comes to the track. She couldn't care less about the world championship. But, despite all this, she said she wanted to come this time. I couldn't inflict a whole weekend on her and, besides, she can only stay one night because of the children. In the meantime, her sister Renate will babysit. I wasn't able to find someone to fly my Learjet, so I asked Nelson Piquet to send his Citation to Ibiza and have his crew pick Marlene up. She arrives at the circuit around mid-morning. She is a bit fluttery but doesn't make me nervous.

As noon approaches, I start to feel more and more tense. I put on my helmet. Whether it is pure joy or an indescribable feeling of power I don't know, but tears come into my eyes. I have never felt as strong as this in my whole life. I drive out of the pits and onto the grid. I am very, very calm and I know I won't do anything stupid.

I have programmed myself to play a waiting game for the first couple of laps to make sure I get clear of the heavy traffic. I hold the centre of the track coming into the first corner to ensure that no one can jostle me. The Alfas of Cheever and Patrese are in front of me, the Arrows of Boutsen and Surer behind.

I see Piquet go into a spin and that makes me angry: why the hell can't he watch what he is doing? Does he have to pick today of all days to mess around like this? Surely he must know that I need him around. (Nelson is my only real friend out of the whole bunch and it goes without saying that he will do his best to beat Prost and do me a favour.) Now he is way back down the field and I have the kind of feeling you have when your only friend has suddenly disappeared.

First signal from the pits: twelfth position. That's all right, that's not important. I take the two Alfas, then Tambay. It is difficult to make out the pit signals because the circuit is so bumpy and everything is blurred. On top of this, the final bend is one of the few places where you have a chance of overtaking. I find myself in a group of five that I must break clear of to stop Prost disappearing into the far distance. He is in second place. Then I manage to make out from the blurred signal boards that he has gone into the lead: I can just imagine him up ahead, eating up the track. I am now stuck in ninth position. Johansson is in front of me, and I can't get past because his Toleman is faster than the McLaren on the straights.

I am still completely calm, calm enough to think clearly: if I can't take Johansson, it can only be because my engine is not delivering full power. We are coming up to halfway and I am still chugging away behind Johansson. There is no doubt in my mind why he is putting up such a fight: the TV cameras are locked in on us and this young man is in the process of deciding the outcome of the championship. Every other driver would have done the same in his place.

Time is beginning to run out for me. Now that I know that my engine is under-performing, I have to boost charge pressure – from 2.2 to 2.5. This is taking an enormous risk. At 2.5, I am using far too much fuel. You can only drive that high for short bursts at a time, otherwise you haven't a hope of going the distance.

At long last, Johansson makes a mistake. I pull ahead on the finishing straight, he brakes coming into the next corner, and his wing clips my left rear wheel. It is unintentional, of course, but it is stupid and completely unnecessary. Why does he have to pick now to brake too late and go into the corner with his tyres smoking? (I saw this on the TV replay after the race.)

Things are moving along nicely now. I am reeling them in one after the other every second round. Finally, I overtake Senna. I think I am in second position. A signal comes from the pits. I can just make it out: third position. What a slap in the face. Mansell in the Lotus is between me and Prost. And he is no less than thirty-nine seconds up, which accounts for my not seeing him or sensing his presence.

I drive flat-out, posting one new lap record after another, clipping 1 to 1.5 seconds per lap off Mansell's lead. It should be okay, but it's going to be tight.

I keep battling on and am on schedule until I come up behind a really tough group of lapped drivers. Berger is the only one who moves over; all the others make themselves important, put on a show of being involved in the race for the title. I have to drive off line time and again. I lose six seconds and I am livid. I start driving aggressively again, much more so than I had intended.

Suddenly I see a Lotus just ahead of me. I think I must be coming up to lap de Angelis. There is no way it could be Mansell, he is too far ahead. Then I notice that the front wheel of the Lotus is blocking as the car brakes. Someone has problems. It's Mansell. I am past him.

I am second, second, second, that's all I need. Not quite, I have to finish. Thinking back to when I boosted charge pressure earlier, I start to get worried. I know that I must have used up too much fuel.* I immediately reduce pressure to 1.8, but have to go back up to 2.2 at once because Senna is starting to put the pressure on behind. I adjust my speed to Senna's. I couldn't care less what Prost is doing out in front.

Piquet has been lapped, but I notice that he tucks in behind me, even though I have eased up. There is something touching about this, as if he is standing by to push me over the line if necessary (as if that matters, seeing that it is forbidden). At any rate, the mere fact of his company makes me feel good. Come on little car, sweet, well-behaved little car, don't let me down. A couple of corners to go, then I accelerate out of the last one and know that I will make the line, with or without fuel.

The chequered flag.

As I cross the line and slow down, Piquet pulls alongside and makes an inquiring gesture. He isn't exactly sure that I have placed second, that I am world champion. I signal to him that I have made it and he punches the air in pleasure. Then Laffite comes up, makes the same gesture; I respond, but he doesn't react. He accelerates away. I know, of course, that he and Prost

---

* It was established later that this was not the case. The left turbocharger had been damaged (at its most drastic, this meant that the blades were slowly disintegrating). This meant a loss of 100 to 120 horsepower – which I had sensed when battling it out with Johansson, but which hadn't showed up on my instrument panel. In this instance, data on turbo performance related exclusively to the one that was working well, i.e. the right turbocharger. By turning up the charge pressure I had only contrived to restore approximate values, which meant I was not using up any more fuel than planned. During a race itself, however, it is impossible to determine this.

are close friends. I wave to the spectators and they go wild with delight. I somehow always had the feeling that the Portuguese were pro-Lauda; at any rate, they seem to be pleased that I am world champion.

There is pandemonium when I pull up. They try to drag me off to the podium right away. But I take my time. I take off my helmet nice and slowly. Breathe deeply.

Then we are on the podium. Alain Prost is there already. I can tell by his expression how tough it is for him. He is fighting back the tears. Forget it, I tell him, forget it as soon as you can. That was my year, next year will be yours. Forget all the rest, just look forward to next season. Prost listens to me eagerly and seems grateful for what I am saying (and I really do mean it). I can see the tension go out of his face.

I have difficulty coping with victory ceremonies. You are brutally yanked out of another, distant world where you have been living for the past two hours. The brusque transition from total concentration and self-centredness is too much for the brain to assimilate. Suddenly, you are everyone's property.

The real joy of winning is something to be savoured in silence at the precise moment of victory. I often imagine how fantastic it would be to win a race or become world champion and be able to get out of the car unmolested and sit down somewhere with nobody else around. Instead, you ache all over, you are sweating like a pig, people are pushing and shoving, you are hauled up onto the rostrum like a side of beef. Then they play the national anthem, and you're not ready to *feel* anything. You stand there like a puppet, with no brain and no heart. To get through it, I normally speak to the other two guys up there: at least they live in your world, they are on your wavelength.

That is why the urge to get away from all of it as soon as possible after the race is so incredibly strong. Head for the 'copter, make it to your own plane and get out of there. Then, next morning, you can wake up and really enjoy what is, after all, a genuinely marvellous feeling.

Winning only comes true the morning after.

In Estoril everything was particularly tough, but I knew it had to be, it was part of the job. I was stuck there for three and a half hours giving interviews. It was all rather a farce: if the turbocharger had packed in completely instead of only partly, I would have been sitting alone somewhere.

I finally managed to dash back to the hotel, change, and keep a dinner date with Mansour Ojjeh, who had hired an entire restaurant. There were no speeches or other such formalities. It was all good fun. Prost – who had turned up from Monaco with Stephanie – started to relax again. Willy Dungl had promised to have a few if I won the title. Everyone was anxious to see what kind of face the fitness guru would pull when he downed his first whisky. He made a valiant attempt, but three whiskies were his limit.

We moved on to a disco which McLaren had booked exclusively, but the place was jam-packed. I had bought presents for my eight mechanics (whether I won or not) and there was great hilarity when I handed them over.

At some point, Marlene complained of tummy trouble, so we called it a day at half past twelve. I was still fairly sober when I got back to the hotel and I thought to myself, just as well, you have to fly tomorrow and there is a TV show in the evening.

A quiet end to an eventful day.

CHAPTER ELEVEN

GETTING NOWHERE FAST

MONACO, 1985. IT is the evening after the first day's qualifying. Since tomorrow is a rest day, I can stay up a bit later than usual. I wander down to the Tip-Top Bar and order myself a whisky. Rosberg comes striding in, sits down.

Out of the blue, he turns to me and says:

'Don't you think all of this is stupid?'

'Come again?'

'It's sick how we drive around here in our little bathtubs. It makes me want to throw up. I really felt like walking away from it all today.'

That makes two of us, I reassured him. I was pleased by the fact that he, of all people, had brought the subject up. Keke sometimes drives like a maniac and doesn't give a damn about anything or anyone. I was already beginning to believe that I was getting too sensitive, that all the years in the game had softened me up. That very day, everything had struck me as totally mad. I had just finished my first qualifying lap. I had half accelerated into the hairpin behind Sainte Dévote when the feeling hit me: I was in the wrong place and in the wrong job. This had to be ridiculous, zooming around here like so many trained chimpanzees. One thousand horsepower on this circuit? Madness.

For the first time in my whole professional career I was assailed by doubt: could I make it through the next corner? It was all too tight, too fast, too insane for words. It no longer made sense. That's it, I thought, I've had enough; all I want to do now is get out, walk away, go home. However, I pulled myself together. I reminded myself that I had called it quits once before when I had been in a similar kind of mood. I mustn't make the same mistake again. I would keep going, see if it came good.

I had spent the whole day like that, toughing it out, and along comes Keke that same evening and says the whole business makes him feel sick. At that moment, I felt some empathy with him – which is saying a lot, if you know the man.

This exchange came right in the middle of a series of non-events. Up to that point in the season, not one race had gone smoothly: computer trouble, piston trouble, electrical failure. (As it turned out, in Monaco itself I spun out on an oil slick from a shunt involving Piquet and Patrese. The engine died on me and there was no way I could get it to fire again.)

Then came Montreal, another of my least favourite circuits. It had become increasingly obvious by then that there was something wrong with the rear axle on the McLaren. The wheels would shudder in slow corners and develop a nasty wheel spin. Barnard had acknowledged this and said a solution was imminent.

Training was traumatic. Nothing went right. I even chose the wrong qualifying tyres. I was on the crucial qualifying lap when the yellow flag came out. I eased off and, just at that moment, I noticed a beaver sitting by the side of the track to my right. He was staring straight at me and I thought to myself, please, don't get yourself killed, just stay where you are. As it happened, he didn't budge and I flashed past, missing him by inches.

I qualified in seventeenth position. When I mentioned the beaver to Ron Dennis, he simply smiled at me sympathetically, as if to say: poor old Niki, he's reduced to telling tales to explain away his lack of speed. The next day one of the track photographers started showing round shots of the beaver. Dennis must have felt a sudden twinge of conscience: 'You know, I really thought you made that up.'

When you are back in seventeenth place on the grid, you begin to have second thoughts. Even the view is terrible. You don't get a glimpse of fresh air – all you see are cars, cars, cars, all the way to the horizon, and you have a very strong sense of being at the back, far away from it all. What is more, there is no point in playing the hero. All you can do is tag along with the field, otherwise your chances of a collision are too great.

Once the race gets going, I work my way slowly through the back-markers – that seems to be par for the course this season – until, yet again, it is suddenly all over. This time, it is a bolt which detaches from the air cooler mounting.

In Detroit, the brakes go.

At Le Castellet, the differential.

At Silverstone, the electrical system.

At Nürburgring, a loose wheel.

At Österreichring, a defective turbo.

It is unbelievable. And there is nothing you can do about it.

You start imagining things. It is clear that Dennis and Barnard are all out for Prost this year and that all their efforts are justified by his strong challenging position in the championship race as of mid-season. It is frequently alleged – usually by the press – that my long run of bad luck can be attributed to Ron Dennis taking his revenge. That, of course, is utter nonsense. Dennis is not everybody's sweetheart, but he is certainly no criminal, and he wouldn't have arranged all these defects intentionally. The plain fact is that I am caught up in an insane series of setbacks which are oppressive in their consistency and which seem to develop a sort of inner dynamism which preys on my mind.

Is the fault not mine? I wonder. Ten cases of 'bad luck' in a row* is something I wouldn't accept from any driver in the world: I would tell him that he too had to be at fault somewhere along the line. I have to judge myself by this same criterion. Does this funny old car somehow sense that my heart is no longer in it? Do the mechanics think that? Have I lost the vital spark that keeps things running properly?

I must admit that, at the time, there were precious few sparks coming from me. I had had to psych myself up unduly before the very first race of the season, in Rio, and had done the same thing in Monaco, in Montreal and, from then on, in practically every subsequent race. There was no sense of novelty. The same Prost (perhaps just a shade faster than before), the same Dennis (even surlier than before), the same car, the same faces.

When I looked back at my first retirement in Montreal in 1979, I thought that I had gone about it wrongly. Simply

* Although I placed third at Imola and fifth at Nürburgring, in both races there was something wrong with the car that precluded a better result.

getting out of the car during training and saying *that's it* had seemed the right thing to do at the time but, by 1985, I took a different view: I wanted to probe my feelings more deeply and examine my reasons thoroughly.

One strong indication that I should retire was the fact that I frequently found myself thinking about the dangers inherent in the sport. I remember a conversation with Piquet during Silverstone. He told me about his mother and his brother, how closely knit his family was, and how he was supporting them. In passing, he dropped a remark to the effect that, deep down, he had come to terms with the fact that he would die in a racing car. His mother knew as much also. I wouldn't let go: had he *really* come to terms with that? Was that possible? He thought about it for a while, then he said:

'Yes, I believe so.'

By 1985 this sort of attitude was totally foreign to me. The conversation with Nelson made such an impression on me because it pinpointed the extent to which I was oriented towards survival; it made me realise how important it had become for me to get out in one piece. I wasn't like Piquet any more: I was one of the ones who think they have made it. All I had to do was take my helmet and go home – when the time was ripe.

An image from Montreal. As I drive away from the pits I see my fellow competitors streaming past flat-out, scorching into the first corner, swooping round at 155mph. I am in a completely different time frame as I edge out of the pits; I am just another spectator, divorced from the proceedings. All I can see are these midgets scrunched down in their cars, careening across the uneven circuit, their heads twisted first this way, then that. As an outsider I can only think: they must be absolutely deranged. If the slightest little thing happens to the car, the midget will be lifted and swatted as if by a giant hand. Then I have to pull myself together, urge myself on: *Get going, old son, put your foot down, get a move on.* And, one lap later, I'm back in the swing of things: just one mad midget among many.

This was not the sort of thing I could talk over with Prost, of course – there was nothing to be gained from handing him my weakness on a platter. But I suppose that he doesn't think about it, doesn't care, just gets coolly behind the wheel and puts his foot down as far as it will go.

I made a point of scrutinising my feelings and reactions, asking myself questions all the time and making sure I gave honest answers. After a while, I came to the conclusion that what was hurting most was my lack of matter-of-fact spontaneity; and that it would be pointless to drive if my rational self instructed me otherwise. There were other factors – the chilly atmosphere in the McLaren camp (Alain being one of the few exceptions), and the ridiculous series of mechanical failures. The bottom line was that I would retire.

I didn't foresee any problems in driving the remaining races of the season. I had enough experience and training to psych myself up sufficiently to avoid making a fool of myself in the couple of races left.

I told Ron Dennis on the Friday before Nürburgring that I wouldn't be driving the following season, neither for him nor for anyone else. He accepted my decision but asked me to keep it quiet for the time being. Once my retirement was made public, all the team bosses would immediately put pressure on their albeit too few star drivers to sign for the following year. It would be decent of me if I could let him have a chance to buy himself someone new. I agreed. A week later, he rang me up and told me: 'I have Rosberg. He has signed. Now you can do and say whatever you want.'

It was rather convenient for me that the next stop was the Österreichring, since this meant I could announce my retirement in my own country. I asked Marlboro's press attaché to call a press conference for nine o'clock on the Saturday. I had an announcement to make.

'What are you going to announce?'

'If I tell you now, I won't have anything to announce tomorrow. Maybe I'm pregnant.'

Ron Dennis was there within five minutes: 'You called a press conference for tomorrow?'

'Yes, why?'

'Okay, if Marlboro is giving a press conference, I'll be there.'

'Come if you like, but it's a Lauda press conference, not a Marlboro affair.'

The next morning the press tent was packed with reporters, The difficulty for me was to give a plausible explanation for something that seemed a little bit strange even to myself: I was calling it a day, but not right away. Anyhow, I simply explained how things were: that I didn't have the same motivation as formerly; that I was increasingly preoccupied with developing Lauda Air. In short, I was changing jobs.

Since Ron Dennis was standing beside me, nothing could have been more natural than to thank both him and McLaren. I asked if there were any questions. It didn't take long.

'What is going to happen at McLaren?'

Dennis took the mike, but didn't answer the question. Instead, he went into a diatribe. Pointing to the rear, where John Barnard was standing, he said: there is the really great man, the one who has been responsible for all these spectacular performances, but his contribution is never recognised and it should be, now, once and for all.

Not a word about me. Just Barnard and McLaren. It was stupid and embarrassing – you could see as much in the reporters' faces.

Qualifying started immediately afterwards. I had problems with one of the turbochargers and had to come in. Dennis came up to me in the pits. I told him he was an idiot and that he'd made a fool of himself in front of all those people. His only reply was the old chestnut: 'Nobody is perfect, everybody makes mistakes.' I turned on my heel and left him standing there. As the weekend progressed, it gradually filtered through to him that he had brought a wave of ill-feeling down upon himself, even in the British press. He apologised. He had had a few the night before, had got a little confused, and had been thrown by the bilingual press conference.

He was obliged to speak to me again just before the Dutch Grand Prix at Zandvoort, when he had to ask me to cede to Prost the car I was due to qualify in. That was a reasonable request, given the situation in the title race, and I didn't make an unnecessary fuss about it. As we talked, however, his real problem surfaced.

Lauda with teammate Clay Ragazzoni, Maranello, 5 February 1974.

Regazzoni, Lauda and Emerson Fittipaldi at the Spanish Grand Prix, Jarama, 28 April 1974.

Niki Lauda, in the Ferrari 312B3-74. Monaco, 26 May 1974.

Niki Lauda and Clay Regazzoni, Ferrari 312T, Grand Prix of Spain, Montjuic, 2 May 1975.

Lauda wins the Monaco Grand Prix in his Ferrari. Prince Rainier III of Monaco and Princess Grace are there to present the trophy, 11th May 1975.

Niki Lauda is flying in his Ferrari during practice for the fateful 1976 German Grand Prix around the Nürburgring track nicknamed 'The Green Hell'.

The crash at Nürburgring. The Ferrari was doing some 150 mph, 1 August 1976.

The burnt-out wreck was never officially investigated.

Lauda returns to race at Monza just six weeks after his crash, 12 September 1976.

Grand Prix of Italy, Monza, 12 September 1976.

Lauda in the McLaren-Ford MP4/1B, Grand Prix of Great Britain, 18 July 1982.

Stefan Johansson ahead of Lauda during the decisive race of the world championship in Estoril, 21 October 1984.

Raising the trophy at the 1984 British Grand Prix at Brands Hatch circuit in Kent, 22 July 1984.

Lauda, poses in front of a turbine during the delivering ceremony of the first executive jet 'Legacy 190' model to fly Niki airlines, at Embraer's headquarters, in Brazil, 14 May 2009.

Niki Lauda jokes with his protégé Lewis Hamilton in the Mercedes garage before the Australian Grand Prix, the first race of 2016 and another championship year for the British driver.

'Barnard and I work fifteen hours a day, 365 days a year for this car, this team. But when a race is won, it's always Prost or Lauda who has won it, nobody mentions us. That's wrong and it's unfair, we should get at least as much press coverage as the drivers. That's why the press conference in Zeltweg should have been McLaren's and not yours.'

Then he lost his temper again: 'You go off to Ibiza and laze around in the sun while we're working, and when you come back all the photographers are round you.'

I told him he had an inferiority complex and that I felt that discussions with him were stale and stupid. There was simply a barrier between us. Forget me, I told him.

Zandvoort. I psych myself up again, trying to find some motivation. It is liable to be a bloodbath out there if it rains and I am not sure if I could face up to that. But it should be fun if the circuit is dry, and there is no doubt that the McLarens are the best cars for this super-fast circuit.

The reason for this is the McLaren underbody, one of Barnard's true strokes of genius. Ever since the rules were changed to outlaw wing-cars by prescribing a flat bottom, all designer variants have focused on the final section of the bodywork, behind the engine. Here, you are permitted to increase the gap between underbody and track, and this works ideally in the case of the McLaren. The narrow engine and the configuration of the exhaust system make for the extremely advantageous bottle-like shape that is the be-all-and-end-all of underbody aerodynamics. Barnard has managed to generate considerable downthrust without having recourse to huge spoilers that adversely affect top speed. To put it in a nutshell:

Zandvoort – like the Österreichring – is a circuit where aerodynamic design takes precedence over all else. And that strongly favours the 1985 McLaren.

Technical problems during qualifying had forced me back into tenth place on the grid, but they were sorted out and did not re-emerge during the race proper. I drove the fastest warm-up lap and I sensed that I could win – even from tenth position. It suddenly was very important to me that I should seize one of my rare opportunities of the season, not least because I had just announced my intention to retire.

The start of the race is absolutely chaotic. Boutsen is ahead of me on the grid. He inches forward and comes to a standstill. I swerve out right, only to find Piquet there, also stalled. Somewhere along the line Mansell is also stranded. I zigzag like crazy and, one way or another, come through in one piece. I make it to the first corner. I am in sixth position.

A sudden flash of alarm: the car is oversteering. I have made a poor choice of tyres. The problem must be the hard tyre rear left. The arrangement with the pit crew is as follows: if I come in after only a couple of laps, it will be for harder tyres; if I come in to change tyres later on in the race, then they have to fit four softs (instead of three softs, one hard, as at present).

I come through into fourth position, then third – behind Rosberg and Prost. I close up on Prost, only to drop back again: I can't match his speed because the car is handling increasingly badly. There is no option – I have to change tyres as quickly as possible, even before the halfway point. By this point in the race, the arrangements call for four softs. So be it. And, just to make sure that the pit crew has no second thoughts,

I come in without signalling. The pit lane is long enough for them to realise what is happening. The tyre change goes beautifully smoothly. I drive back out. Eighth position.

What is this? The car is still handling badly. I am very, very careful about accelerating and I take it very gently through the slower corners so as to avoid wheel spin and damage to the tyres. Despite this, the damn thing is oversteering. The cars ahead of me suddenly are no longer there. They have gone in for a tyre change too, of course. All at once, I'm in the lead, ahead of Senna and Prost. There is no pressure from Senna but I know only too well that Prost will make a move. By the halfway point I have nine seconds in hand over Alain.

What I have no way of knowing is this: Ron Dennis has mounted another hard compound rear left whereas Prost, who comes in a couple of laps later, now has four softs. Prost keeps coming closer and closer, every lap bringing him a few tenths of a second nearer. Piquet looms up ahead of me. Because of his disastrous start, Nelson has never really got into the race, but his car is running so well now that he can avoid being lapped. In the faster corners he throws up turbulence which irritates me and forces me to brake. If only he knew how much this is cramping my style! Eventually, the penny drops: he speeds up, increasing the gap between us just enough to let me profit from his slipstream.

By this time, Prost is well past Senna and closing up behind me. With six laps to go, he looms large in my rear-view mirrors: all I can see behind me is *Marlboro.*

I take stock of the situation. There is no doubt that Alain can lap faster than I can – his car is oversteering less than mine. The classic place to take me has to be at the end of the long straight but, to outbrake me successfully, he has to be in a strong position coming into the straight. Instead, he seems to lose contact fractionally at precisely that point. I know that he can only take me somewhere else on the circuit if I make a mistake.

My course of action is clear: I have to concentrate particularly hard on driving the corner before the long straight so cleanly that I can drive flat-out away from the corner as early as possible. I have to watch what I'm doing in the chicane also: driving the ideal line means swinging right to left, but the defensive line is right down the middle.

There is no way I am simply going to let Prost through: I haven't driven all this way risking life and limb only to hand it to him on the last few laps. What is more, as far as the world championship is concerned, he probably won't need any help from me or, if he does, then only in the last couple of races; certainly not now, in September.

On the last lap he puts everything into an incredibly strong challenge, trying to force through on the inside coming through the chicane. I've been expecting this, however, and I hold the middle line. Prost is forced onto the grass verge with his two nearside wheels. Only two corners to go. Don't blow it now. One final burst of acceleration into the straight. I take the flag two car lengths up.

As Prost climbs out of his car he signals his congratulations, but looks a bit sour. The McLaren supremos also look a bit crestfallen, but there are some happy faces about. It is fairly obvious how the land lies: I have developed a feeling for this sort of thing during the long Ice Age at McLaren.

Alain says that I drove a pretty tough race. Well, of course, I reply, why not? You wouldn't want it said that World Champion Prost had to rely on Lauda's help. But if it gets really tight later on, I add, you don't have to worry, I'll be right with you. At that, he is his usual pleasant self again.

Ron Dennis congratulates me and says how pleased he is. I don't believe him for one minute. Anyway, I couldn't care less whether he's pleased or not.

CHAPTER TWELVE

FROM 400 TO 1,000 HORSEPOWER

Formula 1 1972–1985

THE 1972 MARCH delivered some 400 horsepower; the 1985 McLaren-TAG delivered around 1,000 at full charge pressure. Between 1972 and 1985 I had first-hand experience of the 12-cylinder BRMs, Ferraris and Alfas, the gradual demise of the 8-cylinder Cosworth, and the supremacy of the turbos. New materials came on the scene – the most notable being carbon fibre – and all manner of aerodynamic trickery. There was also the grotesque aberration known as the wing-car era.

In order to gain some impression of the absurdity of today's 1,000hp cars, you need look no further than Monaco: qualifying there is just about the most perverse experience imaginable in motor racing today, because the rpm intervals are so much tighter than anywhere else. Under normal driving conditions, there is an rpm interval of some 2,300 revs when changing up; since maximum revs are at 11,500, the next gear down should be somewhere about 9,000rpm. Not so in Monaco: there you have about 1,000 revs to play with at most – you are hitting 10,500rpm and, as a result, already coming up fast to the 11,500 limit.

Eventually, the whole procedure gets on top of you. As you accelerate, you find you can't shift fast enough to keep up with the tight rpm interval and the sudden turbo surge. You are slammed up against the rev limiter – literally: as the revs build up, the turbo kick forces your head back, then you hit the limiter and your head is jolted forward, then you shift gear and your head is yanked backwards again, and so on – three times in a row.

Fortunately for me, the McLaren-TAG had a rev limiter which operated progressively, with the result that the power did not cut out as abruptly as in other engines. Watching the BRM drivers in 1985 was particularly bizarre: you heard the rev limiter go hmmmm-pap-pap-pap, then you saw the driver's head being jerked forward. The whole sequence of movements was so disjointed that there was no way the driver could properly coordinate it all – steering, shifting gear, accelerating, adjusting to turbo surge: his reflexes simply couldn't cope. On top of this, there is the feeling of sheer terror as you thread the needle through Sainte Dévote and zoom up the cratered street towards Casino, or as you take the tunnel or the chicane. All of this happens at full boost, usually with other cars getting in your way. Believe me, the experience has to be lived to be appreciated.

Extreme situations like these – 1,000hp qualifying laps in Monte Carlo – have precious little, if anything, to do with driving in the conventional sense. As far as real driving is concerned, however, there is not all that much difference between a 400hp and a 1,000hp car. One's subjective 'feel' for the limit remains the same over the years (apart from the fact that, in the wing-car era, you couldn't hold your head straight). The most remarkable feature of that era was not that you could suddenly drive a 110mph corner at 135mph – you didn't even notice the difference – but that, when something went wrong, you would hit the guard-rail 25mph faster. For me, driving *per se* has always been a more or less straightforward affair, irrespective of the horsepower at my disposal.

The cars of the early and mid-seventies had narrower tyres and less wing, which is to say less downthrust and, as a result, more response. You could sideslip and drift. That all disappeared when the wing-cars came on the scene: they clung to the asphalt as if they were on rails.

The limit is the same whether you are driving at 70mph or 190: you lose front axle or rear axle and have to get it back again. The incredible power of today's cars gives rise to wheel spin and tends to favour rear-axle loss, the result being that the cars oversteer considerably more than they used to. In cold weather and with tyres that have not yet warmed up, you can have wheel spin all the way through to fourth gear; even in standard conditions, you get wheel spin in second and third. Frequent wheel spin and pronounced oversteer will cause the rear tyres to deteriorate rapidly – something you can't afford to let happen in the race itself. Accordingly, you have to drive as cleanly as you possibly can, avoiding rear-axle loss, sideslipping or straying off the perfect line. If you let the rear wheels drift, the turbo power will make mincemeat of the tyres. This differs from the old days, when there was less need to be so painstaking and exact – if you went into a drift now and again, it wasn't the end of the world.

The driver's subjective impressions are extremely important when it comes to setting the car up and assessing how well it is handling. This said, however, it must be added that the driver's input has very distinct limits. I can accurately detect front-axle slide or rear-axle drift and, generally speaking, take steps to counteract either by judicious adjustment from the cockpit. Then I have a car that is handling neutrally and responding obediently, but it may well be two seconds slower. The driver doesn't sense those two lost seconds, nor does he sense that he has lost 50 horsepower or that he has less than perfect ground-effect. In other words, the driver's subjective impressions are valuable and valid only to the extent that they are confirmed by his actual lap times.

My days with BRM were particularly fruitful in this respect, in that I felt that I could make a positive contribution to the car's performance. The BRM had a good chassis that was very responsive to physical adjustment. If you moved the front wing up or down a notch, you at once changed the handling characteristics of the whole car. Equally, if you re-designed the stabiliser, you immediately sensed the difference. The only drawback with the BRM was the engine: for all its twelve cylinders, it simply didn't come up to scratch and, when we hit the straight, the other marques left us standing.

During my early days at Ferrari, the situation was exactly the reverse: the engine was beautiful, but the car understeered atrociously. You could do what you liked with the stabilisers, springs or wings, you could adjust the wings by three degrees or five notches; it didn't really matter – understeer was built into the Ferrari. To put things right, Forghieri was obliged to re-design the car and to make radical changes in such fundamentals as weight distribution. It was only then that the Ferrari slowly began to respond. I must say that, if it hadn't been for my time with BRM, I would never have known how a car can and should be set up – if you have been driving understeering cars all your life, you probably start believing that that's how it should be.

The fact that I was able to test drive regularly at Fiorano made genuine progress possible and meant that Forghieri could be encouraged to experiment and eliminate shortcomings. Up until the time of my first retirement (at Brabham), this was always my *modus operandi*: a willingness to work hard alongside the technical crew allied to a talent for motivating them. I *knew* how a car should feel, and working with someone like Gordon Murray meant that we could turn out a car that was fast. At Brabham, of course, we had to contend with the Alfa engine and, because of this, we didn't get the best results.

When it came to the wing-cars, the situation was something else again. I suppose it was my misfortune that my comeback happened to coincide with that era – it would have been nice to have missed out on it. I alluded earlier to the sensational ground-effect generated by special underbody design and lateral seal. This meant that we could corner at incredible speeds; g force in the corners was so pronounced that we couldn't hold our heads straight. For the whole ground-effect principle to work effectively, you had to have brutally hard springs, the result being that driver comfort became a thing of the past. When you hit a bump or dip on the circuit, the suction effect and the hard springs multiplied the impact. At Monza, for example, the ride was so rough on the straight that you were jarred simultaneously up through the spinal column and into your head: you felt like screaming out loud with pain and sheer frustration. There was hardly any discussion as to how the car should be set up: the sole consideration was ground-effect and, because handling was so de-emphasised, the technical contribution made by the driver was minimal. We only had one task to perform – to hold on desperately like bronco-busters in a rodeo. Fortunately, this nonsense came to an end in 1982 when the regulations were changed and we were again given sensible cars to drive.

The McLaren approach to Formula 1 technology was totally different to what I had experienced in all the other racing stables. John Barnard takes the view that one genius in the squad is enough and that he adequately fits the bill: he doesn't need to consult with drivers and sundry other ancillary personnel. Any important questions he has will be resolved by the computer and the wind tunnel; that's where all the necessary answers are to be found. Right now, I wouldn't like to say one way or the other whether I think he is a genius or not – I would say that he has to keep designing the best car around for a couple of seasons more. What I will say is that he is essentially on the right track: his methods work and his superior attitude vis-à-vis the drivers would appear to be vindicated by results to date. He comes up with an idea, keeps tight-lipped about it, develops a design, builds the car and, one fine day, is gracious enough to let the driver sit behind the wheel of a new machine which, as a rule, is fabulous. And McLaren has another winner. As yet, any individual weak points have been so insignificant that they have not threatened to jeopardise overall prospects for success.

A case in point was the rear suspension in 1985. There was something awry from the very first race of the season. The drivers had no say in the matter other than to confirm that there was a problem. Take it easy, said Barnard. Then he began revamping the rear suspension – and taking an inordinate amount of time over it. In fact, the rear axle was a problem all season in the slower corners. At the same time, however, the car was set up so beautifully for fast stretches and had such an impressive top speed that the rear suspension problem in no way threatened McLaren's world championship prospects. Nevertheless, this does show that even Barnard has his limits.

For another thing, we waited two whole seasons for a six-speed gearbox which never materialised. Once it does, of course, it will certainly be perfect, just like almost everything else that Barnard finally makes available. Those cars are absolute gems, straight from the master craftsman's atelier, marvels of design, detail and finish. Whether this will always remain so is hard to say. One of these days, the computer may feed Barnard some data that is wide of the mark – and he won't have a driver around to put a finger on what is wrong or come up with an alternative solution. I had a habit of keeping the pressure on, and even caused some friction by forcing the pace on the development side; Prost and Rosberg will perhaps be less active in this respect.

To recap once more, I think Barnard is right in this day and age to discount driver input in the design of a new car. The parameters are now so complex that sophisticated theory and computer and wind-tunnel analysis are essential; there is no place for helpful suggestions from the likes of me. However, if the new design has some flaw or other, there is still a case for the driver putting in his ten cents' worth.

The upshot was that, over the last few seasons, I did much less test driving than, say, in my Ferrari days. Not that I regret this – I was grateful for the extra time off. Today, a driver's technical know-how is best employed in selecting for himself the team with the best designer. That is the long and short of it. As far as setting the car up is concerned, however, there are still a few areas where the driver can make a contribution, namely as regards springs, shocks, stabilisers, wings and ride height.

Let's take ride height – clearance – which nowadays is as important again as it was during the wing-car era. If the aerodynamics are to work properly, the car's angle of inclination must be spot on. Even when you have calculated the optimal angle and tested it in practice, you still have to reach an empirical compromise between driving with full and driving with almost empty tanks: if you set up for full tanks, you will (as the race progresses) gradually develop too much clearance and this will distort the aerodynamics and reduce ground-effect. For this reason, it is better to accept driving the first few laps so near the ground that you actually bottom out. The monocoque itself is not resilient enough to take that sort of pounding; accordingly, magnesium blocks are fitted. These abrade in the course of the race (and explain the spectacular showers of sparks coming from underneath the car in the initial stages of a Grand Prix). By the time the fuel load starts to decrease, these magnesium blocks have already abraded and you should be able to drive the remainder of the race at optimal aerodynamic ride height.

The importance of ride height implies fresh emphasis on the springs. Here, too, a compromise must be found. The springs have to be rigid enough to keep the car from bottoming out at high speed but, at the same time, have enough 'give' to allow you to take the slower corners without being plagued by excessive understeer.

As far as the stabilisers are concerned, there have been no appreciable changes over the years. The front one is adjusted by the mechanics, whereas the rear one can be adjusted to one of five variant positions directly from the cockpit.

The most delicate task today's drivers have to perform is that of synchronising angle of inclination and front-wing setting. This is really a very delicate business, but tolerances have become so fine that good drivers in the same marque will inevitably arrive at the same setting. There was scarcely ever any difference in settings chosen independently by Prost and myself.

The rear wing proper is no longer variable, but you can tinker around with the flip-up which is attached to it by means of half a dozen screws. In effect, the flip-up can be made steeper or shallower, thereby creating a certain change in the ground-effect generated.

One of the most dramatic changes in Formula 1 over the past few seasons has been the switch from steel to carbon brakes. You exert even pressure on the brake pedal and, even without pushing down harder, the braking effect builds as the discs heat up to around 800°C. As a result, the brakes start to bite progressively and the sensation of build-up is almost indescribable. In training, you choose a braking point about 100 yards out, then gradually work down to 80, 70, 60, each time finding it harder to imagine that it is going to work. You really have to overcome your natural instincts and put your faith in something that years of experience tell you is impossible. It is also something that your body cannot always take: in Monza, I dislocated a rib because of this and, if I hadn't had Willy the miracle-worker on hand, I would never have made it past qualifying.

The next big breakthrough in Formula 1 must surely be the introduction of the anti-blocking system: there are no immediate prospects, but it is bound to come about one of these days.

One pleasing aspect about recent seasons is that Formula 1 is once again performing a pioneering role over a wide range of technical issues. This is particularly true as far as new materials are concerned – notably light-weight high-strength alloys – and as regards progressive turbo sophistication in the face of reduced fuel loads. Agreed, using fourteen gallons for every sixty miles is not exactly frugal, but today's fuel restrictions are putting designers under increasing pressure to accord high priority to reduced fuel consumption within the overall design framework. What is more, their successes to date are every bit as impressive as turbo technology *per se.*

The first TAG–Turbo that I drove on the Porsche test circuit only performed between 9,500 and 11,500rpm and cut in as abruptly as the crack of a whip. Today's TAG starts to build up power from 6,500rpm and still manages to develop a good 200 horsepower more than the old whip-cracker. There is still turbo lag – you still feel a small jolt – but it is minimal by comparison with 1983. All you need now is a little bit of routine and a sense of anticipation – you have to accelerate with absolute precision and allow for a fraction under one second for the turbo to react. It really isn't much of a problem any more.

What is a problem, on the other hand, is getting off to a decent start in a turbo. With a naturally aspirated engine you are only obliged to concentrate on striking a balance between too much power (wheel spin) and too little (stalling); once you get the revs just right (around 10,000rpm), all you have to do is synchronise clutch and green light. Mind you, even this is tricky enough when you have twenty-five others around you all trying to do the same thing and 100,000 spectators watching. However, things really get difficult when you are on the grid in a turbo.

When a turbo engine is in neutral it builds up only minimal charge pressure because there is no counter-pressure. If I hold at 10,000rpm, the engine will behave like a naturally aspirated one until there is a brutal transition into the turbo mode. Wheel spin will result. Because of this, I have to get the initial revs in the turbo up higher – up around 11,000 or 11,200, say – to build up some charge pressure. Clearly, I now have the narrowest of margins between initial revs and the 11,500rpm imposed by the rev limiter; the danger is in hitting the rev limiter right away or over-revving the engine.

What happens next is as follows. Holding my foot down in neutral to keep the revs up at 11,000, I let in the clutch, feel charge pressure building, and get off the accelerator at once to avoid the full thrust of 1,000 horsepower. This is the crucial moment: if you let the power fall away too much, you find yourself bang in the middle of no-man's land between turbo and naturally aspirated engine – the latter has died on you before the former can take over. There is nothing for it but clutch in, build up revs again, clutch out, and build up charge pressure without over-revving.

Getting all this synchronised to within a tenth of a second is a complicated affair, especially in a 4-cylinder turbo – the ones that are prone to being left on the grid. There are other things to think about too: the car in front, the cars alongside, the cars behind. For the time being, however, you simply have to ignore them – your first priority is to get off to a flying start and hope that the others will get a move on too. There is no way of rehearsing or planning what comes next.

If the car in front doesn't get away cleanly, you have to make your mind up in a split second which side to pass him – again ignoring what the others are doing. In the fraction of a second you have in which to react, you don't have time to extrapolate what their intentions might be. It is total chaos. You head for a gap that isn't there, doors open and shut ahead of you.

By some miracle, you usually find a way through. Occasionally, however, you don't.

CHAPTER THIRTEEN

COLLEAGUES AND COMPETITORS

PERSONAL RELATIONSHIPS ARE not particularly close within the small group of drivers who comprise Formula 1. Friendships are rare, contacts superficial. In many instances, all I know about my fellow competitors is what they look like and what sort of behaviour I can expect of them behind the wheel.

Over my years in Formula 1, four drivers have made an especially strong impression on me: Piquet, Hunt, Villeneuve and Prost.

If asked whom I consider to be the best driver in the world, I need go no further than the first of these: Nelson Piquet. He has everything that a world champion requires: stature, poise, an ability to concentrate on essentials, intelligence, physical strength – and speed. He seldom makes a mistake, he is always fast, he is always on form: I can see absolutely no reason why he shouldn't become world champion for the third time in 1986. On top of all this, I like Nelson as a person. I am attracted by his open, self-assured manner, and I admire his lifestyle. I also envy him because he does so many things better than I do.

Initially, Nelson was something of an enigma for me. He used to tell me how he would take his boat out and fish, swim and skin-dive, how splendid it was spending a whole day doing nothing. It was never quite clear to me how a person can develop skills and self-discipline when he spends the whole week doing quite the opposite, namely relaxing completely. For me, private life and profession have always gone hand in hand – perhaps because that's the way I was brought up or because I never knew any different. I have always gone from one stress situation into the next, incessantly, as if that were the only way to live. Not so Nelson: the calm and confident way he contrives to organise a very intense and very efficient professional life as a racing driver and to keep this separate from his private life is something to which I have often given serious thought. Now that I have settled in Ibiza, of course, much of my own life is more relaxed, more 'private'. In this, Nelson was very much my model – although I can never hope to live up to him, since he is, quite simply, a totally different type of person from myself.

Some of Piquet's characteristics also apply to James Hunt, who, a few years back, was as good to get along with as Nelson is today. We were in each other's company a lot back in the Formula 3 days – when we were both broke – and I can still picture James doing the circuit in his Ford Transit, complete with pit crew and tent. James and I shared a one-bedroom apartment in London for a while. With him around things were always pretty hectic, and there were always a couple of girls about. Hunt played hard – I imagine that Innes Ireland must have been a similar type fifteen years earlier: game for anything and taking life as it came. For all that, Hunt was an open, honest-to-God pal – and one helluva driver. In 1976, when he snatched the title away from me, he drove incredibly well and peaked towards the end of the season, when he showed superlative form to catch up with and overtake me in the title race.

One impressive aspect was his decision to retire when the time was ripe – halfway through the 1979 season – when he felt that he (or his car) was no longer fast enough. He had earned enough money to live well for the rest of his days and he is making the most of it.

Gilles Villeneuve was someone I took a great liking to. I liked everything about him, although I questioned the risks he used to take. It was always on the cards that Gilles would come out of the pits for the first lap and immediately spin out, simply because he drove flat-out in every situation – and cold tyres didn't make any difference to him. His fighting instincts were admirable and contrived to build an image which persists today, long after his death: the Villeneuve legend keeps on growing. He was the craziest devil I ever came across in Formula 1.

A typical Villeneuve episode: I am in my hotel room in Zolder. It is ten o'clock in the evening or even later; at any rate, it is pitch dark outside. Suddenly, I hear the chatter of a helicopter. I throw open the window and see a chopper hovering outside, using its headlights to find a suitable landing pad. Absolutely crazy! Illegal, impossible, mad. Of course, who should it be but Gilles. Next morning, I ask him what on earth was going on: 'I miscalculated by a couple of hours when I took off in Nice, but it all turned out okay. As you can see, I made it.'

There were all kinds of incidents like this – in the air and on the track – where he really went beyond the limit. Perhaps he viewed this sort of thing as a reaffirmation of his lifestyle, to the extent that he took extreme risks whenever and wherever possible. The fact that, for all this, he was a sensitive and lovable character rather than an out-and-out hell-raiser made him such a unique human being.

Villeneuve's death at Zolder in 1982 can be seen in the context of his willingness to take risks, but it came about as a result of a very special kind of misunderstanding. I pieced together what happened that day from the video recording. True, the camera doesn't follow the cars right through the corner, but you can make out how Jochen Mass – who was on a pit-stop lap – chose the last possible moment to move out right, off the ideal line. Obviously he had seen Villeneuve coming up in his rear-view mirror and was trying to do him a favour; on the other hand, this kind of manoeuvre always has the makings of a misunderstanding. To my mind, when you are coming in, you should either edge out towards the grass verge or clearly adhere to the ideal line, so that the driver coming up behind you knows what's what. Moving over at the last moment simply takes the man behind by surprise. I don't think Jochen Mass did the right thing but, having said this, I must say that Villeneuve was perhaps the only driver around who would have chosen the risky option of overtaking a slower car going flat-out off the ideal line. The chances of a mistake or a misunderstanding were simply too great.

Mention has been made of Alain Prost in earlier chapters. He is a nice, likeable, warm-hearted person, and I took to him more and more the longer I knew him. I have already said that I had some initial doubts about him. I was very, very disconcerted by the fact that he had so much over me during qualifying for the first few races of the 1984 season: I was really down, and I had to make a special effort to drive that much better in the races proper. There, he was not better than I was, although he got stronger as the season wore on.

Prost has an astonishing ability to adapt in the shortest conceivable time to any circuit, regardless of weather conditions. During qualifying in the rain at Estoril – the race that was to decide the title in 1984 – he was absolutely magnificent, and I really had to pull myself together to avoid being totally demoralised. The fact is, it took me much longer than Prost to get used to driving a new circuit in the capricious turbo. He really was a golden boy in that respect.

For a long time I had the feeling that Prost was watching my every move, checking out everything I did to see whether he could learn something. Apparently, he learned a lot – as he himself readily admits.

Prost has good technical judgement, but perhaps some nuances escape him. He has a habit of saying that something is either 'good' or 'bad'. When it came to setting up, we virtually always arrived at the same solutions and we discussed everything openly, neither of us trying to put one over on the other. In all our time together, he only once mounted a different stabiliser without letting me know.

We were together on a long promotional trip for Marlboro after the end of the 1984 season, the kind of situation where you can easily get in each other's hair and on each other's nerves, but the relationship between us got better and better. Then came the 1985 season, when we saw a world champion at his brilliant best – Prost was fast in qualifying and impeccable on the day. There was no trace of the nerves which had gnawed at him in previous seasons when he was put under pressure.

There we are then: the four colleagues and rivals that made the most lasting impression on me during my career. Let me add a few comments on one or two of the others (I have already dealt with Peterson and Regazzoni in earlier chapters).

Emerson Fittipaldi: once very good indeed, but he has failed to mature further. Setting up your own team – as Fittipaldi did after he left Lotus – is not such a bad idea, but you do have to be good enough to get yourself the best designer. Once you hire a chief designer, the die is cast – one way or another. In Fittipaldi's case, there was never any hope of things working out.

Carlos Reutemann: no bouquets for this one. A cold, unappetising character. When we were together at Ferrari, we made no bones about it, we simply couldn't stand each other. It was impossible trying to work with him on the technical side because he would always look for a tactical answer that might conceivably work to his advantage during setting up. After my shunt in 1976 he was something of a problem for me to the extent that he tried to win over the entire Ferrari camp, but I soon settled that. A good driver, but nothing spectacular.

Mario Andretti: a shining example of a top-class racing driver. For decades, he has always been up among the leaders, always fast. Andretti lives for racing and involves his whole family in the sport. Irrespective of what he turns his hand to – sports cars, Indianapolis, Formula 1 – he always makes good. He'll continue to be a big draw in the States for years to come.

John Watson: one of the nicer drivers. I usually came out ahead of him, not least because I tended to qualify faster.

When it came to race day, let it be said, John was capable of pulling out all the stops. He was not consistent enough, however, to be a really front-rank driver. Nevertheless, his performances in places like Detroit and Long Beach were something to marvel at.

Keke Rosberg: a fast driver. Takes himself so unbelievably seriously that he overlooks the really important things, the result being that he never seems to appreciate what is going on around him. I have noticed that you can never look him straight in the eye.

Michele Alboreto: a good man in every respect. Very fast, but possibly with too weak a personality to handle Ferrari politics. To cope with those, you have to be tough – you have to know what is right for the firm and how to achieve it. I think that Michele knows which way things should go but is not strong enough to assert himself. Otherwise, he is a sweet guy: fast, good, doesn't make mistakes.

Ayrton Senna: probably the greatest talent to emerge in recent years. By this, I don't just mean his fast lap times, but also the way he has come to grips with the whole business. He simply understands what is going on. I am particularly impressed by the speed with which he has matured without making mistakes along the way.

Gerhard Berger: the talent is there, no question. Everything now depends on how he develops. Perhaps he has to take things a little more seriously, although that may sound somewhat avuncular coming from me. I like him; he is a first-rate guy.

CHAPTER FOURTEEN

THE LAUDA SYSTEM

IT IS ONLY fair to expect an autobiography such as this to contain some comment on how I view myself, how I apportion my time, how I approach life. This kind of soul-searching – discussing the 'Lauda System' – is easier for me if I have an interlocutor who knows me well, one who not only asks questions but also brings his own insights to bear. Accordingly, the following thoughts are set out in interview form. The man asking the questions is Herbert Völker.

A dear friend and colleague of mine, Helmut Zwickl, recalls your first retirement in 1979. He was anxious to say something pleasant by way of farewell, but what he actually said went something along the following lines: 'We'll probably have less to write about in future, but never mind. Please, don't ever, ever make a comeback.' He wasn't sad to see you go because he thought you were a 'dyed-in-the-wool egotistical bastard'. Now that you are retiring a second time, six years on, he is saddened. He thinks we will all miss you. Does this suggest to you that you have mellowed with the passage of time?

I hope so. I think that the decisive year in that respect was 1981, just before my comeback. That was when I realised that the system I had developed over the years to divide my time rationally had only served to bolster my own self-centredness.

Before, I really had been a 'dyed-in-the-wool egotist' – everything had revolved around yours truly. I had hangers-on and limelight-seekers in my retinue and I tried to force everyone I came across into my way of doing things. Everything had to be geared to packing more success, more excitement, more fun into my life, regardless of what it cost. I was on the point of giving a false direction to my whole life but, at some stage or other, I came to my senses …

… which also helps you influence and keep a tight rein on your emotions – which is probably one reason for the 'computer' image you present to the world at large.

I am not prepared to allow my feelings to run riot. I'm too sensitive, too emotional as it is, to let that happen. That would be the end of me.

You really mean that? Emotional? Sensitive?

Yes, deep down, certainly. I am afraid to let myself go. I think that, if I did, I would exhibit a remarkable aptitude for coming apart at the seams. That is why I have developed what I call my 'system' – to protect myself and to apportion my time and energy. And part of that system – as you have already said – is keeping my feelings under control. That doesn't mean to say I have to be some kind of robot, just because I try to channel my emotions and make the best out of them.

This all sounds like the old adage: think positive! Can a person really handle his emotions all that easily?

Who said it was easy? In fact, it is often very complicated. The first step is to take a good hard look at yourself. You have to be quite frank with yourself and make sure you aren't deluding yourself. As soon as I detect something that has negative overtones, I take time out to get to the bottom of it. As soon as I have figured out the whys and wherefores of the situation, I either take steps to change it or try to dismiss it as not worth worrying over.

That isn't exactly a panacea. Obviously, you have to develop a certain knack to ensure that your brain overrules your heart. I suppose there must be marginal situations where the system breaks down?

Of course. When you're in love, the system is shot to hell. But, in most situations, it can be applied. Clearly, it all depends on how honestly you analyse the situation and how intelligently you resolve it.

Do you think you are an intelligent person?

I have a certain peasant cunning. A bit of good old common sense.

Have you any special aptitudes? Mathematics, for instance?

No, certainly not. At best, I have a certain gift for languages, but that only applies if the motivation is right. I have to persuade myself that a foreign language will be useful to me; then I am a quick learner. Such as English, which I started to pick up as soon as I started racing. Or Italian, during my first year at Ferrari. But I draw the line at Spanish, even though I do live on Ibiza and Marlene's first language is Spanish. For me, it's enough to be able to order a cup of coffee in Santa Eulalia. *Con leche* [with milk], that's important.

I'm sorry, but mediocrity and lack of talent don't account for your personality. Even your detractors would admit that you have some unusual qualities ...

The ability to think fast, maybe, and logically. I often seem to grasp a situation faster than other people. I do seem to be one step ahead. In a business discussion, I often find that the man across from me is still elaborating the problem whereas I am already casting about for a solution to it. When people start spelling things out, it really bothers me: I think to myself, get on with it, why are you being so slow? I also believe that I am good at discerning how things connect up. I have the faculty of seeing things in very concrete terms. For example, it fascinates me to see someone who has gone off in utterly the wrong direction: I can actually see him going the wrong way and I ask myself, 'Why doesn't *he* see it?'

There are some people around who think you have taken off in the wrong direction in your Boeing 737.

Those must be the gentlemen from Austrian Airlines.

Let's get back to your system. You really do seem to have built a framework on which to hang your life. The most striking feature is how you organise your time. As if you had transposed yourself from the race track to day-to-day living – but taken a stopwatch along with you. Some people might find that rather disagreeable. You might even say that you're something of a tearaway yourself and that it's time you came in for a pit-stop.

Appearances can be deceptive. It is true, however, that time-saving is a cornerstone of my so-called system. Time goes down on my balance sheet as a very valuable asset and I am much more careful what I do with it than most other people. That's why, in my professional life – as a racing driver or as an entrepreneur – I always keep the pressure on and continually take stock of how much time I spend on something. I am as tight-fisted about time as a miser is about money. To an outsider, that might give the impression that I'm always going flat-out, always under stress, always at the limit, but – for me, at least – the opposite is the case. Inside, I'm quite calm, because I want to do things that way, for the simple reason that it leaves me that much more time for myself.

One manifestation of this is that you have an almost bourgeois preoccupation with punctuality. You don't seem capable of waiting for anyone or anything.

It's not a question of patience or impatience, it's a question of efficiency. I've been accustomed to working quickly and effectively and condensing as much work and as many meetings as possible within a specific time-frame. That being the case, everything falls apart if you are not punctual. Quite apart from that, it is both pleasant and practical: if I turn up ten minutes early for a meeting, I am one step ahead of the game, I'm in better shape than the guy who turns up out of breath at the last minute.

As a boss, you have the reputation of being an early riser – and one who usually gets out of bed on the wrong side …

Early riser, late riser, what difference does it make? The main thing is to organise the time available to you. I wake at seven each morning and I'm ready for action. When I'm in the Vienna office, I get in at 7.30 and it grates on my nerves if an employee comes in at 8.32 when he is supposed to start at 8.30 on the dot. And, if he trots out some excuse about working three hours' overtime the previous day, I tell him, fine, send me a bill, but work starts here at 8.30 prompt.

Those who have had the honour of flying in your private jet know how tight-fisted you can be.

It's ridiculous spending a fortune for a Learjet only to hang around wasting time. That's one reason why Marlene hardly ever comes along. She prefers having a cup of coffee before take-off or wandering through the duty-free shop – and being able to smoke after take-off …

You're a tyrant – and a poor host into the bargain. You don't serve anything to drink and you won't let anyone use the toilet.

Wait a minute. I play the host on Lauda Air and there you can have as much to drink as you want. But, in a private jet, I am on a business trip and, if somebody comes along for the ride, he simply has the good luck to save himself some time. That's all there is to it. As for going to the toilet in a small jet, that's simply not a practical proposition.

So that's why you don't serve any booze?

I wouldn't like anyone to feel uncomfortable. In any case, it's very rare that anyone comes along, so it isn't such a big deal. It just infuriates me to spend a lot of money trying to save some time by flying your own private jet – and, believe me, a Learjet costs a penny or two – only for time to be wasted because of some clown. Willy Dungl has a real talent for leaving his passport in one of the suitcases that my co-pilot loaded hours previously . . .

And this is the kind of drama that unhinges the legendary Lauda? Willy Dungl at Passport Control saying, 'Whoops. I left my ID on the plane'?

Willy is getting better all the time. Apart from that, I always check to see if he has remembered his passport.

Fine. Every minute is precious. You save time by using the most expensive mode of travel around today, you save time by perfect organisation, you save time by arranging meetings one after the other in strict succession, you save time by pushing everything along, by keeping the pressure on your partners and employees. The obvious question is: what do you do with all this time you're so keen on saving?

Nothing. Absolutely nothing. And with no regrets. I jet back to Ibiza, delighted that the effort has paid off: I have earned myself a day off, maybe two, even – on the odd occasion – three. I can't last out much more than three days, however, because I start getting fidgety. I need the action. Ibiza is marvellous, but I would feel hemmed in, lost, if I had to be there all the time …

… quite the opposite to Marlene?

Marlene is happy on Ibiza, she enjoys it. I'm in a completely different world. For me, life is all about achievement. I need the pressure, and the quiet days off in between.

That's another way of saying that you allow the pressure to build up enormously in order to secure a few days' rest that you wouldn't really need if you lived life at a more normal pace?

That's putting it a bit too neatly. In fact, this approach allows me to achieve a lot and, at the same time, to retain a certain measure of independence. I can walk, jog, sleep, do anything or nothing, go out somewhere in the boat, drop anchor, do some serious thinking or simply doze off in the sun. That is very, very valuable. I can get away from the oppressive grind of business life, preserve my own identity, reserve myself some time for reflection. It's also a way of keeping myself physically in shape despite the pressures of work. And I always have something to occupy my mind. By organising my life like this – concentrating on working hard one day and relaxing totally the next – I find that things work out better than lumping it all together. I hate fiddling around, doing a little of this and a little of that, kicking my heels or wasting time. Balancing pressure and leisure, that's what it all comes down to in the end.

To what extent is your life affected by being famous? On the whole, do you find that an advantage or a disadvantage?

I know that a lot of people will probably consider my reply to be condescending or arrogant. The fact is that being well known is detrimental 95 per cent of the time. Being recognised and occasionally fawned upon means nothing to me, absolutely nothing. The compulsion to be somebody is something you are born with – it doesn't have anything remotely to do with what you have actually achieved in life. In my case, there is very little trace of this sort of compulsion, the upshot being that I get very little out of the glamorous side of being famous.

This is not to say that there aren't some useful spin-offs, that some things don't come easier or a little more readily my way than they might, say, for you. If the police pull me over for driving too fast, I have a better chance of getting away with it than you might have. I might say, 'Sorry, officer, I'm in training for the next Grand Prix. How do you expect me to improve if I have to creep along the motorway at 70mph?' The odds are that he will laugh and let me off the hook. But this kind of advantage is outweighed twenty times over by the disadvantages of being permanently on show. One marvellous exception to this is the United States, where practically no one knows me. I remember once, at the reception desk in the Westin Hotel in Seattle, being asked if Niki was my surname or my Christian name: I felt like hugging the receptionist right there and then.

A typical situation might be as follows. I can see out of the corner of my eye that people are nudging each other, talking about me. Then one of them takes out a scrap of paper, hesitates, wondering if he should come over right away or leave it for later. Just as I pick up my coffee cup, I see him on the move. I put the cup down. I notice that he only has this scrap of paper – nothing to write with. He turns to the person next to him: I don't suppose you could lend me a ballpoint? Isn't that Lauda over there? Yes, he says, that's right, that's Lauda, I'm just going over to ask for his autograph. And so on. The whole business gets really involved. No one simply comes over and says a quick Please-and-Thank-You, there always has to be some sort of pantomime.

You were – and still are – a sports personality who was constantly surrounded by the media, even when you weren't winning. Does the Lauda System make provision for dealing with reporters?

I try to keep the time involved to a minimum, but I also try to get the important points across at the opportune moment and as succinctly as possible. There really is no point in rattling on for hours on end, coming out with all kinds of trivia, as some of my colleagues tend to do. I have a sneaking admiration for Prost, namely for the way he never tires of chatting on ad infinitum just to keep a couple of scribbling reporters happy. When we were on the road doing PR work for Marlboro, he answered each and every question in so much detail that we fell completely behind schedule. I suggested to him that he keep it shorter, and showed him what I meant. It was intriguing: his answers got shorter each time, and we used to vie with each other to see who could say as little as possible.

Considering the extent to which you have been in the public eye – thanks to your directness, your unwillingness to pull punches and your entrepreneurial flair – you seem to have been fairly well treated by the media over the years. Were you in a position to set this up in some way?

Not in the slightest. There is no magic formula. I simply made a concerted effort to say little, but to say what little I did with a certain emphasis. I never tried to worm my way into a reporter's good graces. And I always kept my personal life out of the media as far as possible. Marlene doesn't know how to handle the press at all: she gets really flustered.

CHAPTER FIFTEEN

FLYING

IN 1974 I happened to be given a lift in a single-engine Cessna; from that moment on, flying was in my blood. Two years later, just after my shunt at Nürburgring, I was granted my pilot's licence. By this time I had already bought myself a Golden Eagle. Then came the various other qualifications – instruments, commercial second class, commercial first class and, eventually, full airline status.

It may come as a surprise that someone who was a complete dunce at school should suddenly be able to cope with the complexities of commercial flying. The fact that flying was something I wanted to do made all the difference. At school I could never see the reason for having to learn, couldn't see any point to it and, because of that, I simply declined. Flying was something else: it interested me, I wanted to be able to do it. The fact that I grasp subjects very quickly in a visual sense proved to be a bonus. In addition, you have the best possible motivation: when it comes to flying, the more you know about the subject, the safer you are. Every new piece of information helps. Of all the various examinations I took, I had to resit only one – which I did promptly and successfully. By the way, there are no concessions made to celebrities when it comes to flying.

Over the years I have owned or had available to me as a private plane the Cessna Golden Eagle (two), a Citation (now belonging to Nelson Piquet), a Learjet, a Falcon 10 and a Falcon 20. Today, I'm back to a Learjet.

The commercial side of flying intrigued me, particularly in Austria, where, in the seventies, Austrian Airlines had a virtual monopoly. I chanced on the information that a certain Herr Hinteregger was selling off flying rights for around £200,000 so I jumped in quickly, bought the concession and set up Lauda Air. I was entitled to operate planes with a maximum forty-four-passenger capacity. Our first move was to purchase a German Fokker 27 – which had exactly forty-four seats – and use it principally to fly Austrian Club Méditerranée guests on the short haul south. Then one of the major Austrian tour groups, Touropa, said they would like to use our services. We secured financing (from the same bank that had sponsored me in 1971 in Formula 2) and spent just over £3 million on a second Fokker. My aim was to serve that sector of the market immediately below Austrian Airlines; in other words, to operate short- to medium-haul routes using smaller aircraft.

It was never my intention to set up in competition with Austrian Airlines – that would have been ludicrous in any case – and that was why I opted for the forty-four-seater as an ideal solution. What I did envisage was that we could exist side by side for the time being, with perhaps the possibility of a cooperative venture at a later date, inasmuch as I was in a position to complement the AUA network in a variety of ways. After all, DLT makes a living in Germany in the shadow of Lufthansa, and Cross Air survives alongside Swissair; the David and Goliath configuration is not all that unusual in the airline business.

The first indication that I had approached the issues with a certain naiveté came as early as 1978, at a Mercedes 'do' in Salzburg. I had bought my first two Golden Eagles from Herr Pölz, an ex-wartime flyer who had gone into the aircraft business after the war. Pölz was well connected to Austrian Airlines and to AUA's Dr Heschgl in particular. At one point, Pölz came over to me and said, 'I hear you're going commercial with a Fokker 27?' I told him that was so.

'During the war, we used to take people who didn't conform, put them up against a wall, and – rat-a-tat-tat – that was it. Times have changed. When we want to get rid of someone today, we do it by putting them out of business, by ruining them financially. I would advise you against coming into the airline business, because we're not in favour.'

I was staggered. I said I couldn't grasp what he was getting at, he couldn't be serious.

'Don't do it.'

On the drive home I pulled off the road somewhere and tried to sort things out in my mind. The situation was absurd. On the one hand, there was my own euphoria at the prospect of my first plane, Lauda Air, getting a thousand and one projects off the ground; and, on the other, there was the ex-wartime pilot, crooking his finger round the trigger of an imaginary machine-gun. Had I dreamt the whole episode? What was happening?

If that's how the system works in Austria today, I said to myself, then I'm going to fight it. At the same time, however, I was convinced that Herr Pölz was merely exaggerating.

As things turned out, Pölz knew the system very well indeed. Co-existence alongside Austrian Airlines was out of the question, let alone cooperation with AUA. This was a matter of sheer power politics, spearheaded by Dr Heschgl, one of the two chief executive officers at AUA. I met with him on several occasions to see if we could put things back on an even keel. I particularly recall one of his remarks: 'I'm like a fox stalking a rabbit. If you stick your nose out of the hole, I'll snap you up.'

Naturally, I asked him what was behind all this hostility. Had I done something, had I said something wrong, had I hurt AUA in some way, had I simply been impolite? Back came the answer: no. He was simply opposed.

I can only imagine that this attitude had its roots in Dr Heschgl's own personality. In the course of every conversation with him, it would come out that he was the son of a railway worker. I didn't find this information particularly germane to the subject under discussion. Perhaps it was intended to underline that the railway worker's son was laying down the law to the son of a company president? Who knows? At any rate, his antagonism towards me seemed to be rooted in his subconscious. And, because that way of looking at things is so foreign to my own nature, I was never really able to plumb the depths of Dr Heschgl's psyche.

By the end of the seventies, Austrian Airlines held absolute sway over everything that went on in the aerospace division of the Austrian Ministry of Transport: AUA was in a position to force through any measures which helped safeguard its monopoly. Permits for Lauda Air routes were a long, long time in the pipeline and, when all else failed, AUA triggered a price war designed to put me out of business. When Lauda Air announced that it would operate flights to Venice, AUA immediately brought out the big guns and flew DC 9s on the Venice run – at a loss; as soon as Lauda Air cancelled Venice as a destination, AUA did likewise.

I then devised a bold plan to come into the market upstream of Austrian Airlines by offering DC 10 flights. That may sound hare-brained today, but it was not as wild as one might think, given the then dramatically undervalued US dollar on the one hand and a tourist boom on the other. This project was very much on the cards at the time I announced my first retirement. I was fascinated by the possibilities, so much so that this may well have been a subconscious reason for my lack of enthusiasm for Formula 1 – after all, a DC 10 is a damned sight more exciting.

Lauda Air laid out $300,000 on a DC 10 option, and we began working on the financial aspects of this huge project. In the spring of 1980 fuel prices rocketed and interest rates shot up, however, with the result that prospects dimmed. When the real recession set in, the project was written off – together with the $300,000 we had shelled out for the option.

Although we indulged in such flights of fantasy, we never forgot the fact that we still had our two trusty Fokker 27s. The problem there was that we couldn't secure attractive enough destinations. The Vienna–Klagenfurt run would have been ideal for a forty-four-seater, particularly as Austrian Airlines were only using a Metropolitan – a patently inadequate machine which the passengers promptly christened 'the terror tube'. It could take only ten passengers, offered no in-flight catering and was regularly overbooked. Denying Lauda Air rights on the Klagenfurt run was a case of sheer bloody-mindedness.

It has been said that my appeal to Federal Chancellor Kreisky was improper, but I defend it to this day. I should say immediately that I am not a political animal and that the very last thing I would do is publicly hitch my wagon to any political star. I am interested in people, not parties. Sport and politics don't mix. As a result, I had no political ties to Dr Kreisky – or any other politician, for that matter. However, it did seem perfectly reasonable to me to let the Chancellor know what was going on in his Transport Ministry.

Kreisky called a meeting. Transport Minister Lausecker, Finance Minister Salcher, AUA chief executive Heschgl and yours truly would attend. As it happened, the meeting was slightly delayed, so the four of us sat together for a few minutes in the Chancellor's antechamber. The icy silence which prevailed gave me a fair idea of how the other three gentlemen felt at the thought of being called in before the Chancellor because of me.

Kreisky pointed out that a comparable situation had arisen once before, when Austria had made the mistake of treating rather badly a certain gentleman called Porsche, effectively driving him into exile. The Chancellor did not want the same thing to happen in the case of Herr Lauda: there surely had to be some reasonable way to settle this business of two tiny Fokkers?

Klagenfurt was the central issue. Dr Heschgl came up with the argument that Lauda Air couldn't be permitted to fly across the mountains in between because the Fokkers weren't pressurised. Of course, every Fokker 27 is pressurised: it was disgraceful that the Chancellor had to listen to that sort of nonsense.

Finance Minister Salcher also came up with a wonderful argument. In what particular legal form was Lauda Air incorporated? I told him that it was a *GesmbH und Co. KG*, in other words, a limited liability company established as a partnership.

'In that case, you have no real cash at risk – why don't you file for bankruptcy?'

I answered that I owed the bank over £3 million to pay off the two planes. To this the Finance Minister – in the presence of the Chancellor – gave a remarkable reply: 'The banks have enough money as it is.'

I informed Salcher that I had been brought up in a peculiar kind of way – paying outstanding debts was something I considered axiomatic, even if the creditor in question did have enough money.

The Transport Minister's contribution to the discussion was equally nugatory. Lauda Air had submitted twenty-four flight destination applications in all, he pointed out, and eighteen of them had been approved. I was given leave to reply that the six that had not been approved just happened to be those for winter routes, and that they made all the difference between commercial survival and going out of business.

At this point Dr Kreisky lost his temper slightly. He turned to the other three and said that he was not particularly impressed by their arguments. For heaven's sake, he added, there has to be some way of putting this situation right. Good day, gentlemen.

Before any notification came my way that matters were on the mend, the opportunity arose to lease the two Fokkers to

Egypt Air to operate two new, urgently needed domestic routes. The F 27s were exactly what they were looking for in terms of seating capacity. I telephoned Dr Kreisky to thank him for his help and to inform him that, under the circumstances, I felt it more prudent to operate abroad.

The deal with the Egyptians worked out perfectly; I was able to scale down Lauda Air and wait for better days, without having to accept crippling financial losses. Whatever the future held for Lauda Air, one thing was clear: it would only be viable under different political and economic conditions.

The period that followed was calm and orderly. We kept the firm ticking over in Vienna by operating two or three executive jets; meanwhile, the two Fokkers were doing sterling service over in Egypt. As I said earlier, I didn't need to make a Formula 1 comeback to cover my losses.

On the morning of the 1982 Austrian Grand Prix I received a phone call from my secretary in Vienna: 'Lauda Air's licence is being revoked with effect from tomorrow's date.'

A senior civil servant in the Transport Ministry had – thank God – been indiscreet. The enemy was at the door. If they take your licence away, irrespective of their reasons for doing so, then your aircraft are grounded – even if they are far from home in Egypt – and it takes an eternity going through the courts to have the order rescinded.

I called the Transport Ministry first thing on the following Monday. Dr Vogl was on holiday. Dr König was on holiday. Head of Department Halbmayer was on holiday. Transport Minister Lausecker was on holiday. It was August, after all.

I finally got through to one of the secretaries, who didn't know the first thing about it but would check the files. He called back to read me the text of a letter just about to be mailed. There it was: licence revoked 'on economic grounds'.

Irrespective of the underlying complaint – insufficient registered capital, for example – surely the firm in question had to be informed accordingly, given concrete details, and allowed an opportunity to redress the situation? It cannot be fair simply to paralyse a company like that, completely without warning. At any rate, I was able to persuade the secretary in question to delay sending out the letter until the official responsible could be reached; in the meantime, the notice of revocation would stay on his desk.

I immediately flew to Majorca, where Chancellor Kreisky was on holiday. I secured an appointment to see him right away. He at once telephoned Transport Minister Lausecker and asked him to make absolutely certain that no mistake was being made: the whole affair should be gone over again very carefully.

A few weeks later I was called to the Transport Ministry. All the officials responsible were present. What was I thinking about, making all that fuss?

'Didn't you intend revoking my licence?'

'No,' said Dr Vogl, 'you're simply imagining things.'

When I told him about my conversation with the secretary, he replied: 'Never mind him, he's only a pen-pusher.'

'At least he can read.'

There wasn't much more to the conversation. However, there was no further talk of revocation. Lauda Air kept going on the back burner and the two Fokkers did their job in Egypt.

The breakthrough came two years later. The constellation was right. Herr Nouza of the Avanto fuel company and Herr Varvaressos of the tour company Itas also voiced misgivings about AUA's monopoly. The three of us got together, chipped in £200,000 each, and set up Lauda Touristik AG. The biggest problem was having my carrier licence extended. We were clearly moving up a gear and my permit was still valid for forty-four-seater-maximum aircraft. It took eight long months to have my application approved. AUA did everything in their power to block it, and it only went through because Austria now had, in Dr Lacina, a new Transport Minister who was objective and thoroughly pragmatic.

We chartered two BAC 1-11s from the Romanian airline Tarom and had a very successful year in 1985. Itas took a 49 per cent stake in Lauda Air, which means that I now have Austria's second-largest tour group in the company. Itas sells 80,000 holidays each year, predominantly in Greece and Spain. On the basis of this payload, we now have access to two Boeing 737s. The 737–300 is the most modern middle-distance aircraft in service today – a 146-seater that cost us $25 million and will be delivered in July 1986. From January 1986, however, we have available a 130-seater 737–200 which we lease from the Dutch airline Transavia. The lease runs for two years three months precisely, the intention being – provided that business develops according to my confident projections – to take delivery of our own (second) 737–300 as soon as the lease expires.

AUA has tried to block us at every turn. Every bank we could conceivably approach for financing was sent a set of figures by

AUA showing that we would never make ends meet, that we would be running at an annual loss of around £1.3 million. It goes without saying, of course, that these estimates are not based on our figures but on those dreamt up by the AUA; needless to say, they do not take account of the high payload that we are guaranteed by Itas.

My business strategy has changed since 1978. At the time I did everything I could to promote cooperation with the AUA and opted for aircraft that would complement Austrian Airlines services. Because of their open hostility then, I now see no need to confront them other than head-on – by operating aircraft that are better and more economical than theirs.

To my mind, the market will decide.

CHAPTER SIXTEEN

IBIZA

MY WIFE LIVES life in her own sweet way and leaves me all the latitude I so urgently need. Because we don't see each other for long stretches at a time and because she is so naturally tolerant and easy-going, I tend to think that our life together is completely satisfactory – that my egocentricity is quite normal and that I am right to take myself so seriously. I am such a compulsive performer that I get caught up in projects and concepts where I am the sole focal point. Marlene is not the type of woman who will bring this up every single day: she lets things simmer over a six-month period then, one day, totally out of the blue, it all boils over.

It doesn't take much to spark things off. Marlene is definitely not at her best in the mornings, and all it can take is some jocular remark over the breakfast table. That early in the day, Marlene is not 100 per cent ready to appreciate subtleties, so there is every chance of a marmalade jar flying past my head and shattering against the wall behind me. (The walls in our home on Ibiza are of the typical Spanish-white variety; marmalade dripping down them creates quite a spectacular effect.)

The minute I raise my voice, Marlene will walk calmly over to the fridge and kick the door until it is bent irreparably out of shape. 'You want more?' she will ask, making her way to the sideboard and scattering plates right and left. Even the clothes iron is in jeopardy. This makes me incredibly angry. The first thing that comes into my mind is that, this time, I won't pay for the damage. 'You can pay for this out of the housekeeping money, do you hear me?'

Of course, Marlene has no grasp of financial matters. I could give her £1,000 or £10,000 as housekeeping money, it makes absolutely no difference; by the 25th of the month it'll be gone and she won't know where it went. All of this is ludicrously at variance with my own precise, disciplined approach to money matters. On the other hand, it cannot be said that Marlene spends money on luxuries – she has no time for furs or jewellery; instead, the children will suddenly have ten new radios. Not surprisingly, someone like myself is cut to the quick by the demolition job on the fridge door and clothes iron. I immediately work out how much damage has been done in terms of cash; not so Marlene – she lives on a totally different plane.

Once the area in question has been wrecked to Marlene's satisfaction, a sense of calm sets in. It will be a couple of days before the incident is discussed – typically, when I've gone early to bed because I am flying off the next morning. In the middle of the night, when I'm still half asleep, I will be informed that things can't keep on like this. I tell myself to get back to sleep: I need sleep, I need rest. But, suddenly, her arguments are so precise, so reasonable, that I have to pull myself together and concentrate.

The switch from flying marmalade jar to succinct analysis fascinates me. By now, I am wide awake. At most, however, I can challenge one third of what she says; as to the remainder, I have to admit that she is right.

The key point at issue is inevitably my egocentricity, my lack of empathy, my lack of consideration. I immediately capitulate, hoist the white flag, and promise – in all sincerity – to try harder in future. And, for hours, days, weeks, months thereafter, I turn over in my mind how I can change for the better. And I do my level best.

That is another striking difference between Marlene and myself: my propensity for self-criticism and her obstinacy. If Marlene were to wrap her car round a tree tomorrow, she would insist that the tree was at fault for the rest of her days. Any attempt on my part to demonstrate the tree's innocence will only end in disaster.

Every now and then, for example, I do try to explain to her that she is not completely blameless when it comes to some argument or other. She is not particularly keen on housekeeping, for example, which wouldn't be all that much of a problem except for the fact that our housekeeper is not particularly keen on it either. Milla is a Filipino who speaks next to no English, a bit of Spanish and excellent Tagalog. When Marlene is in a mood, Milla can't bring herself to prepare breakfast, lunch or dinner for me. There will be absolutely nothing to eat in the entire house.

For someone like myself who is obliged to travel a lot and who really suffers because restaurants are too inflexible to prepare a particular diet – in my case, to Willy Dungl's specifications – a defeat such as this on the home front is particularly hard to accept.

The real crunch comes when there is no yoghurt. Marlene will never admit to forgetting to buy any (it would take the wind right out of my sails if she did admit as much). Instead, she will inform me, 'There was no yoghurt. It was sold out. All the shops were shut. There is no yoghurt to be had on Ibiza. There were no deliveries from the mainland. That's the problem when you live on an island.'

Willy Dungl's formula is as follows: go down to breakfast each morning feeling positive. Breakfast is yoghurt and strawberries. Nothing else but yoghurt and strawberries all year round. And, if it so happens there aren't any strawberries to be had, then yoghurt on its own. Some mornings I leave Marlene dead to the world in bed and go downstairs to follow the Dungl ritual, positively motivated by the prospect of yoghurt and strawberries. When I go into the kitchen, what do I find? A dozen empty wine bottles (we keep a very open house and our Spanish friends are big-hearted enough not to be offended if the host goes off to bed and leaves them to it), innumerable ashtrays (all full), the odd piece of stale fish, a thousand flies, and a Filipino wearing flip-flops that slap on the tiles as she walks, her hair set in red rollers. Milla explains in her broken Spanish: '*Nada* yoghurt.'

One such morning I decided that I would have to do something about it because my anger had reached breaking point. I informed Marlene that she was incapable of organising a household and the housekeeper attached to it: Milla would have to go. Marlene agreed at once. An advertisement would be placed in an Austrian newspaper: German-speaking housekeeper required for pretty house on Mediterranean island.

There was no shortage of replies. The plan was that Marlene would travel to Vienna to select the lucky candidate for the post, but she suddenly didn't feel quite up to it when it came to getting onto the plane. Instead, she asked her sister Renate – who, at the time, was living in Geneva – if she would deputise. A lady from Kärnten was deemed suitable. She flew back to Ibiza with me and proceeded to cook Willy Dungl vegetables to perfection. Unfortunately, she was less than perfect when it came to housework: gradually, the whole house filled up with sand which crunched underfoot. When I next flew back to Vienna, she was a passenger. Marlene, meanwhile, had found a fantastic solution to the problem.

Anyone who knows Marlene and her generous nature will have no trouble in guessing what the solution was: back came Milla. I appended a few conditions to her contract, notably that the flip-flops and the hair rollers had to go. These harsh terms were accepted and, since then, there has been a 5 per cent improvement in how the house is kept.

One of the problems is that I need clean clothes – sweaters, shirts, socks, slacks. I buy five or six Hugo Boss sweaters every couple of weeks or so, and I still don't have enough. Every time I walk into Albi's Bar ('La Villa') there is somebody sitting there – male or female – wearing my clothes. Even the Marlboro sweaters, which are reserved exclusively for team members to wear at press conferences, find their way out of my wardrobe. My brother-in-law Tilly wears my slacks, Marlene wears my tee-shirts, and all Ibiza wears my sweaters.

My sister-in-law Renate and her two children are usually staying with us, so we're not exactly lonely, what with our own two kids, two dogs, two ponies and the guinea pigs (which require elaborate protection against our dog Tasso). Tilly also likes visiting. He is a fiery thirty-two-year-old Chilean who is a superb painter and a man who can do anything he turns his hand to. Horses are his great passion. He has three of them, and prefers to ride at night, with a lamp attached to his forehead, just like a coal miner. I have asked him why he doesn't ride during the day and he tells me it's too hot for the horses.

If you go down to Albi's Bar in the middle of Santa Eulalia around two o'clock any morning, the first thing you are liable to see is a horse parked outside. It's like something out of *High Noon*. The horse has an artistically hand-tooled leather Chilean saddle with a white lasso coiled over it. Behind the saddle is a blanket roll for sleeping outdoors, together with saddlebags big enough for a three-month ride. Tilly's dog stands guard.

Tilly himself is inside the bar, wearing a gigantic Chilean sombrero and riding boots, looking for all the world like Clint Eastwood. What are you up to? I ask, and he nods towards the bar. There are at least a thousand bottles lined up on the bar and I am not too sure what he is trying to tell me. Once I take a closer look, however, I notice the miner's lamp plugged into a socket to charge the batteries. Half an hour later, he clips the lamp onto his sombrero, whistles up the dog, whistles up the horse, jumps into the saddle and rides off into the night, the horse's hooves striking sparks from the asphalt and the dog loping along behind him. Tilly doesn't feel like having a place of his own for the moment: he either dosses down for the night at Albi's, stays out at our place or sleeps under the stars.

Tilly bought Mathias a pony on his fourth birthday – against my wishes, because I couldn't for the life of me imagine who would actually take care of the creature over the longer term. However, Tilly and I brought the pony back from the other side of the island. Mathias was over the moon, but Lukas had his doubts about a one-pony family. We also had to have a little cart for the pony, but the farmer who had just what we wanted would only sell if we bought another pony besides. I knew it was only a matter of time before we had two ponies, so I reckoned we needed a stable.

Next to our house is a huge meadow which I am continually encouraged to buy. Since the asking price is about four times the current market value, I have repeatedly declined the offer, although Marlene thinks I should jump at the opportunity. While I was off driving the 1985 Grand Prix season, Tilly masterminded the erection of a stable right on the perimeter of the meadow. Every time I came back after a race, the walls would be that much higher. It finally dawned on me that the stable was taking on the dimensions of a mansion – a huge heap of masonry which was blocking our view to the sea. Tilly had designed the stable in such a way that it would house the two ponies and, as it happened, his own three full-grown Chilean thoroughbreds. One fine day the neighbour dropped in and adduced proof that we had built too close to the limits of his property: he was convinced that, finally, he would be able to sell the meadow to me for four times the going rate. I refused to buy. Accordingly, we ripped down the monster stable. I was given the go-ahead to build my version, and we now have a cute little stable that is just big enough for the ponies. It's still standing and everyone seems very happy about the outcome.

As a matter of fact, all our differences seem to resolve themselves eventually and everyone seems to be happy. Even when there is a real ding-dong row and Marlene goes on the rampage, there is never any talk of divorce. We have been married close on ten years and have a fantastic relationship. The sole purpose underlying any argument is to change me for the better. I think it is a miracle that two people who are temperamentally so different should be able to put up with each other. I view myself as a calculating, egotistical, goal-oriented person – and Marlene is diametrically the opposite. She takes every day on its own merits and is completely contented and unstructured. She never does anything unless it appeals to her, and she has absolutely none of the self-discipline that seems to have been bred so effectively into me. What I have too much of, she has too little of, and vice-versa; the result being that we are strangely and splendidly complementary.

This is not to say that I have any illusions: there is no way that we could live a solid bourgeois day-in-day-out existence. The fact that I have to travel so much, that I work in Austria and live in Spain, automatically precludes our being stuck in each other's company to the point where our contrasting temperaments might clash too strongly.

Ibiza was the best thing that could have happened to us. I have fewer problems on the fiscal front, Marlene is blissfully happy in her Spanish environment, with her mother and sister Renate living close by, and the children are growing like crazy. Lukas is now six and Mathias is four, and both of them are frank, uncomplicated, generous and likeable, the image of their mother. (By the way, Marlene's scattiness and overall lack of consistency are nowhere in evidence when it comes to bringing up the kids: where they are concerned, she operates on a completely different level.)

The younger one, Mathias, is a real tearaway, totally fearless and ready for anything. If he is up a tree, he'll simply shout 'Catch me' and jump, confident that everything will turn out all right somehow. Lukas, on the other hand, would check the situation thoroughly and make sure that there was someone in position to catch him. Both of them are growing up bilingual in German and Spanish; Lukas goes to a local Spanish-speaking school and Mathias to a Spanish-speaking kindergarten.

My original intention had been to move back to Austria once the children were of school age, but that is out of the question now, because we are all so happy on Ibiza. Also, I don't think it would be feasible to persuade Marlene to pull up roots and move to Austria a second time. She never felt at home in Salzburg – she found the locals too formal (at least by comparison with her circle of friends on Ibiza).

I also enjoy the few days I can occasionally snatch on Ibiza between working and travelling. Our house is just outside Santa Eulalia, built on a gentle rise looking out over the sea some two miles away. We water regularly to keep the garden nice and green. The house itself was a typical Spanish farmhouse which brother-in-law Tilly has extended quite ingeniously. It is light, airy and quite a contrast to the severe lines of the huge place I have at Hof, near Salzburg. Another advantage is that the house on Ibiza is reached via an atrocious unsurfaced path, which helps keep the fans at bay; back in Salzburg they really were something of a plague.

We are very fortunate to have Albi Clary as a neighbour – a dear friend who goes all the way back to the first days of Lauda Air. Albi runs the charming bar called 'La Villa' in Santa Eulalia, together with a restaurant which is annexed to Ibiza's biggest discotheque, Pacha. Albi always knows what's on and where the action is.

Life on Ibiza is also made richer by the presence of Tilly. Although he had great success as a painter about ten years ago and made a considerable amount of money, he has been living on Ibiza for a couple of years now and rarely paints any more. Not so long ago, I asked him why. He replied: 'I'm happy here without doing any work, and that's bad for an artist. An artist needs to be confronted by reality, he needs worries and a sense of dissatisfaction. You can derive pleasure from being dissatisfied, providing you can translate that dissatisfaction into art. I suppose being in prison might be best suited to this. But being on Ibiza is fatal: it is too beautiful, too carefree, and I live too well here. There are no artists on Ibiza. A lot of painters have moved here, but hardly any of them have kept on painting for any length of time.'

Incidentally, Tilly believes that some of the above also applies to me: 'Being able to derive pleasure from dissatisfaction by turning it into an art form holds true for you and your driving. Once you are completely content, you won't race any more.'

Instead of painting, Tilly has worked as an antique expert and restorer, but also as a mechanic and as an architect. He can do anything. Four years ago he decided to devote himself to horses, and went about it in his usual way – with total dedication. It was as if he had gone into a whole new profession: he studied everything there is to know about horses and he is now as gifted in veterinary medicine as he is in the blacksmith's craft.

Tilly often says, however, that his eternal passion is agriculture. I am convinced that, one day, he will go back to Chile and take up farming: in other words, he will go and do what his father tried unsuccessfully to do back in the fifties. But Tilly will approach it in a completely different way, substituting professionalism for enthusiastic idealism.

CHAPTER SEVENTEEN

THE LAST LAP

THE ACCELERATOR PEDAL blocks coming in from qualifying for the Belgian Grand Prix. It all happens so quickly that there is nothing I can do – neither switch off the ignition nor take my hands off the wheel. Doing about 110mph I angle off line and plough into the guard-rail, which is only a couple of yards back from the track at this point. No big deal, but Ron Dennis reacts just the way I would expect him to. As if I had been daydreaming and simply let the car go.

There is one consolation – I won't have to put up with Ron all that much longer. There is no way I can change gear with such a badly bruised hand, so I fly to Vienna and have a doctor and Willy Dungl take a look at it. As a result, no Lauda at Spa, no Lauda at Brands.

In the meantime, Bernie Ecclestone puts in an appearance and makes me the kind of offer that belongs in the movies: $6 million to drive the Brabham for one season, the kind of money that is impressive even for a high-earner like myself. Technically speaking, the 1986 Brabham is liable to be highly interesting, and I have always had great faith in Gordon Murray as a designer. This is not the sort of deal to dismiss lightly and I am annoyed to find that I keep turning the pros and cons over in my mind. The public will think I'm a money-crazed idiot if I vacillate yet again, and Marlene will have me committed to a psychiatric ward. Apart from that, I won't be able to look myself in the eye. At any rate, I need some time to think it through.

It was obvious what had driven Ecclestone to make such a ridiculous offer. Bernie had taken a gamble on Piquet, had miscalculated, and had lost him to Williams. A top team like Brabham, with powerful partners and sponsors such as BMW, Pirelli and Olivetti, needs an international star driver – and, by autumn 1985, there wasn't one free. That was why this incredible sum was being mooted – about twice as high as my own assessment of my current market value (Piquet had been lured away for $3.3 million).

I was out for five weeks because of my injured hand, but I didn't feel I had lost anything. I was quite relaxed when I got to Kyalami. Because of jet lag I was awake early and at the track well ahead of time. As the sun came up a few mechanics appeared and started to work on the cars; it was quiet and beautiful. The lads greeted me as if welcoming me back into the bosom of the family, and I suddenly had a feeling that I would miss all of this, that I must be a fool to want to give up this kind of life.

Strictly speaking, Ron Dennis should have showed himself and welcomed me back. It would have been a nice gesture to do so and to show me to my qualifying car. (The third team car was available in turn to Prost and myself. Training with two cars is an enormous bonus, because you don't have to hang around while one car is being modified or repaired. As from Zandvoort, however, I had waived my turn with two cars in order to back up Prost's bid for the title. Now that he had the title locked up, I automatically assumed that we would revert to the original arrangement, and this time it was my turn.)

At any rate, Ron Dennis did not say 'Welcome back' or 'Here's your qualifying car.' Instead, he told me I should count myself lucky to have even one car to drive: being out for five weeks had inevitably made me less sharp and he couldn't let me have the second car. I told him that he was on the point of making a lifelong enemy and that he should think it over carefully.

He went into a huddle with the engineers and pit crew, then he came back and said that I could have the second car just to make sure that I didn't have any excuses afterwards for being too slow. I told him what a charming person he was and in what high regard I held him.

After this build-up, I stormed out onto the circuit. I needed the second car right away, because the first wouldn't build charge pressure. I was faster than Alain right through qualifying. There was no point in trying to match the other marques, because we had a definite 100hp less than the Hondas and the BMWs – Porsche somehow couldn't adjust the turbos to the extreme altitude in Kyalami.

I was very pleased with my performance, happy that I had found my old edge again. Overall, I felt so elated that I couldn't imagine what life would be like without Formula 1. If only Bernie Ecclestone had chosen to come up and be nice and friendly then, if only he'd asked again, I would have signed for another season right there on the spot.

Bernie had no idea what was going through my mind, so he didn't come over. It was only when we were back in Europe that he started calling me again but, by that time, I was back in control and thinking rationally again. The magic and excitement of Kyalami had gone. Three days later I called Bernie and said no. That's a pity, he replied, not knowing how close we had been to reaching agreement.

The last race: the Australian Grand Prix in Adelaide on 3 November 1985.

Even at Melbourne airport I was struck by how racing-mad the Australians are and how delighted they were to have their very own Grand Prix. The whole country was behind it and the atmosphere was electric and contagious.

As for myself, I was drained by the long flight and annoyed that I had to put in an appearance the evening we arrived at one of those McLaren parties that grate on my nerves. I gulped a couple of glasses of wine, chatted with Ron Dennis (who was having one of his better days), then had a couple more and another two after that. I fell into bed round about 3am, having just set a record for the worst race preparation in my eighteen-year career. I paid the penalty: next morning, my head was splitting and I felt nauseous during the first training laps. That'll do nicely, I thought – the idea being that everything should be as unpleasant and sterile as possible to make my leave-taking that much easier. Let's keep sentimentality and emotion out of it as best we can, I thought.

Unfortunately, everybody in Australia seemed to have other ideas. Instead of struggling to stage some kind of third-rate Grand Prix, the Aussies put on the best show of the whole season. The circuit was marvellous, everything was beautifully and professionally organised, and I've never in my life seen so many rapturous fans. There were 60,000 of them in the stands during training and the tremendous atmosphere got to all of us.

Everyone you met gave the impression of being happy that these twenty-six clowns had turned up. Whenever you switched on a TV set – from 7am to midnight – every channel seemed to be covering the Grand Prix. It was unbelievable; there was nothing that even the most miserable nit-picker could fault. I remember being irritated and saying to Willy Dungl: 'My headache's gone. My bellyache's gone. Can't you do something about it?'

For all that, training and qualifying went according to plan: one defect after another, nothing seemed right. We had electrical problems, then engine trouble. It was a total disaster. I placed sixteenth on the grid – the ideal position to demotivate any Formula 1 driver. There wasn't much else that could go wrong.

The conditions on race day were superb: hordes of spectators, beautiful weather. Being sixteenth on the grid was the only thing that dampened my enthusiasm.

I started cautiously, but soon realised that all manner of surprises were on the cards. The warm weather combined with abraded rubber to give the circuit more grip than during qualifying. I noticed very early on that the rear tyres on Johansson's Ferrari were disintegrating rapidly. You'd better watch what you're doing, I said to myself. I turned turbo boost down from 3.5 to 3.2* and took great care when accelerating.

* At first sight, these figures seem at variance with those cited in Chapter 10. However, charge pressure on the McLaren-TAG was electronically regulated from the 1985 season onward and is now expressed in absolute values, i.e. inclusive of atmospheric pressure.

Despite this, I worked my way up through the field comparatively quickly and was soon in sixth place. I noted that my tyres were still in excellent condition, so I went back up to normal boost and eased myself into the lead group. It is possible that I was the only driver that day who took sufficient care of his tyres. Rosberg and Senna in particular killed off their tyres in the shortest time imaginable, went in for a change, and drove so wildly when they came back out that their tyres were beginning to deteriorate again after another fifteen laps.

I had no option other than to outbrake Senna and move into the lead. As I did so, I felt that surge of excitement that Formula 1 can bring. Marvellous, I thought, just look how you've managed to put one over on the others simply by using a bit of brain power. I was so delighted with myself and my performance and the feeling of tearing round that fabulous circuit, that things were beginning to look serious again for a moment. But then the brakes made their presence felt.

We had opted for carbon brakes even though we had some trouble with them during qualifying. The unusually good grip during the race itself put more strain on the brakes and the carbon discs had abraded faster than anticipated. You had to pump like crazy – sometimes it worked, at others it didn't. This is what we call 'knock-off': when the discs wear thin unevenly and begin to spin the brake linings don't make contact; the pounding they take on the long straight does the rest. When you apply the brakes nothing happens at first; you have to pump several times (if necessary, with your left foot while accelerating with your right) to get them to react at all. It is alarming being in that situation, because you know that your brakes can pack up on you at any moment.

I am obliged to bring my speed up because Rosberg, who is sixteen seconds behind, has just come out of the pits with fresh tyres and is bound to drive like a maniac. I have no choice other than to go flat-out myself to stop him closing the gap too quickly. We are doing about 190mph at the end of the straight. I hit the brakes. Nothing happens. I pump again – still nothing. A third time – only the rear brakes hold. And block. The car is thrown out left.

A wall.

The nose of the McLaren shaves the concrete and the bodywork scrapes along the wall. The car comes to a standstill. I jump out. I feel angry with myself, but I suppress my irritation almost immediately: 'Take it easy, who cares, it's your last race, it's over, you made it.'

The spectators applaud and wave, and their cheers follow me all the way back to the pits. It's a nice place to finish, here in Adelaide. All the mechanics are on hand to say goodbye. There are dozens of reporters around me and the doyen of the German-language motor-sport press, Ernst Graf, has tears in his eyes. 'That's the end of a legend,' he says. Rather than collapse in tears myself, I run over to the 'copter. Ron Dennis says thank you on behalf of McLaren; I thank him back.

He tries to convince me to stay for a big celebration in the evening: the whole of Formula 1 has been invited. But I don't want any fuss – the chopper is waiting.

Adelaide – Sydney – Honolulu – San Francisco – London. Bernie Ecclestone is on the same flight. He comes up with an extra hundred thousand dollars or two to make yet another offer. No, I'm through. It is my good luck that I am sitting next to an attractive coloured girl rather than Bernie. The in-flight movie is *Gandhi*.

My co-pilot Samy is waiting with the Learjet in London. We take off for Ibiza and arrive in the evening. I can only stay one night because I have to be in Nice the next day to make a film. I've been en route for two days and two nights, I am all in.

My car is at the airport. I console myself that I'll be in bed in half an hour's time. As I drive through Santa Eulalia I notice funny lights to my left. I drive through the town, turn off the asphalt onto the gravel path, fishtail through the right hander, turn left up our driveway. A rocket zooms up into the sky above our house: the Ibiza clan has gathered.

Marlene has organised a 'retirement party'. All the tension and frustration have gone out of her; she is happy, effervescent. I could have sworn that all I would want to do after that long haul is stumble into bed. No way.

Dinner is a dream. The hostess is delectable.

We wake up next morning. Marlene turns to me and says: 'Now for the bad news. *Nada* yoghurt.'

POSTSCRIPT BY *KEVIN EASON*

POSTSCRIPT

'THE WORST TIME OF MY LIFE'

THE SLEEK JET nosed carefully into position on the outskirts of Vienna airport, close to the lounge where businessmen would wait to board their private planes to make deals all over the world. This gleaming Bombardier Global Express 7500, more than $70 million worth of the most luxurious transport in the skies, was the first to be delivered to Europe and to the most exacting of owners, the Laudamotion company launched in 2018.

But for the first time in his forty-year aviation career, Niki Lauda was not there to see this addition to his fleet. He had always collected his new planes in person from the manufacturer, whether from Boeing in Seattle or Bombardier in Montreal, to fly them home to Austria himself.

There was good reason for the personal touch, for Lauda never missed the chance of a deal. He would go over his new plane with a forensic eye, looking for clumsy paintwork or nicks in the leather seats. 'That way I could say to the airline, "Hey, come on. You can give me a discount for this or that because it isn't perfect."' He could also push the limits of the deal further. When he acquired a new 777 aircraft from Boeing in 1997, he pointed out it had no fuel to fly back to Austria, so he demanded that the manufacturer fill the tanks. The airline business was going through a rough period at the time and Lauda knew Boeing needed every sale they could get. Reluctantly, executives offered enough fuel to get the 777, with Lauda at the controls, to Vienna, but then he pointed out that there also had to be enough spare in case he was re-routed. Lauda got his full tanks – at a cost to Boeing of an estimated $40,000. It was a victory as good as any on the track.

Lauda would have been at the controls of this stunning Bombardier, too, but for the illness that would eventually claim his life. He had personally ordered the beautiful cream leather and dark wood cabin from the designers Hannes Rausch and Veronique Ferrari and overseen the fitting of the full-size kitchen, where chefs could make his favourite Wiener Schnitzel and potatoes, and four living spaces that would ease the pain of travelling between countries and continents almost weekly. He had built a close relationship with Bombardier, becoming a figurehead for the business, and that propelled him to the front of the European queue when the new, long-distance jet was ready to fly. Less than two months after it touched down in Vienna, Lauda was dead.

'He never saw it,' Bernie Ecclestone said, recognising the poignancy of that jet's arrival in Vienna at the end of March 2019. The friends had flown together many times, Lauda in the cockpit for take-off and landing, while Ecclestone languished in the leather armchairs in the passenger cabin. 'Niki loved his planes and his flying and he always liked to bring the plane back himself, but this one he never got to see. It was very sad.'

There is a dreaded moment that faces every athlete, when everything that they have known and practised every waking minute of their lives comes to an end. They say that athletes have to die twice – the first time when they retire. Racing drivers live on the extreme edge, an adrenalin rush of speed and danger that cannot be replicated in almost any other sport. Ordinary life seems one-dimensional and horribly slow when the time comes to hang up their racing helmets and join the rest of the world.

But Niki Lauda never had any doubts about his future. He was quite simply crazy about planes – big planes, small planes, jets or good, old-fashioned planes with propellers – and he saw a new career in the air. Paddy Lowe, who worked with Lauda towards the end of Niki's life, remembered: 'He was mad about his planes and flying. I used to sympathise with his pilots because he would do the fun bit of taking off and landing and they would have to do the boring bits. He knew about planes technically, but also operationally. If you mentioned planes, he would be off. If you asked about engine failures, he would start a talk on engines and routes. He knew every type of aircraft, how many passengers – everything, in fact.'

When Lauda quit Formula 1 for the first time in 1979, walking out on Bernie Ecclestone's Brabham team with two Grands Prix of the season still to run, he was already making moves into the aviation business. At the same time as his return to the track in 1982 with McLaren, he was trying to set up his fledgling airline, Lauda Air, while travelling to all points of the globe to race. He was to win the world championship for a third time in his career in 1984, but his heart wasn't in the sport the following season. He was teammate to a younger, faster driver called Alain Prost and he endured a miserable year, suffering eleven retirements in fourteen races and breaking his wrist. His relationship with McLaren's team principal Ron Dennis was also at breaking point and he decided that with three world championships and twenty-five victories behind him, there was nothing left to race for. He quit McLaren and Formula 1 after the final race of the 1985 season. That was enough; his life would be in the skies from now on.

But it was a struggle, as he recounts in detail. Austrian Airlines, the national carrier, didn't want competition from this upstart operation, founded on a shoestring budget and a good deal of hope. In fact, the biggest asset Lauda Air possessed was the man himself – Niki Lauda. As one Austrian newspaper once observed: 'Niki Lauda's greatest strength is selling himself.' For Niki Lauda, this was like Formula 1, only with wings instead of wheels. There was nothing he liked better than the odds being stacked against him so that he could take on the Big Boys and win.

He rose to the challenge in Formula 1, constantly regarding failure as a lesson before moving on. Twelve years after founding Lauda Air, he discovered that failure in the airline business can have much greater consequences.

At 23:02 on 26 May 1991, the Lauda Air Flight 004 took off from Don Mueang International Airport in Bangkok bound for Vienna. There was a full complement of 213 passengers aboard the Boeing 767 and ten crew, under the command of Captain Thomas J. Welch. The plane was barely two years old and carried the name of *Mozart* as an aviation tribute to one of Austria's most revered sons.

Six minutes into the flight, Captain Welch and his co-pilot Josef Thurner, who had sat alongside Lauda in the cockpit several times, spotted warning lights indicating that the thrust reverser on the number one engine threatened to deploy in flight. After checking the plane's handbook, they decided that it was no more than an advisory message, but nine minutes later, the warning became stark reality. The reverse thruster did deploy and the Boeing was sent into a terrifying, supersonic dive, breaking up at about 4,000 feet. Wreckage was strewn over a kilometre-square area of dense forest 160 kilometres north-west of Bangkok. There were no survivors.

Niki Lauda was at home in Vienna when the phone rang at 9:45 that evening. It was Austrian television calling to tell him that one of his aircraft had disappeared in Thailand. Lauda was both cautious and dismissive because he was often the victim of bogus calls of one kind or another. As he told Will Buxton for his book, *My Greatest Defeat*: 'They had called me a couple of weeks before when I had been in a restaurant and said, "Thank God we are speaking to you because we've just had a message that you were killed in a car accident." So, I said, "What is this bullshit? I'm sitting here. I am not dead."'

But the awful facts of Flight 004's fate soon became clear and Lauda rushed to his office to take charge. The corporate reaction among his executives was predictable and they wanted Lauda to stay in Vienna to deal with a media he knew well and which would be sympathetic to such a charismatic and famous figure in Austria. But Lauda was on a quest to discover what had happened: this was his aircraft, his airline, his crew and his passengers. He had stared death in the face as a man, but this was bigger and something beyond even his courage and determination.

In an interview with the UK's *Guardian* newspaper, Lauda put it this way: 'People always think that the worst time of my life must have been after the German Grand Prix in 1976, which put me in a coma and left me with severe burns. But it wasn't. When I was motor racing, I took the decision to risk my life, but when you run an airline and more than 200 people want to go from A to B and they don't arrive, that is a different responsibility.'

Ecclestone had been at Lauda's side at the Monza racetrack for his comeback Grand Prix in 1976 and watched as his friend took off his racing helmet and fireproof balaclava to reveal the blood-soaked bandages covering his scars. 'I told him, "You can't go out onto the track like that, covered in blood." He said absolutely nothing. He just replaced the bandages, put his helmet back on and raced again as though nothing was a problem. It was him, alone. But this aircraft crash, that was massive for him. He felt personally responsible, even though he wasn't involved and wasn't there. It affected him very deeply indeed for the rest of his life. He could never forget the crew and passengers and what he saw on the ground in Thailand.'

What Lauda saw at the site of the crash was horrific: bodies were scattered far and wide across the jungle; Captain Welch was found, still strapped into his pilot's seat. Lauda had travelled to Thailand with a Boeing expert and asked him what to expect, but there could be no adequate preparation for the smell of burning bodies and the torn wreckage of a once gleaming airliner. There was paper everywhere, scorched pieces hanging from branches and piles scattered across the forest floor, but it was only when Lauda studied some of the fragments that he could make out the logo of Lauda Air; they were napkins that would have been issued to the passengers for their in-flight meal as they had started to switch on the entertainment systems after take-off, unaware of their fate just minutes later.

Lauda watched with revulsion as villagers looted the belongings of the dead, even taking rings from the fingers of stricken bodies. Stalls started to appear as the locals sold the electronics, clothes and keepsakes they found in the jungle that might have been dear to relatives. Recovering the bodies became more macabre by the day as they were collected and sent to a hospital in Bangkok that had no refrigeration facilities. The bodies decomposed and had to be identified by dental records. Some bodies were never identified.

Lauda realised he had to be forensic, and the 'computer brain' he had used to such effect in motor racing was triggered into action among the trees of the Thai forest. He had spotted one engine before finding the other a couple of kilometres away, and realised that the thrust reverser had been deployed on one and not the other. When he asked Boeing's team on the ground, they fobbed him off, but Lauda was already curious and homing in on a possible cause. The black-box recorder was destroyed, but the voice recorder was intact, so that Lauda could hear the panic in the cockpit as the thrust reverser deployed and sent the Boeing into its fatal dive. It was obvious to Lauda that there had been a catastrophic failure, something so out of the ordinary that Welch, an experienced American pilot based in Vienna, and Thurner could not regain control of their aircraft.

The investigation by the Thai authorities and the Boeing Corporation, the world's biggest airline manufacturer, was painfully laborious. There was much at stake, not least the reputation of Boeing, which sold planes to almost every airline in the world, many with dozens of aircraft like the 767 that now lay stricken and in a million pieces.

Lauda, meanwhile, had to steel himself for the gruelling round of funerals. He met families of his lost crew, including the boyfriend of the aircraft's purser, who was suicidal and had to be talked into accepting what had happened. Then, Lauda attended the ceremony for the 25 unidentified passengers, watching tearfully as a small boy threw marbles into the open grave, clattering onto the coffins below. Lauda discovered the marbles were a gift from the child's parents, but both died on Lauda Air Flight 004. Lauda told Buxton: 'This was the worst time of my life.'

He started using the mind of a pilot and all his experience in the cockpit, sitting for hours in a simulator at Gatwick Airport, south of London, trying to figure out whether the thrust reverser was the culprit, as seemed to be indicated in the initial findings of crash investigators. He became more and more convinced that Captain Welch had been taken by surprise by the sudden reverse thrust, but he needed to convince Boeing that this was the case and that it was their fault that his aircraft had been brought down.

He was furious with Boeing's stubborn insistence that they would not accept the blame and argued that he must run tests personally on the company's own simulator in Seattle. They gave in under the intense pressure of Lauda's anger, and he conducted flight after simulated flight, proving each time that no pilot could overcome a sudden burst of reverse thrust at altitude.

Boeing executives warned, however, that their lawyers might need three months to sort out the correct legal wording of any statement, anxious not to concede that the 767 might have a crucial fault, but Lauda could not countenance delays when he and the bereaved families needed answers. He issued the ultimatum: he would call a press conference and challenge Boeing to fly a 767 with him on board to test the reverse thrusters for real. Boeing executives were at his hotel immediately and a statement was drafted. Airlines later carried out modifications to a range of Boeing aircraft to fix the faulty valve system that led to the reverse-thrust deployment.

Today, there is a shrine to the dead of 004 near the crash site in the Suphanburi region of Thailand, marked by a simple wooden sign. Some fragments of the aircraft remain, neglected and left to be swallowed up by the intense greenery of the forest, a final, bleak reminder of that awful night.

Lauda refused to be deflected from his quest for the truth. For months, he had slogged through bureaucracy and corporate obstinacy, all the while promising that he would close down Lauda Air if the cause was pinned on him or his company. Finally, Lauda had his answers and his justice, although that would never wipe clear the memories of 004 that followed him to his own grave.

In the heated aftermath, there were accusations that the Lauda aircraft was not airworthy and that crucial maintenance documents had gone missing, while long memories and a series of problems with his various businesses meant that a suggestion to rename Vienna airport as the Niki Lauda Airport quickly ran into criticism. Yet few could doubt the sincerity of Lauda's anguish over Flight 004, and few could doubt his determination that it would not force him out of the airline business, no matter how turbulent that would prove to be.

Operating out of a headquarters in Schwechat, a town close to Vienna's international airport, Lauda had rapidly expanded from two leased BAC 1–11 planes to a fleet flying to Cuba and Miami, as well as Australia and the Far East, including Hong Kong and Thailand, where Flight 004 would meet its end. This was a business very much centred on the reputation and charisma of the boss, the big red 'L' on the tail and the letters spelling out LAUDA in red along the fuselage of his aircraft. He loved to fly his own planes, occasionally joining the passengers in the cabin for a chat and to sign autographs and pose for photos with fans, a habit he retained throughout his career.

Lauda was somehow able to recover from the tragedy and all seemed to be going well when he floated the business on the Vienna Stock Exchange and then struck a deal to cooperate with the German carrier Lufthansa in 1992. But rising costs and the oppressive presence of Austria's national carrier would always be at the forefront of his mind and, finally, in 1999 he saw his airline make a loss for the first time in a decade. There was nowhere to go, so he sold a 36 per cent shareholding in Lauda Air to Austrian Airlines, a company whose monopoly of his home market he had tried so hard to break with his low-cost operation. He attempted to recover losses by selling and leasing aircraft, but, in 2001, Austrian Airlines acquired Lufthansa's 26.5 per cent of the company and the scene was set for conflict between the corporate and correct Austrian Airlines board and the straight-talking Lauda with his mantra: no bullshit. He sold his 30 per cent shareholding to Austrian and then didn't have long to wait, for it could only end badly ... for Lauda.

According to a report in the UK's *Daily Telegraph*, the end was quick and cruel. Lauda was told that, at fifty-two years old, he was too old to fly, a devastating blow for a man who adored his life in the cockpit, and he was ordered to clear his desk and get out of the company he had founded. Lauda was beyond bitter and lashed out, as well as packing for a new life in London. He accused Austria of not being fit to be in the European Union because politics and personal connections had become more important than the ability to run a business, and told the *Daily Telegraph*: 'Why should I stay [in Austria]? They have brutally driven me out like a dog, just because I wouldn't let myself be trained to heel. I started as a lone fighter 20 years ago and just because in all that time I get one bad result, because of the high price of fuel and the rate of the dollar, I am forced to give up.

'If I had not been the biggest critic of the heads of Austrian Airlines, I would still be part of this system, but I could not see my life's work destroyed. I thank God I am not tied to Austria and that I can move to London where my countrymen's idea of an economy based on who you know and not what you know doesn't exist.'

In the event, it did matter who Lauda knew, and that someone was Bernie Ecclestone, the controversial controller of Formula 1, who had a plan for his lifelong friend, not in the air but back on the racetracks of the world.

CHAPTER NINETEEN

BREAKING THE RULES

THE FIRST CALL after Lauda's dramatic and bitter exit from his airline came from Bernie Ecclestone. The diminutive boss of Formula 1 was not just the brains behind the sport's burgeoning finances, but also the master manipulator, switching drivers from team to team and gently cajoling auto-industry executives to take up his suggestions – like taking on Niki Lauda, a three-times world champion and one of his closest associates, as team principal.

It seemed a perfect fit to Ecclestone: he had a pal out of work and a new team that added much-needed lustre to Formula 1, but that was struggling to establish itself. Jaguar, one of the most respected car brands in the world, had been catapulted into Formula 1 to the sound of the loudest fanfare in recent Formula 1 history just as Lauda was being ejected from his airline office in Vienna. Although owned by the American multinational Ford, the Jaguar name still carried cachet and the British Racing Green livery evoked memories of victories at the fabled Le Mans 24-hour Endurance Race.

Lauda had tried returning to the sport once, as a consultant to his old chum and mentor, Luca di Montezemolo, who had taken over as president at Ferrari in 1991 when the team was a shambles and at its lowest ebb. It was a largely undistinguished return to Maranello, although Lauda claimed to have recommended that Montezemolo hire Michael Schumacher from the Benetton team where he had won two world championships in 1994 and 1995.

'In 1995, I made the first contact with Schumacher, who was with Benetton. I spoke to his manager [Willi Weber] in Brazil,' Lauda told *Opus World*. 'I called Luca from Brazil and told him, "Schumacher is the guy we need, but we have to start now, before any of the other teams start talking to him."' Weber needed convincing: the Ferrari cars were hopeless and Jean Todt, the new sporting director, was battling the scepticism of the Italian nation insulted that their national team was being run by a Frenchman, as well as trying to reorganise a team that had hit the depths and was lacking a world champion since Jody Scheckter in 1979. But Lauda had dangled the carrot – and Weber bit. Then Lauda discovered that Todt had taken over the negotiations, deciding firmly that he was in charge, not the consultant, no matter how famous and close to the president. Meticulous and wedded to detail, Todt was anxious and didn't want Lauda on his turf claiming the credit. A reckoning was inevitable. 'Todt decided that they didn't need me any more and put so much pressure on Luca that they didn't renew my contract,' Lauda told *Opus*. 'That was it. But, of course, they were very successful together. Whatever happened between Todt and me, I would never deny that he was the right choice to lead Ferrari. With Schumacher driving, he did a great job and the results were unbelievable.'

They were indeed. Todt propelled Ferrari to a run of six consecutive world championships as a constructor, while Schumacher became the first world champion for the Maranello team in twenty-one years and went on to a total of five titles in the colours of the *Scuderia*.

Jaguar was a different proposition, though. Ford spent a reputed £100 million buying Sir Jackie Stewart's eponymous team, based at Milton Keynes in the South Midlands of England. The Stewart team was in existence for only three seasons, but had achieved one pole position and a victory, and finished the 1999 season fourth in the constructors' world championship, an incredible achievement for a fledgling outfit. It seemed ripe for success, which is why Ford executives pounced to buy out Stewart and rename the team Jaguar to bring the Big Cat into Formula 1.

The launch at the world-famous Lord's Cricket Ground in London was lavish and awash with optimism. Johnny Herbert, who had won the 1999 European Grand Prix for Jackie Stewart, was to partner Eddie Irvine, a hugely expensive purchase from Ferrari where he had finished as runner-up in the 1999 world championship. His contract was said to be worth £18 million over three years, a figure that dazzled his old bosses in Italy, who believed he was no more than a support driver for Michael Schumacher, and led to Edsel Ford, then chairman of the family business, asking who exactly 'this Irvine guy' was because he was the company's highest-paid employee.

Wolfgang Reitzle, a Ford insider who was chairman of Ford's Premier Automotive Group, was to run the team. Reitzle was stiff, correct and corporate, and he had no chance against the wily Ecclestone and the rest of the team principals, who called themselves 'The Piranha Club' because so many were ripped to shreds in this hostile world. Jaguar finished its maiden season in an embarrassing ninth place of eleven teams and Reitzle left.

Ford's executives across the Atlantic in Dearborn, Michigan, 3,700 miles from Milton Keynes, turned to Bobby Rahal to be team principal. Rahal was a renowned racer and team owner in the USA Cart and IndyCar series, but he was too open and charming for a sport run by the most aggressive and ruthless team owners in sport. The answer, according to Ecclestone, was straight-talking Lauda, a man who knew Formula 1 from the inside and wasn't an infiltrator from the USA.

Lauda couldn't wait to start. 'When Jaguar offered me the job, Bernie advised me to take it. The offer came just at the right time. Jaguar hadn't won anything yet and that is why I decided to accept the challenge.'

Lauda immediately made a bold statement of intent, typical of his bullish approach to any problem, no matter how tricky. 'I am going to put Jaguar at the top of Formula 1,' he declared to Reuters. He brought experience from Ferrari where Enzo – *Il Commendatore*, the Commander – ran his team and his company like an emperor; then Brabham where Bernie Ecclestone, as the owner, made his word law. Next came McLaren, a team built and dominated by Ron Dennis.

It was fraught from the start. In January 2002, Lauda had his first chance in seventeen years to drive a Formula 1 car, taking the new Jaguar for a spin at the Valencia test circuit. Literally. He spun the car and, somewhat shame-faced, was towed back to the pits. When he did complete a lap, he was fifteen seconds off the pace. Typically, only weeks before, he had told anyone who would listen that monkeys could drive a modern Formula 1 car with all of its gadgets and technology. Now he was eating his words.

The test had seemed a jolly idea, but was, perhaps, a metaphor for what was to come. Lauda had probably thought he could be a natural successor to Enzo, Ecclestone and Dennis, but he hadn't reckoned on the power and panic of corporate America. Just like Austrian Airlines, Ford was run by men in suits and they controlled the finances and, in the end, they controlled Jaguar Racing. John Hogan, who was to pilot Jaguar's Formula 1 team into new ownership, said: 'Ford thought they could run it from the USA when they had Niki on the ground trying to deal with the problems. It could never work.'

Ford believed money was the answer until the bank account started to run dry. Lauda and Rahal clashed frequently, not least when the American attempted to sell Irvine to the Jordan team to offload his massive salary. Lauda knew nothing about it and was incandescent when he found out. Then there was a ham-fisted attempt by Rahal to lure Adrian Newey, Formula One's pre-eminent designer, from McLaren that ended with lawyers, lurid headlines and failure, and an apology issued by Lauda on Jaguar's behalf. Meanwhile, results on the track were woeful.

Rahal quit and, sixteen months into his tenure, Lauda was gone, too, along with seventy staff at Milton Keynes who were made redundant, and Hogan moved in to organise the sale of the team. Ford said that Lauda lacked 'technical depth', which he did because Formula 1 cars had moved on apace since he had last driven in 1985. But Lauda's departure was no surprise to observers in the paddock, who had watched the mounting tensions between Ford's corporate executives, who were increasingly worried about the soaring costs of running a Formula 1 team, and a recalcitrant Lauda, who insisted on wearing his uniform of red cap, sweater and blue jeans even when he turned up for meetings at Ford's plush headquarters in Berkeley Square in London's Mayfair.

'When I started working there,' Lauda told *Motor Sport* magazine, 'the finance guy at Jaguar called me and said he had to give me this book. He called it the "Ford Compliance Rules" and said it means whatever you do, it has to comply with what's in this book. I asked him for an example. He said: "Okay. Let's say you are staying in a hotel and you take a sparkling water from the mini bar, you have to pay for it. But if you take a still water, you don't have to pay for it." I asked him if he was serious and when he said he was, I told him to keep the book.'

This was about Ford rules and the whole point of Niki Lauda – and why Ecclestone backed his appointment – was that he didn't do rules. He made rapid, quickfire decisions, just like Ferrari, Ecclestone or Dennis, that would tie up conventional company boardrooms for months. That was how Formula 1 worked at its best.

Lauda decided the Ford way was, inevitably, 'bullshit' and that he would pay his own expenses, using his private credit card, but that caused panic among Ford's accountants when Lauda waited for the next tranche of money on his contract. 'Suddenly there were people rushing over from America, running into Jaguar and demanding to have the accounts for Niki Lauda. I said I had no accounts. "What do you mean? You must have expenses." I said, "There are no expenses." "But there must be." They just could not believe it. Can you imagine? These people had come all that way, looking for this fucking mineral water. After six months' fight, I got my money. And they found no mineral water.'

Ford threw in the towel at the end of 2004, handing over the team to Red Bull Racing for a symbolic $1 and a commitment to invest up to $400 million over the following three years. Ironically, it was Lauda who recommended Dietrich Mateschitz, Red Bull's co-owner and a close friend as well as a fellow Austrian, as the new boss.

Five years after taking over, Red Bull Racing won both the world drivers' championship with Sebastian Vettel, and the world championship for constructors, the first of four consecutive years of domination of Formula 1, while still employing many of the mechanics and engineers who had served under Sir Jackie Stewart ... and Niki Lauda.

CHAPTER TWENTY

THE FINAL VICTORY

Sunday, 3 November 2019

NINETEEN OF THE world's best drivers clambered from their sleek Formula 1 cars to acknowledge the last of their number to arrive in the seething pit lane at the end of an intense US Grand Prix.

There was no victory for Lewis Hamilton today, no winners' trophy to add to the eighty-three he had already captured at the time and that were taking up space in his father's loft back home in Hertfordshire. But he had achieved his ultimate goal: the world championship. He nosed his silver Mercedes between his rivals to the space marked out in white letters on a black background, saying: RESERVED PARKING. 2019 WORLD CHAMPION. This was Hamilton's sixth world title, but five were achieved since he joined Mercedes in 2013, a run of success that placed him ahead of some of the greatest names in the history of Formula 1, from Juan Manuel Fangio, a five-times winner considered by many to be the best of all time, to Ayrton Senna, a three-times champion and Hamilton's boyhood hero.

Hamilton leapt from the claustrophobic cockpit of his car into the sunshine and threw himself into the arms of those he loved and had lived with on the racetracks of the world, such as his race engineer Pete Bonnington. Waiting, too, was his father Anthony, who set his son on the road to Formula 1 when he bought him a go-kart for his eighth birthday. For the first time, Hamilton's entire family – his father, stepmother, and mother and stepfather – were united at the racetrack to join the celebrations.

Only one familiar face was missing from the smiling, cheering crowd.

In the deserted Mercedes garage, still hanging in their allocated box as they were for every Grand Prix, was a pair of headphones. On the hook above was a bright red cap with the logo of Parmalat, the company that sponsored the career of Niki Lauda for decades. The headphones were the ones that Lauda used at each race to monitor his drivers and engineers as they broke record after record with an unprecedented six consecutive world championships as a constructor, plus six drivers' world titles for Hamilton and Nico Rosberg.

The ghost of Niki Lauda is with Hamilton and Mercedes whenever they are at the racetrack and Hamilton is acutely aware of the presence of the man he came to regard as mentor and friend. Since Lauda's death, Hamilton had paused at the headphones on his way to his racing car to remember the man who had used his own experience of glory to persuade a young, but mercurial, Englishman to leave a successful McLaren team and gamble on the ambition of the squad he was trying to create.

As the crowds ebbed from the Circuit of the Americas and into the nightlife of the Texas capital of Austin after this US Grand Prix, Hamilton reflected on the impact Lauda had on his career. He had not realised just how great a blow Lauda's death would be to him, but he couldn't help smiling when he remembered their banter and how Lauda would have chided his £40 million-a-year driver after the qualifying session for the US Grand Prix, in which Hamilton could manage only fifth place on the grid for the race. 'He would have told me he was paying me too much,' Hamilton said. But then Lauda would have removed his red cap on Sunday to acknowledge a battling second place that was enough to clinch the world championship.

'I didn't think I would miss him as much as I have,' Hamilton added, attempting to summarise his grief. 'I wouldn't have been able to do this without Niki. Losing him was a pivotal point, but he's here with us in spirit.'

It is impossible to know just how much Niki Lauda influenced a Mercedes team that became a force unmatched in the history of Formula 1. The technical intricacies of supercomputer programs, laptop-generated strategies and complex aerodynamics dreamt up by PhD graduates escaped Lauda, and the internecine battles over finance in the Formula 1 boardroom were probably beyond his patience, but there was no doubting his ability to galvanise and focus those around him when it mattered. And he remained himself throughout, unbowed by corporate correctness and unwilling to toe the PR line. As one paddock observer put it to me: 'No matter how much pressure he was put under by the public relations department, he insisted in telling it the way he saw it.'

Yet the way back into Formula 1 as executive chairman of the Mercedes Formula 1 team in 2012 was as unexpected as it was driven by the grandmaster of the sport's chessboard, Bernie Ecclestone.

After his brief and disastrous spell with Jaguar, Lauda switched his attention back to airlines, starting a new business, Fly Niki, in 2003 to realise his dream of a low-cost airline that still offered all the comforts of scheduled flights, such as free drinks and meals. That kept him busy until the business was absorbed by Air Berlin in 2011, and he started to make plans for the launch of Laudamotion, another low-cost carrier, seven years later. Meanwhile, he had been lured back to the Formula 1 paddock as a pundit and commentator for the German television station RTL. His views were trenchant, no-holds-barred and, occasionally, hilarious. And he was back alongside the old chums and confidants he had known throughout his decades in the sport – such as Ecclestone.

As Lauda spoke to German Formula 1 fans on television, Ecclestone was struggling in the backrooms where negotiations over a series of commercial deals with the sport's ten teams were growing increasingly fractious and Mercedes would become a powerful player.

Ross Brawn had pulled off the seemingly impossible by guiding his own team to the 2009 world championship after Honda pulled the plug on the outfit based at Brackley in Northamptonshire. He refused to give up and negotiated a one-off $100 million payoff from Honda to keep the team running. First, though, he needed an engine and a last-minute appeal to Norbert Haug, the head of Mercedes Motorsport, had his engineers trying to shoehorn a Mercedes power pack into the rear of what should have been a Honda. However difficult it was, it worked a treat. Thanks to some design brilliance that stole a march on the rest of Formula 1 and Mercedes power and reliability, Brawn GP and Jenson Button ran away with the world championship.

Haug, a gruff, burly German and former motor-sport journalist, had taken Mercedes back into Formula 1 after an absence of four decades, forging a successful partnership with McLaren from 1995, and winning world championships with Mika Häkkinen and then Hamilton in 2008. But the relationship was souring as McLaren took the plaudits and Mercedes was 'just' the engine supplier, while the British team had ambitions to build their own supercar for the streets, effectively competing against their partners in Stuttgart in the lucrative market for sports cars. As Haug watched the Brawn miracle unfolding, he sensed a chance to break free to allow Mercedes to find its own glory and persuaded the board of Daimler, the Mercedes parent business, to buy the team.

Ambitions were on the grand scale with Michael Schumacher, now a seven-times world champion, brought out of retirement on a £20 million salary to lead the team. Ecclestone quickly discovered, however, that the financial clout of a global multinational such as Mercedes could not be ignored – as he found out when talks started with Brawn and Nick Fry, his chief executive, to tie the new team into a commercial deal in 2012. Talks were deadlocked because Fry and Brawn believed the deal was in Ecclestone's interests, but not their team's. Ecclestone's way out of the deadlock was simply to encourage Dieter Zetsche, the chairman of the main Daimler board, to take on a new boss ... someone such as Niki Lauda, his former driver and good friend.

Bodo Uebber, the Mercedes-Benz chief financial officer, was already an enthusiastic supporter and drafted in Lauda. 'Bodo called me and asked me what I thought about Niki,' Ecclestone told me in the quiet sanctuary of his office, which faces London's Hyde Park in the exclusive district of Knightsbridge. 'I said he would be good with people and stop them doing silly things. He will do a first-class job because he will tell them as it is. The important thing is to know when something is wrong and quickly put it right. And if you did something wrong, he would tell you immediately. That was Niki's strength.'

But Lauda's weakness was the speed of his appointment at such a critical time in Formula 1 when the teams were squabbling viciously over money. Lauda was plunged straight into the hurly-burly of negotiations, according to Brawn in his memoir, *Total Competition*. Brawn was at his holiday home in Cornwall when he discovered Lauda and Uebber were in talks with Ecclestone at his headquarters in Knightsbridge, but neither were intimately familiar with the detail and started a series of phone calls to Cornwall for advice. 'They would keep leaving the meeting and ringing me,' Brawn recalled. 'I was picking up the phone every fifteen minutes with the latest on what they should or shouldn't accept. Understandably, it's difficult for Niki to walk in and understand it all.'

Maybe it was the Lauda touch, or the depth of his friendship with Ecclestone, but somehow he emerged with a deal that eventually proved highly lucrative: Ecclestone had offered a £40 million annual bonus if the team won two consecutive world championships, something he believed could not happen – but it did until there were six world championships with the bonus fixed to pay out every year until 2020.

Lauda was only the first of the men to arrive as part of the management shakeup. In 2013, Mercedes also recruited Toto Wolff, an Austrian tech entrepreneur. Brawn could see that he was being squeezed out by the men from Vienna and chose to leave, followed by Haug, allowing Lauda and Wolff to forge a team in their own image. They brought in their own technical head, Paddy Lowe from McLaren, and Lauda's direct approach was crucial yet again. According to Lowe: 'Niki was assigned by the Daimler board to sign me up. I signed in January 2013, but I then faced eleven months' gardening leave. I had worked for twenty-five years without more than two weeks off, so I was looking forward to quiet time, but he phoned in the middle of May and said, "I've done the deal. You start in two weeks." He had phoned McLaren and bought me.' In fact, Lauda had cut through the red tape and paid McLaren about £1 million to get Lowe out of his contract.

'Other people might have ummed and ahhed because it's a lot of money,' Lowe added, 'but Niki's attitude was, let's get on with it, do it and move on. I have worked places when there was so much haggling that the notice period would have been consumed before the negotiations and the lawyers had been through the morass of details.'

Lauda was the conduit between Formula 1, Ecclestone and the remote Daimler board, who understood his value as a figurehead and decided not to wield the dreaded corporate 'compliance rules' with quite the same brutality as Ford, although his free spirit caused problems as he plunged into the job as chairman.

The key season for Mercedes would be 2014 when Formula 1's technical regulations underwent a revolution, ditching traditional petrol power for a futuristic hybrid package, comprising a small, 1.6-litre combustion engine linked to a complex battery system. It was hugely complicated and expensive, but Brawn had planned more thoroughly than any other team in the sport, which meant that the Mercedes power plant was way ahead of its rivals when the season opened. That gave Lauda, Wolff and Lowe the chance to capitalise and transform Mercedes from a mid-grid outfit to serial winners.

Their toughest competition would be Red Bull, still owned by that other Austrian, Dietrich Mateschitz, who were entering the new era on the back of four consecutive world championships. But Red Bull had a significant problem: they were parting company with Renault, their engine supplier, and wanted a Mercedes power pack for 2014. Lauda met Mateschitz – a member of Formula 1's Austrian 'mafia', according to Ecclestone – but without consulting Wolff or Lowe. The result was that Mateschitz thought he had a deal.

Wolff was aghast that Mercedes' most deadly rival might have even the remotest opportunity to share his team's greatest strength and went to each member of the Daimler board to warn them that not only would Red Bull be the fiercest competition, but he believed that the secrets of Mercedes' technology would eventually be passed to their closest showroom rivals at Audi, who were assessing the idea of entering Formula 1. The deal was quickly pulled.

Lauda insisted he had not given any guarantees, but there was enough smoke to turn the issue into a Formula 1 wildfire. Yet the outcome somehow turned out for the best again, Lowe said. 'It turned out to be a genius manoeuvre because we spent two months trying to undo this handshake, at board level and below, and eventually we got Red Bull to understand they weren't getting an engine,' he explained. 'After that they went to Ferrari and they also refused. We are heading into October and Red Bull didn't have an engine and had to go cap-in-hand back to Renault at the last minute, which set them back a long way for the following season. So, in one way, Niki's deal worked.'

The rumpus had a happy outcome for Mercedes, but had put Wolff on a collision course with his chairman. 'The first six months were rough,' Wolff told me just days before Mercedes would celebrate their haul of six drivers' and six constructors' world titles at the 2019 season-ending Abu Dhabi Grand Prix. The relationship between the cautious businessman Wolff and the headstrong racing driver Lauda was so uneasy that they were called to the Daimler headquarters in Stuttgart for a dressing-down to quell their regular rows. They arrived in Stuttgart ready to face the music, but Lauda headed off a confrontation. 'Right outside the toilets in the terminal at Stuttgart airport, Niki turned to me and said, "This is stupid. Let's sort this out ourselves." We shook hands there and then before we even went to see the board and we spoke almost every single day after that,' Wolff said.

Lauda's strength, as Ecclestone pointed out, was to recognise a mistake and learn from it. He also appreciated the value of teamwork, in which every member of the team plays to their strengths. Wolff's strength was organisation, and Lauda realised that Wolff should carry out the day-to-day running of a team with almost 1,500 employees over two bases, at Brackley and Brixworth, both in Northamptonshire. And Wolff, now head of Mercedes Motorsports, had no doubts about Lauda's qualities: 'His sheer presence was inspirational because he was a powerful force in the team and in the paddock during races. He was almost like our envoy to the rest of the sport, able to communicate and deal with any problems between people.'

Lauda also quickly understood his gifts could be employed better elsewhere, as a persuasive figurehead and a voice of authority gained through three world championships, and where Wolff and the Daimler directors could be circumspect and prone to dithering, Lauda was decisive.

'You need a man to worry about the details,' Paddy Lowe told me, 'but you also need someone who can cut through the nonsense, see the big picture and tell everyone, "That's what is happening. Just do this. No bullshit." It is a very helpful and a useful combination. I learned a lot from Niki, who basically didn't worry about any detail, which is a great skill if you can make it work.'

Wolff also discovered the power of his chairman's decisiveness. In the early days of their relationship, Wolff had set up a meeting over with potential sponsors in Shanghai before the Chinese Grand Prix. Lauda hated official dinners and would often point at Susie, Wolff's wife, and say: 'We shouldn't be long because Susie will be tired so we need to get away as quickly as we can,' although it was actually Lauda who wanted to be early to bed. After much persuasion, they set off with Wolff trying to talk Lauda through a sponsorship deal that would be worth $10 million. At the dinner table, Lauda was seated opposite the chief executive of the sponsor company, but even before the menus were handed round, Lauda looked him in the eye and blurted out: 'Right, are you going to sponsor Mercedes? Because if you are not, we are wasting time here and we can all go home.' The room was electrified for a few seconds, while the chief executive sat silently. 'I thought, "Oh no, Niki has wrecked the whole thing,"' Wolff said. But the chief executive suddenly smiled and reached across the table to shake hands and the meal went ahead. The deal was done in typical Niki style.

As Lowe put it: 'He would like nothing better than times when we needed agreement from all of the team principals in the paddock. He would go down the paddock into every motorhome to browbeat everyone into signing what he regarded as his deal. And it worked every time. He loved that chance to do a deal. Nothing gave him more pleasure because he could engage. Niki liked doing deals and anything that looked like a deal was great fun for him.'

There was one deal, though, that not only marked the turning point in the life of a young driver, but was of such significance that it will be forever entered into the history of Formula 1.

When Lauda attended his first board meeting as a guest in 2012, the Mercedes trophy cabinet, which was situated in the foyer of the Mercedes factory, was embarrassingly bare. There was a single winners' trophy for Nico Rosberg's victory at the

Chinese Grand Prix that season. Michael Schumacher had not just been signed for his high profile, but also for his genius. Sadly, that appeared to have deserted him; he joined Mercedes at the age of forty after three seasons out of Formula 1, and a single podium was all he had to show for three frustrating years as an also-ran.

Lauda sensed that the great driver was running out of road and intervened to ask who would drive in 2013. Haug replied, 'Rosberg and Schumacher, of course.' But it didn't seem so clear cut to Lauda, who believed Schumacher's commitment was waning and he might be tempted to announce his second retirement. Lauda convinced Haug to let him explore the chances of signing the man he believed was the best in the world – Lewis Hamilton.

'I knew from day one he would be one of the greats, and I knew he would inspire the whole team,' Lauda said.

It was a long shot, given that Hamilton had been signed by McLaren at the age of thirteen and most pundits agreed that his loyalty would tie him to the team that had brought him up to be a world champion in 2008. Hamilton was deeply unhappy, though, and had poured out his heart to Ecclestone, who naturally tipped off his friend and ally. Ecclestone was so worried that Hamilton – his biggest box office star – would quit the sport that he telephoned Dieter Zetsche to offer to pay half his salary demands. Meanwhile, Lauda waited to pounce.

His opportunity came in the dead of night in Singapore. Hamilton led the 2012 Grand Prix around the streets of the city state until his gearbox – ironically, made by Mercedes – failed him and Sebastian Vettel romped unchallenged to victory. It was not just the loss of that single race but the knowledge that Vettel was on his way to a third consecutive championship in a vastly superior car that seemed set to condemn the McLaren driver to a career marooned on a single world title. Martin Whitmarsh, the McLaren chief executive, had arrived in Singapore clutching a new $22 million-a-year contract for Hamilton to sign, but Hamilton hid in his luxurious suite at the Conrad Centennial hotel overlooking the Marina Bay Street Circuit, alone and depressed – until there was a knock at the door and he found the dishevelled figure of Niki Lauda outside, still in his rumpled jeans and red cap. They talked long into the night, Lauda trying to convince Hamilton that Mercedes' ambitions would take the team beyond anything McLaren could achieve – and equipped with the knowledge that, thanks to Ecclestone, he could happily offer $10 million more than McLaren. 'Lewis was going to re-sign for McLaren on the Monday after Singapore, but I convinced him in his hotel room, in the middle of the night, to join Mercedes,' Lauda said with a chuckle.

Wolff believes Hamilton was blown away by the force of nature that was Niki Lauda, a personality who could not be denied. 'Niki was like a cruise missile. He just fired straight into things because his attitude was not to waste time on formalities. Just get it done,' Wolff said.

Formula 1 was aghast when news leaked that Hamilton was leaving McLaren, an established team with a pedigree as the second most successful outfit in Formula 1, for an unproven Mercedes team. Hamilton, too, must have wondered what he had done during his first season in 2013 when he could manage only one victory, while his new teammate Nico Rosberg won two Grands Prix.

Vindication came with the introduction of the hybrid engine in 2014. Hamilton won eleven Grands Prix and the championship came down to a final-race decider at Abu Dhabi between Hamilton and Rosberg. Having teammates sparring for the same honours was wonderful for the Mercedes publicity department back in Stuttgart and a global audience that was spellbound by the internal competition. Yet Wolff and Lauda were thrust into a managerial nightmare that threatened to tear their team apart, for Hamilton versus Rosberg was a rivalry that compared with any in the history of Formula 1 for its venom and tensions.

The background was this: Hamilton and Rosberg were born just five months apart in 1985, but in radically different circumstances. Rosberg was born into a Formula 1 dynasty as the son of Keke, the 1982 world champion who had raced against Lauda. Blond and handsome, Rosberg Jnr's racing career was funded by a wealthy father and they travelled to the track in Dad's helicopter from their home in Monaco. Hamilton was born into humble surroundings and brought up in a tiny apartment in Stevenage, an unprepossessing 1960s new town in Hertfordshire, to a white mother and black father, who had come from Grenada in the Caribbean. At one time, Anthony Hamilton held down four jobs to finance his son's karting career until he was signed by McLaren.

Rosberg and Hamilton raced side-by-side as juniors, becoming friends, and when they were brought together at Mercedes, it felt like a 'dream team' had been formed. Hamilton moved into the same apartment block in Monaco and the pair played table tennis together.

But their friendship dissolved in the acid of their relationship on the Formula 1 track. From chums, they became enemies, with Lauda and Wolff in no-man's land trying to keep the peace. Rosberg had seemed to be the natural team leader; he was cerebral, able to speak five languages fluently and had been offered a place on an engineering degree course at London's Imperial College, while his teammate was better known for his 'bling' jewellery, a pop-star girlfriend and frequent outbursts of sullen behaviour.

But it was Hamilton who was the more gifted and started to rack up the titles, to the chagrin and intense disappointment of Rosberg, who was desperate to emulate his father. Lauda was having to intervene in their spats and their relationship was consuming more time than was healthy for any team. 'It all started fine, but then it became clear that the world championships would be only between these two, and that is when things went wrong. The competition at each Grand Prix was only between the two of them and that meant trouble because there was jealousy,' Lauda said. 'They had no relationship at all. I don't expect drivers to be friends and eat breakfast together or have dinner, but this was terrible. They wouldn't speak in debrief or have anything to do with each other.'

The 2016 season brought the culmination: they crashed at the Spanish Grand Prix, handing victory to Red Bull's tyro Max Verstappen. And then the blame game started, with Lauda attempting to referee. He called Hamilton to his home in Ibiza to sit him down for a heart-to-heart.

'Lewis would listen to Niki more than anyone else because he was a three-times world champion and Lewis knew what he had been through,' Paddy Lowe said. 'Niki's strength was that he was talking to the drivers on their level and could make them see sense.'

The season went to a final-race decider in Abu Dhabi again. This time Rosberg was leading the championship after a Herculean effort to beat his more talented teammate, but Hamilton was in no mood for favours and never was character more revealed than during those fifty-five laps around the glittering, floodlit Yas Marina Circuit. Rosberg had to finish on the podium to become champion and was cautious from the outset, while Hamilton drove like a man possessed, leading the entire race and knowing that his only chance to snatch back the world championship was to back Rosberg, following him in second place, into the chasing pack and hope that he would be swallowed up.

Against furious orders from Lowe and Wolff, Hamilton slowed his pace until Rosberg was firmly in the sights of the onrushing Ferrari of Sebastian Vettel. The tension on the Mercedes pit wall was unbearable, for here was a driver deliberately attempting to wreck his teammate's race – and the world championship he had craved since childhood.

Rosberg made it safely home, but the fallout was extreme. Wolff threatened to sack Hamilton, while an emotional and drained Rosberg quit the sport a week later, unable to continue his gruelling war with Hamilton. Lauda was shocked and angry at Rosberg's decision, but powerless to stop him. Hamilton, though, was still his driver and once again he had to use his considerable powers of persuasion to prevent the Englishman walking out on Formula 1. He succeeded and the result was three more world championships for the man who almost quit.

'It was good cop, bad cop,' Wolff said. 'I had to be tough, but Lewis respected Niki because of what he had achieved. Lewis knew that Niki thought like a driver and I often would ask Niki for advice, how a driver would think, before we went into these difficult meetings. Niki had a credibility that no one else could bring to the discussions. There was also a bond between Lewis and Niki, something they didn't talk about, but you knew it was there.'

If the relationship counselling could be tricky, it was meat and drink to Lauda, who loved the cut-and-thrust of the paddock, the smell of the garage and the fearless speed of the drivers. He often used to dismiss modern Formula 1 as too easy because of the huge progress in safety, which had transformed the sport from the killing ground of his era. But he knew just how much skill and courage were required to drive at more than 200mph without dwelling on the potential consequences.

'He was hard-wired into what happened at the track,' according to Lowe. 'He wouldn't miss a single race. He hated the summer break because he wanted to get to the races. He even came to the tests. In fact, any time the car was running he wanted to be there when most team principals couldn't be bothered.'

His passion, though, could be an irritant; he loved to be up early and at the circuit almost as the gates opened. Lowe said:

'He shared a car with Toto and it was always an issue because he would be up and ready to get out at 7am when the Formula 1 cars wouldn't be running until 11am or even later.'

Wolff solved the problem by ordering an extra car to take Lauda to the track. 'He wanted to be at the track before anyone else,' he remembered. 'He would arrive when there was only the cleaning staff in the motorhome and the paddock was empty. He simply loved his racing, he loved Formula 1. It was his life.'

EPILOGUE

NIKI LAUDA LOVED a Grand Prix. It was his oxygen, mixing with his beloved drivers and meeting old friends, swapping stories and gossip. He would sit for hours, and his only demand of staff in the lavish Mercedes hospitality centre, where guests would meet and Lewis Hamilton would give his press conferences after each session, was for a ready supply of coffee and that the air-conditioning was turned up to 25°C to ward off the chill of his increasingly failing health.

But once the race was over and the formalities were completed, whether he was in Monza or Melbourne, he would have his briefcase in his hand and be dashing for the exit, chivvying along anyone who expected a lift in whichever new Bombardier plane he was flying that weekend. The reason? Breakfast.

Lauda's routine was immovable when he was in Vienna. He would be at the Café Imperial, an elegant Viennese coffee shop beneath the Hotel Imperial, sandwiched between the city's museum and the concert hall, for breakfast. He was such a regular that the Café Imperial came up with the *Niki Lauda Frühstück* – the Niki Lauda breakfast – frothy, creamed coffee, a soft-boiled egg, toasted sourdough bread and organic yoghurt with raspberries and stewed apple, all for 21 euros.

There, tucked away on a red velvet banquette, Lauda would sit among smart-suited businessmen, wearing his trademark red baseball cap, ordering the same breakfast he had enjoyed for years. He would wave and nod to those who recognised him, but keep himself to himself. Lauda had eaten here under the brilliant chandeliers since he was a child, when he was expected to conform to his family's strict code of behaviour. 'When I was young my family would always celebrate Christmas Day at the restaurant of the hotel,' he once told *Motor Sport* magazine. 'We children were required to be on our best behaviour and to honour the place's long tradition.' He ate alone with his thoughts after what was usually a hectic Grand Prix weekend.

Toto Wolff once saw an unexpected side to the man he worked alongside for almost six years. In an interview with the *Daily Telegraph*, Wolff recounted this anecdote: 'After we won our third world title in Japan, we flew back from Nagoya, and Niki was shedding a tear. "What's going on with you?" I asked. "You know I have no friends," he replied. "If I was to call at three in the morning, lying on the side of the road and waiting for help, I wouldn't be able to reach anybody. No one would pick up the phone. But if there is such a thing as a half-friend, well, it would be you."'

It was as sad and revealing as any story about Niki Lauda, yet curious given the deep friendship of people such as Bernie Ecclestone and Gerhard Berger, the former Ferrari driver and a fellow Austrian, and his ex-wife Marlene, who remained devoted despite their divorce in 1991 after almost fifteen years of marriage. Wolff had started out as an adversary in the Mercedes boardroom but he, too, become a close confidant. The outpouring of grief at Lauda's passing around the world also revealed a well of goodwill that few others could ever engender.

And his private life had appeared happier than ever as he split his time between Vienna and his beautiful home in Ibiza. His ventures into the airline business were turbulent to say the least, but Laudamotion was on its way as a successful business carrier and was to become a subsidiary of Ryanair, Europe's biggest airline.

He had been alone since splitting up with Marlene because of an affair, which led to the birth of an illegitimate son, Cristoph. But it turned out that being an airline magnate had its blessings when he met a young flight attendant called Birgit Wetzinger. Thirty years his junior, she was bright and devoted, as Lauda was to find out in the most dramatic of circumstances when he needed a kidney transplant. Lauda had asked his son Lukas if he would donate, but he was not a match. Then Birgit, whom he had been dating for just eight months, stepped in. 'Birgit then said she would do the test. I asked her why she would do it. She said she wanted to do it because she loved me. She was never frightened or worried. She just did it for me.'

A year after their 2008 marriage came twins, Max and Mia, to add to the extended Lauda family, which became increasingly reconciled and rallied around a man they all loved. Lukas and Mathias accepted the twins, and Cristoph was welcomed and added to Lauda's will. And then there was his beloved Mercedes team, conquering all before it, with his visits to the tracks around the world like a home-from-home.

It was destined not to last. Lauda had hidden his ill health from all but those closest to him, going racing just as he had for years up until July 2018, when he was admitted to hospital. Lewis Hamilton was charging towards his fifth world championship with Mercedes, but Lauda would not witness the climax where he would have wanted – at the track with his beloved team.

Doctors in Vienna revealed he was just days from death when they carried out their initial examinations. His lungs – exposed to that toxic combination of smoke, heat and fumes in the Nürburgring crash forty-two years before – were finally giving up the fight. He was diagnosed with haemorrhagic alveolitis, an inflammation that led to bleeding and an inability to absorb oxygen. He was put on a ventilator while doctors scoured Austria for lungs they could transplant. The transplant surgery was a success – even though Lauda claimed it felt worse than the recovery from his 1976 accident – and he started to bounce back, training for up to six hours every day. He never lost touch with his beloved team, phoning the garage during Grands Prix, and getting regular updates from Toto Wolff. Hamilton sent texts and Sebastian Vettel, a rival at Ferrari, sent a handwritten note of encouragement, while fans from around the world posted messages on social media. The world really did love Niki Lauda, after all.

Niki Lauda clearly had an ego or he wouldn't have achieved what he did, but he seemed strangely unable to see himself as others did. Perhaps the first time it occurred to him that he was special was when Ron Howard, the Hollywood director, brought the story of the Nürburgring to cinemas with his movie, *Rush*. I sat with Lauda and Howard in a cramped room at the Circuit of the Americas in Austin, Texas, before the film's 2013 release and there was just a trace of tears as Lauda discussed what he had seen.

Daniel Brühl's portrayal of Lauda was uncanny, as near to the man as you could get, although their relationship started warily. Brühl recalled in an interview with *The Times*: 'The first conversation we had on the phone, Niki said, "Please just bring hand luggage to Vienna in case we don't like each other."' There was regret that the friendship and respect Lauda enjoyed with Hunt had not been fully reflected in the script, and there was a tinge of sadness when he thought of his rival, dead at just forty-five as a result of a life lived to excess. But the film brought back the rawness of the crash, the pain of the recovery and that comeback at Monza. For the first time, he understood why people couldn't look him directly in the eye, perturbed by the intense scarring around his eyes and ears.

'It was the first time I was outside looking in,' Lauda told me at that interview for *The Times* in Austin. 'At the time, I was concentrating on fighting. That was all. Fighting to live and then to race again. When I went through the mess at the time, I honestly didn't care. I was burnt, but I got up and drove again. I never had side-effects, I just got on with it. But when I saw Danny Brühl filming, the way he looked with all the blood and the cuts on his head, I was shocked. Was that really the way I looked at the time? Yes, it was.

'How could I turn up and race like this, half-dead? It really affected me, much as it must have affected other people at the time.'

The movie brought Lauda's story to a new audience and suddenly casual observers understood the scars and the red cap, and gave new credence to the opinions expressed so honestly and bluntly.

Lauda wanted to be back at the track to give those opinions again as he recovered at his home in Ibiza. But then, when all seemed set for recovery and another miracle, Lauda fell victim to a bout of flu and was hospitalised again, eventually for specialist treatment in Zurich. He never recovered.

Lauda died on Monday, 20 May 2019, a day when Formula 1 and Austria stopped and paid tribute. He had seemed invincible, the eternal warrior who came through the inferno, but the Nürburgring had finally claimed him after more than four decades.

His family – his wife Birgit and ex-wife Marlene; sons Mathias, Max, Lukas and Christoph and daughter Mia – were there throughout. Their statement said: 'His unique successes as a sportsman and entrepreneur are and remain unforgettable. His tireless drive, his straightforwardness and his courage remain an example and standard for us all. Away from the public gaze he was a loving and caring husband, father and grandfather. We will miss him very much.'

The funeral took place on 29 May at St Stephen's Cathedral in Lauda's home city of Vienna. There was a who's who attending, from Arnold Schwarzenegger, a fellow Austrian, movie star and former governor of California, to Bernie Ecclestone and Lewis Hamilton, the driver Lauda groomed, cajoled and inspired to five world championships and a position, arguably, as the greatest of all time.

All 3,000 seats were filled to see Birgit Lauda place the familiar red racing helmet onto the lid of the coffin, along with a victory laurel wreath, before the Austrian President Alexander Van der Bellen and Gerhard Berger delivered eulogies and

Alain Prost, Lauda's last teammate at McLaren, read from the Bible. Lauda was then buried beside his mother at the Neustift Cemetery, dressed in the red overalls he wore at Ferrari. He had driven for Brabham and McLaren, but his heart had remained forever with the *Scuderia*, which gave him his chance to become a world champion for the first time and which cemented his name into legend.

Three days before the funeral, Lewis Hamilton had won the Monaco Grand Prix in a Silver Arrows car decorated with silver stars. In among them was a single red star, symbolising Niki Lauda. It will remain on the car as long as there are Silver Arrows to race.

There were hundreds of heartfelt tributes from around the world, but perhaps the most poignant came from Daniel Brühl, the man who had become the mirror image of Lauda on film. They had spent hours together as Brühl got to know and understand the man he was to play, becoming more spellbound by the day as Lauda's character unfolded.

Brühl published a picture on his Instagram page of Lauda, red cap on, in the cockpit of one of his private jets, with this message: 'The bravest man I've ever met, not only because he was an F1 World Champion in the crazy 70s and had the most incredible comeback in sport's history, but also because of how he treated people. Always honest, straightforward, blunt. Niki told you the truth in your face, no matter how uncomfortable. He was totally unpretentious and incredibly funny. I learned a lot from him and deeply admired him. I know how much you enjoyed flying. Race the sky in peace, immortal Champ. We'll miss you. *Mach's gut* Niki.'

APPENDIX: FOR THE RECORD

NIKI LAUDA
BORN: 22 February 1949
DIED: 20 May 2019

GRAND PRIX CAREER

Debut:	1971 Austrian Grand Prix
World championships:	1975, 1977, 1984
Grand Prix starts:	171
Victories:	25
Pole positions:	24
Podiums:	54
Fastest laps:	25
Teams:	March 1971/72
	BRM 1973
	Ferrari 1974/75/76/77
	Brabham 1978/79
	McLaren 1982/83/84/85
Final Race:	1985 Australian Grand Prix

Non-executive chairman AMG Mercedes Formula 1: 2012–19
World champion constructors: 2014/15/16/17/18/19
World champion drivers: Lewis Hamilton 2014/15/17/18/19; Nico Rosberg 2016

CAREER RACE RECORD

Abbreviations

A Austria
Arg Argentina
Aus Australia
B Belgium
Can Canada
CH Switzerland
CS Czechoslovakia
D Germany
E Spain
F France
GB United Kingdom
H Hungary
I Italy
Irl Ireland
NL Netherlands
NZ New Zealand
S Sweden
SA South Africa
SF Finland
USA United States of America
Yu Yugoslavia
* Class

1968

Bad Mühllacken (A) 15.4.
Cooper 1300, Placed 2*
Hill climb
Herbert Grüsteidl (A), Cooper*
Richard Gerin (A), Porsche 906

Dobratsch (A) 28.4.
Cooper 1300, Placed 1*
Hill climb
Lauda (A), Cooper*
Rudi Lins (A), Porsche 906

Alpl (A) 5.5.
Cooper 1300, Placed 1*
Hill climb
Lauda (A), Cooper*
Richard Gerin (A), Porsche 906

Engelhartszell (A) 26.5.
Cooper 1300, Placed 1*
Hill climb
Lauda (A), Cooper*
Gerhard Krammer (A), Brabham-Alfa

Kasten-Viechtenstein (A) 9.6.
Porsche 911, Retired (crashed)
Hill climb
Dieter Schmied (D), Lotus 23

Koralpe (A) 23.6.
Porsche 911, Placed 1*
Hill climb
Lauda (A), Porsche 911*
Richard Gerin (A), Porsche 906

Tulln-Langenlebarn (A) 14.7.
Porsche 911, Retired (engine failure)
Aerodrome
Klaus Reisch (A), Alfa Romeo GTA

Tauplitzalm (A) 4.8.
Porsche 911, Placed 1*
Hill climb
Lauda (A), Porsche 911*
Giulio de Guidi (CH), Cooper-ATS

Stainz (A) 11.8.
Porsche 911, Placed 1*
Hill climb
Lauda (A), Porsche 911*
Jochen Rindt (A), Brabham F-2

Walding (A) 15.8.
Porsche 911, Placed 1*
Hill climb
Lauda (A), Porsche 911*
Peter Peter (A), Porsche 906

Zeltweg (A) 25.8.
Porsche 911, Placed 1*
Aerodrome
Lauda (A), Porsche 911

Aspern (A) 6.10.
Porsche 911, Placed 3
Aerodrome
Ernst Furtmayer (D), BMW 2002

Aspern (A) 6.10.
Kaimann Formula Vee,
Placed 8
Formula Vee
Erick Breinsberg (A),
Kaimann

Innsbruck (A) 13.10.
Porsche 911, Retired
Aerodrome

P. Kaiser (D), Porsche 911

Dopplerhütte (A) 27.10.
Porsche 911, Placed 1*
Kaimann, Placed 2
Hill climb
Lauda (A), Porsche 911*
Kaimann: Rudi Lins (A),
Porsche 910

1969

Hockenheim (D) 12.4.
Kaimann, Placed 4
Formula Vee
Gerold Pankl (A), Austro-Vee

Aspern (A) 13.4.
Kaimann, Retired
Aerodrome, Formula Vee
Peter Peter (A), Austro-Vee

Belgrade (Yu) 20.4.
Kaimann, Placed 2
Formula Vee
Gerold Pankl (A), Austro-Vee

Budapest (H) 11.5.
Kaimann, Placed 4
Formula Vee
Alfred Vogelberger (D),
Olympic

Rossfeld (D) 8.6.
Kaimann, Placed 5
Hill climb
Alfred Vogelberger (D),
Olympic

Hockenheim (D) 15.6.
Kaimann, Placed 2
Formula Vee
Erich Breinsberg (A),
Kaimann

Nürburgring (D) 29.6.
Kaimann, Placed 2
Formula Vee Hansa-Pokal
Erich Breinsberg (A), Kaimann

Sopron (H) 6.6.
Kaimann, Placed 1
Formula Vee
Lauda (A), Kaimann-Vee

Tulln-Langenlebarn (A) 13.7.
Opel 1900, Retired (engine failure)
Peter Huber (A), Ford Escort TC
Formula Vee
Kaimann, Placed 3
Peter Peter (A), Austro-Vee

Öesterreichring (A) 27.7.
Kaimann, Placed 8
Formula Vee
Helmut Marko (A), McNamara

Nürburgring (D) 3.8.
Kaimann, Placed 2
Formula Vee
Helmut Marko (A), McNamara

Öesterreichring 10.8.
Lauda/Stuppacher (A), Porsche 910, Placed 21
Siffert/Ahrens (CH/D), Porsche 917

Mantorp Park (S) 31.8.
Kaimann, Retired (fuel pump)
Formula Vee
Bertil Roos (S), RPB

Salzburgring (A) 21.9.
Kaimann, Placed 3
Formula Vee
Dieter Quester (A), Kaimann

Innsbruck (A) 5.10.
Kaimann, Placed 2
Aerodrome, Formula Vee
Erich Breinsberg (A), Kaimann

Nürburgring (D) 12.10.
Kaimann, Placed 20
Eifel Cup, Formula Vee
Peter Peter (A), Austro-Vee

Munich-Neubiberg (D)
26.10.
Opel 1900, Placed 5
Kaimann, Placed 1

Aerodrome
Dieter Basche (D), BMW 2002 ti
Lauda (A), Kaimann

1970

Nogaro (F) 29.3.
McNamara, Retired (crashed)
Formula 3
J.-P. Jaussaud (F), Tecno

Nürburgring (D) 19.4.
McNamara, Placed 16
300 km, Formula 3
Freddy Kottulinsky (S), Lotus

Magny Cours (F) 3.5.
McNamara, Placed 5
Formula 3
J.-P. Jaussaud (F), Tecno

Hockenheim (D), 10.5.
McNamara, Retired (crash)
Formula 3
Hermann Unold (D), Tecno

Öesterreichring (A) 17.5,
McNamara, Placed 6
Formula 3
Freddy Kottulinsky (S), Lotus

Brno (CS) 24.5.
McNamara, Placed 2
Formula 3
Jürg Dubler (CH), Chevron

Silverstone (GB) 7.6
McNamara, Did not start
Formula 3
Mike Beuttler (GB), March

Norisring (D) 28.6.
Porsche 908, Placed 8
Jürgen Neuhaus (D), Porsche 917

Hockenheim (D) 5.7.
Porsche 908, Placed 12
Vic Elford (GB), McLaren-Chevy

McNamara, Placed 5
Formula 3
Gianni Salvati (I), Tecno

Nürburgring (D) 12.7.
Lauda/Herzog (A/CH),
BMW 1600, Retired
6 hours
de Adamich/Picchi (I), Alfa Romeo

Brands Hatch (GB) 17.7.
McNamara, Retired (crash)
Formula 3
Mike Beuttler (GB), Brabham

Diepholz (D) 19.7.
Porsche 908, Placed 1
Aerodrome
Lauda (A), Porsche 908

Karlskoga (S) 9.8.
McNamara, Placed 5
Formula 3
Peter Hanson (GB), Chevron

Porsche 908, Retired (gearbox)
Chris Craft (GB), McLaren-Cosworth

Knutstorp (S) 16.8.
McNamara, Retired (crash)
Formula 3
Ulf Svensson (S), Brabham

Keimola (SF) 23.8.
Porsche 908, Retired (bearings)
Gijs van Lennep (NL), Porsche 917

Zandvoort (NL) 30.8.
McNamara, Placed 4
Formula 3
Jürg Dubler (CH), Chevron

Brands Hatch (GB) 31.8.
McNamara, Retired
Formula 3
Gerry Birrell (GB), Brabham

Zolder (B) 6.9.
McNamara, Retired (crash)
Formula 3
James Hunt (GB), Lotus

Imola (I) 13.9.
Lauda/Kottulinsky (A/S), Porsche 908, Placed 5
Bell/Redman (GB), Porsche 917

Thruxton (GB) 20.9.
Porsche 908, Placed 5
Jürgen Neuhaus (D), Porsche 917

Öesterreichring (A) 11.10.
Lauda/Peter (A), Porsche 908, Placed 6
1,000 km, World Endurance Championship
Siffert/Redman (CH/GB), Porsche 917

Nürburgring (D) 18.10.
Porsche 908, Placed 3
Helmut Kelleners (D), March-Chevy

Öesterreichring (A) 25.10.
Porsche 908, Placed 1
Martha Grand National
Lauda (A), Porsche 908

1971

Mallory Park (GB) 14.3.
March-Ford, Retired (fuel pump)
Formula 2
Henri Pescarolo (F), March-Ford

Hockenheim (D) 4.4.
March-Ford, Retired (clutch)
Formula 2 European Championship (EC)
François Cevert (F), Tecno-Ford

Thruxton (GB)
12.4.
March-Ford, Placed 10
EC Formula 2
Graham Hill (GB), Brabham-Ford

Nürburgring (D) 2.5.
March-Ford, Placed 6

EC Formula 2
François Cevert (F), Tecno-Ford

Jarama (E) 16.5.
March-Ford, Placed 7
EC Formula 2
Emerson Fittipaldi (Brazil), Lotus-Ford

Salzburgring (A) 23.5.
Chevron-Ford, Placed 1
2-litre EC Sports
Lauda (A), Chevron-Ford

Crystal Palace (GB) 31.5.
March-Ford, Did not qualify
EC Formula 2
Emerson Fittipaldi (Brazil), Lotus-Ford

Monza (I) 20.6.
March-Ford, Retired (gearbox)
EC Formula 2
Dieter Quester (A), March-BMW

Rouen (F), 27.6.
March-Ford, Placed 4
EC Formula 2
Ronnie Peterson (S), March-Ford

Nürburgring (D) 11.7.
Lauda/Huber (A), BMW-Alpina Coupé, Placed 3
EC Saloon
Marko/Glemser (A/D), Ford Capri RS

Spa-Francorchamps (B) 24/25.7.
Lauda/Larrousse (A/F), BMW-Alpina Coupé, Retired
EC Saloon
Glemser/Soler-Roig (D/E), Ford Capri RS

Mantorp Park (S) 8.8.
March-Ford, Placed 13
EC Formula 2
Ronnie Peterson (S), March-Ford

Öesterreichring (A) 15.8.
March F-l, Retired (engine)

Austrian Grand Prix,
Formula 1
Jo Siffert (CH), BRM

Kinnekulle (S), 22.8.
March-Ford, Placed 6
Formula 2
Ronnie Peterson (S), March-Ford

Brands Hatch (GB) 30.8.
March-Ford, Placed 7
Formula 2
Ronnie Peterson (S), March-Ford

Tulln-Langenlebarn (A) 1.9.
March-Ford, Retired
EC Formula 2
Ronnie Peterson (S), March-Ford

Albi (F) 26.9.
March-Ford, Retired
EC Formula 2
Emerson Fittipaldi (Brazil), Lotus-Ford

Vallelunga (I) 10.10.
March-Ford, Placed 7
EC Formula 2
Ronnie Peterson (S), March-Ford

1972

Buenos Aires (Arg) 23.1.
March F-l, Placed 11
Formula 1, Argentinian GP
Jackie Stewart (GB), Tyrrell-Ford

Kyalami (SA) 4.3.
March F-1, Placed 7
Formula 1, South African GP
Denny Hulme (NZ), McLaren-Ford

Mallory Park (GB) 12.3.
March-Ford, Placed 2
EC Formula 2

Dave Morgan (GB), Brabham-Ford

Oulton Park (GB) 31.3.
March-Ford, Placed 1
Formula 2
Lauda (A), March-Ford

Thruxton (GB) 3.4.
March-Ford, Placed 3
EC Formula 2
Ronnie Peterson (S), March-Ford

Hockenheim (D) 16.4.
March-Ford, Retired (engine failure)
EC Formula 2
J.-P. Jaussaud (F), Brabham-Ford

Jarama (E) 1.5.
March F-1, Retired (jammed throttle)
Formula 1, Spanish GP
Emerson Fittipaldi (Brazil), Lotus-Ford

Pau (F) 7.5.
March-Ford, Retired (rear axle shaft)
EC Formula 2
Peter Gethin (GB), Chevron-Ford

Monte Carlo 14.5.
March F-1, Placed 16
Formula 1 Monaco GP
Jean-Pierre Beltoise (F), BRM

Brno (CS) 21.5.
Alpina-BMW, Retired (engine failure)
EC Saloon
Dieter Glemser (D), Ford Capri

Crystal Palace (GB), 28.5
March-Ford, Retired (crankshaft)
EC Formula 2
Jody Scheckter (SA), McLaren-Ford

Nivelles (B) 4.6.
March F-1, Placed 12
Formula 1 Belgian GP

Emerson Fittipaldi (Brazil), Lotus-Ford

Hockenheim (D) 11.6.
March-Ford, Retired (engine failure)
EC Formula 2
Emerson Fittipaldi (Brazil), Lotus-Ford

Vallelunga (I) 18.6.
March F-l, Did not start (crashed during training)
Rome Trophy
Emerson Fittipaldi (Brazil), Lotus-Ford

Rouen (F) 25.6.
March-Ford, Retired (engine failure)
EC Formula 2
Emerson Fittipaldi (Brazil), Lotus-Ford

Clermont-Ferrand (F) 2.7.
March F-1, Retired (rear suspension)
Formula 1 French Grand Prix
Jackie Stewart (GB), Tyrrell-Ford

Öesterreichring (A) 9.7.
March-Ford, Retired (engine failure)
EC Formula 2
Emerson Fittipaldi (Brazil), Lotus-Ford

Brands Hatch (GB) 15.7.
March F-l, Placed 9
Formula 1 British Grand Prix
Emerson Fittipaldi (Brazil), Lotus-Ford

Imola (I) 23.7.
March-Ford, Placed 3
EC Formula 2
John Surtees (GB), Surtees-Ford

Nürburgring (D) 30.7.
March F-1, Retired (oil-tank leak)

Formula 1 German Grand Prix
Jacky Ickx (B), Ferrari

Mantorp Park (S) 6.8.
March-Ford, Did not qualify
EC Formula 2
Mike Hailwood (GB), Surtees-Ford

Öesterreichring (A) 13.8.
March F-1, Placed 10
Formula 1 Austrian Grand Prix
Emerson Fittipaldi (Brazil), Lotus-Ford

Zandvoort (NL) 20.8.
Lauda/Hezemans (A/NL), BMW-Alpina Coupé, Placed 3
EC Touring
Mass/Soler-Roig (D/E), Ford Capri RS

Salzburgring (A) 3.9.
March-Ford, Placed 6
EC Formula 2
Mike Hailwood (GB), Surtees-Ford

Monza (I) 10.9.
March F-1, Placed 13
Formula 1 Italian Grand Prix
Emerson Fittipaldi (Brazil), Lotus-Ford

Oulton Park (GB) 16.9.
March-Ford, Placed 2
Formula 2
Ronnie Peterson (S), March-Ford

Mosport (Can) 24.9.
March F-1, Disqualified
Formula 1 Canadian GP
Jackie Stewart (GB), Tyrrell-Ford

Hockenheim (D) 1.10
March-Ford, Placed 9
EC Formula 2
Tim Schenken (Aus), Brabham-Ford

Watkins Glen (USA) 8.10
March F-1, Placed 17
Formula 1 United States Grand Prix
Jackie Stewart (GB), Tyrrell-Ford

Kyalami (SA) 4.11
Lauda/Scheckter (A/SA), March-BMW, Placed 4
9-hour endurance
Regazzoni/Merzario (CH/I), Ferrari

1973

Buenos Aires (Arg) 28.1.
BRM F-1, Retired (engine failure)
Formula 1 Argentinian Grand Prix
Emerson Fittipaldi (Brazil), Lotus-Ford

Interlagos (Brazil) 11.2.
BRM F-1, Placed 8
Formula 1 Brazilian Grand Prix
Emerson Fittipaldi (Brazil), Lotus-Ford

Kyalami (SA) 3.3.
BRM F-1, Retired (engine/pistons)
Formula 1 South African Grand Prix
Jackie Stewart (GB), Tyrrell-Ford

Brands Hatch (GB) 18.3.
BRM F-1, Retired (battery/tyres)
Race of Champions
Peter Gethin (GB), Chevron F 5000

Monza (I) 25.3.
Lauda/Muir (A/AUS), Alpina-BMW Coupé, Placed 1
ETC Touring (4 hours)
Lauda/Muir (A/AUS), Alpina-BMW Coupé

Aspern (A) 1.4.
BMW 2002 Gr. 1, Retired (tyres)

Aerodrome
Dieter Quester (A), BMW 2002 Gr. 1

Silverstone (GB) 8.4.
BRM F-1, Placed 5
Daily Express Formula 1 Trophy
Jackie Stewart (GB), Tyrrell-Ford

Barcelona (E) 29.4.
BRM F-1, Retired (tyres)
Formula 1 Spanish Grand Prix
Emerson Fittipaldi (Brazil), Lotus-Ford

Spa (B) 5.5.
Alpina-BMW Coupé, Placed 1
Coupe de Spa (Spa Trophy)
Lauda (A), Alpina-BMW Coupé

Spa (B) 6.5.
Lauda/Stuck (A/D), Alpina-BMW-Coupé, Placed 7
1,000 km, Championship of Makes
Bell/Hailwood (GB), Gulf-Mirage-Ford

Zolder (B) 20.5.
BRM F-1, Placed 5
Formula 1 Belgian Grand Prix
Jackie Stewart (GB), Tyrrell-Ford

Nürburgring (D) 27.5.
Lauda/Muir (A/Aus), Alpina-BMW Coupé, Did not start (Muir crashed in qualifying)
1,000 km
Ickx/Redman (B/GB), Ferrari

Monte Carlo 3.6.
BRM F-1, Retired (gearbox/clutch)
Formula 1 Monaco Grand Prix
Jackie Stewart (GB), Tyrrell-Ford

Anderstorp (S) 17.6.
BRM F-1, Placed 13

Formula 1 Swedish Grand Prix
Denny Hulme (NZ), McLaren-Ford

Nürburgring (D) 23/24.6.
Lauda/Joisten (A/D), Alpina-BMW Coupé, Placed 1
24-hour endurance
Lauda/Joisten (A/D), Alpina-BMW Coupé

Paul Ricard (F) 1.7.
BRM F-1, Placed 9
Formula 1 French Grand Prix
Ronnie Peterson (S), Lotus-Ford

Nürburgring (D) 8.7.
Lauda/Joisten (A/D), Alpina-BMW Coupé, Placed 3
EC Saloon, 6-hour endurance
Stuck/Amon (D/NZ), BMW CSL

Silverstone (GB) 14.7.
BRM F-1, Placed 12
Formula 1 British Grand Prix
Peter Revson (USA), McLaren-Ford

Diepholz (D) 15.7.
Alpina-BMW Coupé, Retired (engine failure)
Aerodrome
Rolf Stommelen (D), Ford Capri RS

Zandvoort (NL) 29.7.
BRM F-1, Retired (tyres, fuel pressure)
Formula 1 Dutch Grand Prix
Jackie Stewart (GB), Tyrrell-Ford

Nürburgring (D) 5.8.
BRM F-1, Retired (crash)
Formula 1 German Grand Prix
Jackie Stewart (GB), Tyrrell-Ford

Öesterreichring (A) 19.8.
BRM F-1, Did not start (hand injury at Nürburgring)
Formula 1 Austrian Grand Prix

Ronnie Peterson (S), Lotus-Ford

Monza (I) 9.9.
BRM F-1, Retired (crash)
Formula 1 Italian Grand Prix
Ronnie Peterson (S), Lotus-Ford

Mosport (Can) 23.9.
BRM F-1, Retired (differential)
Formula 1 Canadian Grand Prix
Peter Revson (USA), McLaren-Ford

Innsbruck (A) 30.9.
BMW 2002 Gr. 1, Placed 1*
Aerodrome
Lauda (A), BMW 2002*

Watkins Glen (USA) 7.10.
BRM F-1, Placed 18
Formula 1 United States Grand Prix
Ronnie Peterson (S), Lotus-Ford

Öesterreichring (A) 14.10.
Ford Capri RS, Placed 1*
End-of-season trophy
Lauda (A), Ford Capri RS*

1974

Buenos Aires (Arg) 13.1.
Ferrari F-1, Placed 2
Formula 1 Argentinian Grand Prix
Denny Hulme (NZ), McLaren-Ford

Interlagos (Brazil) 27.1.
Ferrari F-1, Retired (engine failure)
Formula 1 Brazilian Grand Prix
Emerson Fittipaldi (Brazil), McLaren-Ford

Brands Hatch (GB) 17.3.
Ferrari F-1, Placed 2
Race of Champions
Jacky Ickx (B), Lotus-Ford

Kyalami (SA) 30.3.
Ferrari F-1, Retired (ignition)
Formula 1 South African Grand Prix
Carlos Reutemann (Arg), Brabham-Ford

Salzburgring (A) 14.4.
Lauda/Mass (A/D), Ford Capri RS, Retired (engine failure)
EC Saloon
Stuck/lckx (D/B), BMW 3.0 CSL

Jarama (E) 28.4.
Ferrari F-1, Placed 1
Formula 1 Spanish Grand Prix
Lauda (A), Ferrari

Nivelles (B) 12.5.
Ferrari F-1, Placed 2
Formula 1 Belgian Grand Prix
Emerson Fittipaldi (Brazil), McLaren-Ford

Nürburgring (D) 19.5.
Lauda/Mass (A/D), Ford Capri RS, Retired
1,000 km, Championship of Makes
Beltoise/Jarier (F), Matra

Monte Carlo 26.5.
Ferrari F-1, Retired (ignition)
Formula 1 Monaco Grand Prix
Ronnie Peterson (S), Lotus-Ford

Anderstorp (S) 9.6.
Ferrari F-1, Retired (rear suspension)
Formula 1 Swedish Grand Prix
Jody Scheckter (SA), Tyrrell-Ford

Zandvoort (NL) 23.6.
Ferrari F-1, Placed 1
Formula 1 Dutch Grand Prix
Lauda (A), Ferrari

Dijon (F) 7.7.
Ferrari F-1, Placed 2
Formula 1 French Grand Prix
Ronnie Peterson (S), Lotus-Ford

Nürburgring (D) 14.7.
Lauda/Glemser/Hezemans (A/D/NL), Ford Capri RS, Placed 2
EC Saloon, 6-hour endurance
Heyer/Ludwig (D), Zakspeed-Escort

Brands Hatch (GB) 20.7.
Ferrari F-1, Placed 5
Formula 1 British Grand Prix
Jody Scheckter (SA), Tyrrell-Ford

Nürburgring (D) 4.8.
Ferrari F-1, Retired (crash)
Formula 1 German Grand Prix
Clay Regazzoni (CH), Ferrari

Öesterreichring (A) 18.8.
Ferrari F-1, Retired (damaged valves)
Formula 1 Austrian Grand Prix
Carlos Reutemann (Arg), Brabham-Ford

Monza (I) 8.9.
Ferrari F-1, Retired (engine failure)
Formula 1 Italian Grand Prix
Ronnie Peterson (S), Lotus-Ford

Norisring (D) 15.9.
Ford Capri RS, Retired (gear-change problems)
Norisring Trophy
Hans-Joachim Stuck (D), BMW 3.0 CSL

Mosport (Can) 22.9.
Ferrari F-1, Retired (crash)
Formula 1 Canadian Grand Prix
Emerson Fittipaldi (Brazil), McLaren-Ford

Watkins Glen (USA) 6.10.
Ferrari F-1, Retired (shock absorbers)
Formula 1 United States Grand Prix
Carlos Reutemann (Arg), Brabham-Ford

1975

Buenos Aires (Arg) 12.1.
Ferrari F-1, Placed 6
Formula 1 Argentinian Grand Prix
Emerson Fittipaldi (Brazil), McLaren-Ford

Interlagos (Brazil) 26.1.
Ferrari F-1, Placed 5
Formula 1 Brazilian Grand Prix
Carlos Pace (Brazil), Brabham-Ford

Kyalami (SA) 1.3.
Ferrari F-1, Placed 5
Formula 1 South African Grand Prix
Jody Scheckter (SA), Tyrrell-Ford

Silverstone (GB) 12.4.
Ferrari F-1, Placed 1
International Trophy
Lauda (A), Ferrari

Barcelona (E) 27.4.
Ferrari F-1, Retired (crash)
Formula 1 Spanish Grand Prix
Jochen Mass (D), McLaren-Ford

Monte Carlo 11.5.
Ferrari F-1, Placed 1
Formula 1 Monaco Grand Prix
Lauda (A), Ferrari

Zolder (B) 25.5.
Ferrari F-1, Placed 1
Formula 1 Belgian Grand Prix
Lauda (A), Ferrari

Anderstorp (S) 8.6.
Ferrari F-1, Placed 1
Formula 1 Swedish Grand Prix
Lauda (A), Ferrari

Zandvoort (NL) 22.6.
Ferrari F-1, Placed 2
Formula 1 Dutch Grand Prix
James Hunt (GB), Hesketh-Ford

Le Castellet (F) 6.7.
Ferrari F-1, Placed 1
Formula 1 French Grand Prix
Lauda (A), Ferrari

Silverstone (GB) 19.7.
Ferrari F-1, Placed 8
Formula 1 British Grand Prix
Emerson Fittipaldi (Brazil), McLaren-Ford

Nürburgring (D) 3.8.
Ferrari F-1, Placed 3
Formula 1 German Grand Prix
Carlos Reutemann (Arg), Brabham-Ford

Öesterreichring (A) 17.8.
Ferrari F-1, Placed 6
Formula 1 Austrian Grand Prix
Vittorio Brambilla (I), March-Ford

Monza (I) 7.9.
Ferrari F-1, Placed 3
Formula 1 Italian Grand Prix
Clay Regazzoni (CH), Ferrari

Watkins Glen (USA) 5.10.
Ferrari F-1, Placed 1
Formula 1 United States Grand Prix
Lauda (A), Ferrari

1976

Interlagos (Brazil) 25.1.
Ferrari F-1, Placed 1
Formula 1 Brazilian Grand Prix
Lauda (A), Ferrari

Kyalami (SA) 6.3.
Ferrari F-1, Placed 1
Formula 1 South African Grand Prix
Lauda (A), Ferrari

Brands Hatch (GB) 14.3.
Ferrari F-1, Retired (brakes)
Race of Champions
James Hunt (GB), McLaren

Long Beach (USA) 28.3.
Ferrari F-1, Placed 2
Formula 1 USA Grand Prix (West)
Clay Regazzoni (CH), Ferrari

Jarama (E) 2.5.
Ferrari F-1, Placed 2
Formula 1 Spanish Grand Prix
James Hunt (GB), McLaren-Ford

Zolder (B) 16.5.
Ferrari F-1, Placed 1
Formula 1 Belgian Grand Prix
Lauda (A), Ferrari

Monte Carlo 30.5.
Ferrari F-1, Placed 1
Formula 1 Monaco Grand Prix
Lauda (A), Ferrari

Anderstorp (S) 13.6.
Ferrari F-1, Placed 3
Formula 1 Swedish Grand Prix
Jody Scheckter (SA), Tyrrell-Ford

Paul Ricard (F) 4.7.
Ferrari F-1, Retired (engine failure)
Formula 1 French Grand Prix
James Hunt (GB), McLaren-Ford

Brands Hatch (GB) 18.7.
Ferrari F-1, Placed 2
Formula 1 British Grand Prix
James Hunt (GB), McLaren-Ford

Nürburgring (D) 1.8.
Ferrari F-1, Retired (crash)
Formula 1 German Grand Prix
James Hunt (GB), McLaren-Ford

Öesterreichring (A) 15.8.
Did not start
Formula 1 Austrian Grand Prix
John Watson (GB), Penske-Ford

Zandvoort (NL) 29.8.
Did not start

Formula 1 Dutch Grand Prix
James Hunt (GB), McLaren-Ford

Monza (I) 12.9.
Ferrari F-1, Placed 4
Formula 1 Italian Grand Prix
Ronnie Peterson (S), March-Ford

Mosport (Can) 3.10.
Ferrari F-1, Placed 8
Formula 1 Canadian Grand Prix
James Hunt (GB), McLaren-Ford

Watkins Glen (USA) 10.10.
Ferrari F-1, Placed 3
Formula 1 USA Grand Prix (East)
James Hunt (GB), McLaren-Ford

Fuji (Japan) 24.10.
Pulled out of race voluntarily
Formula 1 Japanese Grand Prix
Mario Andretti (USA), Lotus-Ford

1977

Buenos Aires (Arg) 9.1.
Ferrari F-1, Retired (fuel injection)
Formula 1 Argentinian Grand Prix
Jody Scheckter (SA), Wolf-Ford

Interlagos (Brazil) 23.1.
Ferrari F-1, Placed 3
Formula 1 Brazilian Grand Prix
Carlos Reutemann (Arg), Ferrari

Kyalami (SA) 5.3.
Ferrari F-1, Placed 1
Formula 1 South African Grand Prix
Lauda (A), Ferrari

Long Beach (US A) 3.4.
Ferrari F-1, Placed 2
Formula 1 USA Grand Prix (West)
Mario Andretti (USA), Lotus-Ford

Jarama (E) 8.5.
Did not start (ribcage injury)
Formula 1 Spanish Grand Prix
Mario Andretti (USA), Lotus-Ford

Monte Carlo 22.5.
Ferrari F-1, Placed 2
Formula 1 Monaco Grand Prix
Jody Scheckter (SA), Wolf-Ford

Zolder (B) 5.6.
Ferrari F-1, Placed 2
Formula 1 Belgian Grand Prix
Gunnar Nilsson (S), Lotus-Ford

Anderstorp (S) 19.6.
Ferrari F-1, Retired
Formula 1 Swedish Grand Prix
Jacques Laffite (F), Ligier-Matra

Dijon (F) 3.7.
Ferrari F-1, Placed 5
Formula 1 French Grand Prix
Mario Andretti (USA), Lotus-Ford

Silverstone (GB) 16.7.
Ferrari F-1, Placed 2
Formula 1 British Grand Prix
James Hunt (GB), McLaren-Ford

Hockenheim (D) 31.7.
Ferrari F-1, Placed 1
Formula 1 German Grand Prix
Lauda (A), Ferrari

Öesterreichring (A) 14.8.
Ferrari F-1, Placed 2
Formula 1 Austrian Grand Prix
Alan Jones (Aus), Shadow-Ford

Zandvoort (NL) 28.8.
Ferrari F-1, Placed 1
Formula 1 Dutch Grand Prix
Lauda (A), Ferrari

Monza (I) 11.9.
Ferrari F-1, Placed 2
Formula 1 Italian Grand Prix
Mario Andretti (USA), Lotus-Ford

Watkins Glen (USA) 2.10.
Ferrari F-1, Placed 4
Formula 1 USA Grand Prix (East)
James Hunt (GB), McLaren-Ford

Mosport (Can) 9.10.
Did not start
Formula 1 Canadian Grand Prix
Jody Scheckter (SA), Wolf-Ford

Fuji (Japan) 23.10.
Did not start
Formula 1 Japanese Grand Prix
James Hunt (GB), McLaren-Ford

1978

Buenos Aires (Arg) 15.1.
Brabham-Alfa F-1, Placed 2
Formula 1 Argentinian Grand Prix
Mario Andretti (USA), Lotus-Ford

Rio de Janeiro (Brazil) 29.1.
Brabham-Alfa F-1, Placed 3
Formula 1 Brazilian Grand Prix
Carlos Reutemann (Arg), Ferrari

Kyalami (SA) 4.3.
Brabham-Alfa F-1, Retired (engine failure)
Formula 1 South African Grand Prix
Ronnie Peterson (S), Lotus-Ford

Long Beach (USA) 2.4.
Brabham-Alfa F-1, Retired (ignition)
Formula 1 USA Grand Prix (West)
Carlos Reutemann (Arg), Ferrari

Monte Carlo 7.5.
Brabham-Alfa F-1, Placed 2
Formula 1 Monaco Grand Prix
Patrick Depailler (F), Tyrrell-Ford

Zolder (B) 21.5.
Brabham-Alfa F-1 Retired (crashed)
Formula 1 Belgian Grand Prix
Mario Andretti (USA), Lotus-Ford

Jarama (E) 4.6.
Brabham-Alfa F-1, Retired (engine)
Formula 1 Spanish Grand Prix
Mario Andretti (USA), Lotus-Ford

Anderstorp (S) 17.6.
Brabham-Alfa F-1, Placed 1
Formula 1 Swedish Grand Prix
Lauda (A), Brabham-Alfa

Paul Ricard (F) 2.7.
Brabham-Alfa F-1, Retired (engine)
Formula 1 French Grand Prix
Mario Andretti (USA), Lotus-Ford

Brands Hatch (GB) 16.7.
Brabham-Alfa F-1, Placed 2
Formula 1 British Grand Prix
Carlos Reutemann (Arg), Ferrari

Hockenheim (D) 30.7.
Brabham-Alfa F-1, Retired (engine)
Formula 1 German Grand Prix
Mario Andretti (USA), Lotus-Ford

Öesterreichring (A) 13.8.
Brabham-Alfa F-1, Retired (crash)

Formula 1 Austrian Grand Prix
Ronnie Peterson (S), Lotus-Ford

Zandvoort (NL) 27.8.
Brabham-Alfa F-1, Placed 3
Formula 1 Dutch Grand Prix
Mario Andretti (USA), Lotus-Ford

Monza (I) 10.9.
Brabham-Alfa F-1, Placed 1
Formula 1 Italian Grand Prix
Lauda (A), Brabham-Alfa

Watkins Glen (USA) 1.10.
Brabham-Alfa F-1, Retired (engine)
Formula 1 USA Grand Prix (East)
Carlos Reutemann (Arg), Ferrari

Montreal (Can) 8.10.
Brabham-Alfa F-1, Retired (Crash)
Formula 1 Canadian Grand Prix
Gilles Villeneuve (Can), Ferrari

1979

Buenos Aires (Arg) 21.1.
Brabham-Alfa F-1, Retired (fuel pressure)
Formula 1 Argentinian Grand Prix
Jacques Laffite (F), Ligier-Ford

Interlagos (Brazil) 4.2.
Brabham-Alfa F-1, Retired (gears)
Formula 1 Brazilian Grand Prix
Jacques Laffite (F), Ligier-Ford

Kyalami (SA) 3.3.
Brabham-Alfa F-1, Placed 6
Formula 1 South African Grand Prix
Gilles Villeneuve (Can), Ferrari

Long Beach (USA) 8.4.
Brabham-Alfa F-1, Retired (crash)
Formula 1 USA Grand Prix (West)
Gilles Villeneuve (Can), Ferrari

Brands Hatch (GB) 15.4.
Brabham-Alfa F-1, Placed 5
Race of Champions
Gilles Villeneuve (Can), Ferrari

Jarama (E) 29.4.
Brabham-Alfa F-1, Retired (water cooler)
Formula 1 Spanish Grand Prix
Patrick Depailler (F), Ligier-Ford

Zolder (B) 12.5.
BMW M1, Retired (damaged shocks)
Procar (Production Car) Grand Prix
Elio de Angelis (I), BMW M1

Zolder (B) 13.5.
Brabham-Alfa F-1, Retired (engine)
Formula 1 Belgian Grand Prix
Jody Scheckter (SA), Ferrari

Monte Carlo 26.5.
BMW M1, Placed 1
Procar Grand Prix
Lauda (A), BMW M1

Monte Carlo 27.5.
Brabham-Alfa F-1, Retired (crash)
Formula 1 Monaco Grand Prix
Jody Scheckter (SA), Ferrari

Dijon (F) 30.6.
BMW M1, Placed 8
Procar Grand Prix
Nelson Piquet (Brazil), BMW M1

Dijon (F) 1.7.
Brabham-Alfa F-1, Retired (crash)

Formula 1 French Grand Prix
Jean-Pierre Jabouille (F), Renault Turbo

Silverstone (GB) 13.7.
BMW M1, Placed 1
Procar Grand Prix
Lauda (A), BMW M1

Silverstone (GB) 14.7.
Brabham-Alfa F-1, Retired (brakes)
Formula 1 British Grand Prix
Clay Regazzoni (CH), Williams-Ford

Hockenheim (D) 28.7.
BMW M1, Placed 1
Procar Grand Prix
Lauda (A), BMW M1

Hockenheim (D) 29.7.
Brabham-Alfa F-1, Retired (engine)
Formula 1 German Grand Prix
Alan Jones (Aus), Williams-Ford

Öesterreichring (A) 11.8.
BMW M1, Retired (clutch)
Procar Grand Prix
Jacques Laffite (F), BMW M1

Öesterreichring (A) 12.8.
Brabham-Alfa F-1, Retired (oil pressure)
Formula 1 Austrian Grand Prix
Alan Jones (Aus), Williams-Ford

Zandvoort (NL) 25.8.
BMW M1, Retired (electrics)
Procar Grand Prix
Hans-Joachim Stuck (D), BMW M1

Zandvoort (NL) 26.8.
Brabham-Alfa F-1, Retired (injured hand)
Formula 1 Dutch Grand Prix
Alan Jones (Aus), Williams-Ford

Monza (I) 8.9.
BMW M1, Placed 2
Procar Grand Prix

Hans-Joachim Stuck (D), BMW M1

Monza (I) 9.9.
Brabham-Alfa F-1, Placed 4
Formula 1 Italian Grand Prix
Jody Scheckter (SA), Ferrari

Imola (I) 16.9.
Brabham-Alfa F-1, Placed 1
Formula 1
Lauda (A), Brabham-Alfa

1982

Kyalami (SA) 23.1.
McLaren-Ford F-1, Placed 4
Formula 1 South African Grand Prix
Alain Prost (F), Renault Turbo

Rio de Janeiro (Brazil) 21.3.
McLaren-Ford F-1, Retired (collision)
Formula 1 Brazilian Grand Prix
Alain Prost (F), Renault Turbo

Long Beach (USA) 4.4.
McLaren-Ford F-1, Placed 1
Formula 1 USA Grand Prix (West)
Lauda (A), McLaren-Ford

Zolder (B) 9.5.
McLaren-Ford F-1, Disqualified
Formula 1 Belgian Grand Prix
John Watson (GB), McLaren-Ford

Monte Carlo 23.5.
McLaren-Ford F-1, Retired (engine)
Formula 1 Monaco Grand Prix
Riccardo Patrese (I), Brabham-Ford

Detroit (USA) 6.6.
McLaren-Ford F-1, Retired (collision)

Formula 1 USA Grand Prix (East)
John Watson (GB), McLaren-Ford

Montreal (Can) 13.6.
McLaren-Ford F-1, Retired (clutch)
Formula 1 Canadian Grand Prix
Nelson Piquet (Brazil), Brabham-BMW Turbo

Zandvoort (NL) 3.7.
McLaren-Ford F-1, Placed 4
Formula 1 Dutch Grand Prix
Didier Pironi (F), Ferrari Turbo

Brands Hatch (GB) 18.7.
McLaren-Ford F-1, Placed 1
Formula 1 British Grand Prix
Lauda (A), McLaren-Ford

Paul Ricard (F) 25.7.
McLaren-Ford F-1, Placed 8
Formula 1 French Grand Prix
René Arnoux (F), Renault Turbo

Hockenheim (D) 8.8.
McLaren-Ford F-1, Did not start (accident during qualifying)
Formula 1 German Grand Prix
Patrick Tambay (F), Ferrari Turbo

Öesterreichring (A) 15.8.
McLaren-Ford F-1, Placed 5
Formula 1 Austrian Grand Prix
Elio de Angelis (I), Lotus-Ford

Dijon (F) 29.8.
McLaren-Ford F-1, Placed 3
Formula 1 Swiss Grand Prix
Keke Rosberg (SF), Williams-Ford

Monza (I) 12.9.
McLaren-Ford F-1, Retired (chassis)
Formula 1 Italian Grand Prix
René Arnoux (F), Renault

Las Vegas (USA) 25.9.
McLaren-Ford F-1, Retired (oil pressure)
Formula 1 USA Grand Prix (West)
Michele Alboreto (I), Tyrrell-Ford

1983

Rio de Janeiro (Brazil) 13.3.
McLaren-Ford F-1, Placed 2
Brazilian Grand Prix
Nelson Piquet (Brazil), Brabham-BMW Turbo

Long Beach (USA) 27.3.
McLaren-Ford F-1, Placed 2
Formula 1 USA Grand Prix (West)
John Watson (GB), McLaren-Ford

Le Castellet (F) 17.4.
McLaren-Ford F-1, Retired (half shaft)
Formula 1 French Grand Prix
Alain Prost (F), Renault

Imola (I) 1.5.
McLaren-Ford F-1, Retired (crash)
Formula 1 San Marino Grand Prix
Patrick Tambay (F), Ferrari

Monte Carlo 15.5.
McLaren-Ford F-1, Did not qualify
Formula 1 Monaco Grand Prix
Keke Rosberg (SF), Williams-Ford

Spa (B) 22.5.
McLaren-Ford F-1, Retired (engine)
Formula 1 Belgian Grand Prix
Alain Prost (F), Renault

Detroit (USA) 5.6.
McLaren-Ford F-1, Retired (shocks)

Formula 1 USA Grand Prix (East)
Michele Alboreto (I), Tyrrell-Ford

Montreal (Can) 12.6.
McLaren-Ford F-1, Retired (spin)
Formula 1 Canadian Grand Prix
René Arnoux (F), Ferrari

Silverstone (GB) 16.7.
McLaren-Ford F-1, Placed 6
Formula 1 British Grand Prix
Alain Prost (F), Renault

Hockenheim (D) 7.8.
McLaren-Ford F-1, Disqualified (reversing in pit lane)
Formula 1 German Grand Prix
René Arnoux (F), Ferrari

Öesterreichring (A) 14.8.
McLaren-Ford F-1, Placed 6
Formula 1 Austrian Grand Prix
Alain Prost (F), Renault

Zandvoort (NL) 28.8.
McLaren-TAG Turbo, Retired (brakes)
Formula 1 Dutch Grand Prix
René Arnoux (F), Ferrari

Monza (I) 11.9.
McLaren-TAG Turbo, Retired (engine)
Formula 1 Italian Grand Prix
Nelson Piquet (Brazil), Brabham-BMW Turbo

Brands Hatch (GB) 25.9.
McLaren-TAG Turbo, Retired (engine)
Formula 1 European Grand Prix
Nelson Piquet (Brazil), Brabham-BMW Turbo

Kyalami (SA) 15.10.
McLaren-TAG Turbo, Retired (electrics)
Formula 1 South African Grand Prix
Riccardo Patrese (I), Brabham-BMW Turbo

1984

Rio-Jacarepaguá (Brazil) 25.3.
McLaren-TAG, Retired (ruptured battery cable)
Formula 1 Brazilian Grand Prix
Alain Prost (F), McLaren-TAG

Kyalami (SA) 7.4.
McLaren-TAG, Placed 1
Formula 1 South African Grand Prix
Lauda (A), McLaren-TAG

Zolder (B) 29.4.
McLaren-TAG, Retired (engine)
Formula 1 Belgian Grand Prix
Michele Alboreto (I), Ferrari

Imola (I) 6.5.
McLaren-TAG, Retired (engine)
Formula 1 San Marino Grand Prix
Alain Prost (F), McLaren-TAG

Dijon (F) 20.5.
McLaren-TAG, Placed 1
Formula 1 French Grand Prix
Lauda (A), McLaren-TAG

Monte Carlo 3.6.
McLaren-TAG, Retired (spin)
Formula 1 Monaco Grand Prix
Alain Prost (F), McLaren-TAG

Montreal (Can) 17.6.
McLaren-TAG, Placed 2
Formula 1 Canadian Grand Prix
Nelson Piquet (Brazil), Brabham-BMW

Detroit (USA) 24.6.
McLaren-TAG, Retired (spark plugs)
Formula 1 USA Grand Prix (East)

Nelson Piquet (Brazil), Brabham-BMW

Dallas (USA) 8.7.
McLaren-TAG, Retired (crash)
Formula 1 USA Grand Prix (South)
Keke Rosberg (SF), Williams-Honda

Brands Hatch (GB) 22.7.
McLaren-TAG, Placed 1
Formula 1 British Grand Prix
Lauda (A), McLaren-TAG

Hockenheim (D) 5.8.
McLaren-TAG, Placed 2
Formula 1 German Grand Prix
Alain Prost (F), McLaren-TAG

Öesterreichring (A) 19.8.
McLaren-TAG, Placed 1
Formula 1 Austrian Grand Prix
Lauda (A), McLaren-TAG

Zandvoort (NL) 26.8.
McLaren-TAG, Placed 2
Formula 1 Dutch Grand Prix
Alain Prost (F), McLaren-TAG

Monza (I) 9.9.
McLaren-TAG, Placed 1
Formula 1 Italian Grand Prix
Lauda (A), McLaren-TAG

Nürburgring (D) 7.10.
McLaren-TAG, Placed 4
Formula 1 European Grand Prix
Alain Prost (F), McLaren-TAG

Estoril (Portugal) 21.10.
McLaren-TAG, Placed 2
Formula 1 Portuguese Grand Prix
Alain Prost (F), McLaren-TAG

Adelaide (Aus) 18.11.
Ralt Formula Pacific, Retired (crash)
Australian Grand Prix
Robert Moreno (Brazil), Ralt

1985

Rio-Jacarepaguá (Brazil) 7.4.
McLaren-TAG, Retired (computer)
Formula 1 Brazilian Grand Prix
Alain Prost (F), McLaren-TAG

Estoril (Portugal) 21.4.
McLaren-TAG, Retired (engine)
Formula 1 Portuguese Grand Prix
Ayrton Senna (Brazil), Lotus-Renault

Imola (I) 5.5.
McLaren-TAG, Placed 4
Formula 1 San Marino Grand Prix
Elio de Angelis (I), Lotus-Renault

Monte Carlo 19.5.
McLaren-TAG, Retired (spin and stall)
Formula 1 Monaco Grand Prix
Alain Prost (F), McLaren-TAG

Montreal (Can) 16.6.
McLaren-TAG, Retired (engine)
Formula 1 Canadian Grand Prix
Michele Alboreto (I), Ferrari

Detroit (USA) 23.6.
McLaren-TAG, Retired (brakes)
Formula 1 USA Grand Prix
Keke Rosberg (SF), Williams-Honda

Paul Ricard (F) 7.7.
McLaren-TAG, Retired (gearbox)
Formula 1 French Grand Prix

Nelson Piquet (Brazil), Brabham-BMW

Silverstone (GB) 21.7.
McLaren-TAG, Retired (electronics)
Formula 1 British Grand Prix
Alain Prost (F), McLaren-TAG

Nürburgring (D) 4.8.
McLaren-TAG, Placed 5
Formula 1 German Grand Prix
Michele Alboreto (I), Ferrari

Öesterreichring (A) 18.8.
McLaren-TAG, Retired (turbocharger)
Formula 1 Austrian Grand Prix
Alain Prost (F), McLaren-TAG

Zandvoort (NL) 25.8.
McLaren-TAG, Placed 1
Formula 1 Dutch Grand Prix
Lauda (A), McLaren-TAG

Monza (I) 8.9.
McLaren-TAG, Retired (vibration)
Formula 1 Italian Grand Prix
Alain Prost (F), McLaren-TAG

Spa (B) 15.9.
McLaren-TAG, Did not start (crashed in training)
Formula 1 Belgian Grand Prix
Ayrton Senna (Brazil), Lotus-Renault

Brands Hatch (GB) 6.10.
Did not start (following crash at Spa)
Formula 1 European Grand Prix
Nigel Mansell (GB), Williams-Honda

Kyalami (SA) 19.10.
McLaren-TAG, Retired (turbo damage)

Formula 1 South African Grand Prix
Nigel Mansell (GB), Williams-Honda

Adelaide (Aus) 3.11.

McLaren-TAG, Retired (brakes)
Formula 1 Australian Grand Prix
Keke Rosberg (SF), Williams-Honda

INDEX

NL indicates Niki Lauda.

INDEX